D1422947

014046590 X

HERBS
&SPICES

HERBS &SPICES

Jill Norman

Photography
Dave King

Penguin Random House

For Paul, who made it possible

DK INDIA
Senior Art Editor Ivy Roy
Project Editor Janashree Singha
Art Editors Sourabh Challariya, Tashi Topgyal Laya
Managing Editor Alicia Ingty
Managing Art Editor Navidita Thapa
DTP Designers Satish Chandra Gaur, Anurag Trivedi
Pre-production Manager Sunil Sharma

DK UK
Managing Editor Dawn Henderson
Managing Art Editor Christine Keilty
Senior Jacket Creative Nicola Powling
Producer, Pre-Production Rebecca Fallowfield
Senior Producer Jen Scothern
Art Director Peter Luff
Category Publisher Peggy Vance

Original 2002 Edition: Project Editor Frank Ritter,
Editor Hugh Thompson, **Project Art Editor** Toni Kay,
Art Editor Sara Robin, **Managing Editor** Gillian Roberts,
Category Publisher Mary-Clare Jerram, **Art Director**
Carole Ash, **DTP Designers** Sonia Charbonnier,
Louise Waller, **Production Controller** Joanna Bull

First published in Great Britain in 2002 by Dorling Kindersley
Limited, 80 Strand, London WC2R 0RL

A Penguin Random House Company

This revised edition published in Great Britain in 2015 by
Dorling Kindersley Limited

2 4 6 8 10 9 7 5 3 1
001 – 259428 – May/2015

Copyright © 2002, 2015 Dorling Kindersley Limited, London
Text copyright © 2002, 2015 Jill Norman

The right of Jill Norman to be identified as Writer
of the Work has been asserted by her in accordance
with the Copyright, Designs, and Patents Act 1988.

All rights reserved. No part of this publication may be
reproduced, stored in a retrieval system, or transmitted
in any form or by any means, electronic, mechanical,
photocopying, recording, or otherwise, without the
prior written permission of the copyright owners.

A CIP catalogue record for this book
is available from The British Library

ISBN 978-0-2411-9876-6

Colour reproduced by BurdaDruck
Printed and bound in China

A WORLD OF IDEAS:
SEE ALL THERE IS TO KNOW

www.dk.com

Contents

Herbs

Spices

Recipes

Blending herbs and spices   266

Cooking with herbs and spices   304

Index   328

Acknowledgments   336

Introduction

Since publication of the first edition of this book in 2002, our willingness to try new foods has grown. Pomegranates and mangoes, fennel, kale, many varieties of potato, salad greens, and fresh herbs are readily available. The range of spices and blends has extended online and in shops. Sauces from Japan and Korea, fresh Mexican chillies, chilli and herb pastes from Peru, khmeli suneli from Georgia are all there, indicating our interest in these cuisines. Wasabi cultivation has spread to the UK and saffron is being grown again near Saffron Walden in Essex.

Geranium

Food scientists are creating new spice colourants without chemical synthesis. These experiments are in their early days, but freeze-dried and ground rock samphire, *Crithmum maritimum*, also known as sea fennel, produces a vivid green powder with salty, aromatic notes of celery, green citrus peel, and ordinary fennel. Pasta flavoured with this powder turns a delicate green and makes a fine dish with a seafood sauce.

In the first edition, I wrote about food companies producing "aroma-fingerprints" (*p.128*). Flavour drops that extract flavour tones from edible plants were developed for the NASA space food programme. Further use of these concentrated, natural products, extended initially to molecular gastronomy, now they are sold to everyone on the internet. The range is extensive, and includes fruits, spices, champagne, and other drinks. A similar range of concentrated natural herb and spice flavour pastes is available too.

I am not recommending that you use these in place of herbs and spices, but you might want to experiment with one or two, if cooking a large quantity of a dish, for which only one drop, much diluted, may be needed.

Information on individual herbs and spices has been updated where necessary; more spice and herb mixtures, sauces and condiments have been added, and a short section on salt. Salts of different colours and textures, from all parts of the world, are now sold widely, and salt is a frequent companion to herbs and spices. The recipe chapter is longer and contains several new recipes, reflecting the wider use of herbs and spices in everyday cooking as well as recipes for dishes from spice and herb producing regions.

What are herbs and spices?

The definition of what constitutes a herb or spice is not as straightforward as it might seem. Broadly, we think of herbs as plants used by cooks for their flavour and aroma. The word herb derives from the Latin *herba*, meaning grass or, by extension, green crop: it was originally applied to a wide range of leaf vegetables in addition to the plants we now call herbs. Most of the culinary herbs we use grow in temperate climates. Spices, on the other hand, are products of tropical plants: aromatic roots, bark, seeds, buds, and fruits, usually used in dried form, whether whole or ground. Again our word derives from Latin, where *species* meant specific kind but, in later use, goods or merchandise – spices certainly being an important commodity even at the time of the Romans.

How the book is organized

I have followed standard European usage in defining herbs and spices, and have grouped both according to their dominant aroma and flavour. Some fitted easily into a specific category; others were difficult to define and could have been put into more than one group. Marigolds, for instance, are basically sweet, yet have a bitter note. Some Asian basils are more piquant than sweet. Ginger is pungent but it is also earthy and warm. Another difficulty is that the way we express our awareness of flavours and aromas varies from individual to individual. Your perception of aromatics may not be the same as mine, and a different term may come to your mind from the one that came to mine.

Lemon balm

Liquorice

Wasabi   Mace

European definitions of herbs and spices are not used worldwide. In Southeast Asia any aromatic plant used fresh is a herb, but once the same substance is dried it is classed as a spice. In the US, the American Spice Trade Association defines "any dried plant used primarily for seasoning purposes" as a spice; this includes dried herbs, even dehydrated onions, but not what we would call spices when these are used in their fresh form.

Health benefits of herbs and spices

The early use of herbs and spices was medicinal, and in many regions where they grow they are still valued for their medicinal properties. Often their use in cooking owed as much to their perceived ability to promote health, combat flatulence, or help digest fatty foods as to their appetizing fragrances. Fresh herbs and spices provided mineral salts and vitamins long before our need for these was understood. In tropical countries, the vitamin C contained in chillies remains just as important to the diet as the lift that the chillies give to it.

Most cultures recognize the importance of providing a balance in food. Indian cooking follows Ayurvedic principles in using herbs and spices to provide flavour and to create physical and emotional well-being. In China, nutrition and medicine have long been integrated. Chinese cooking is based on a theory that well-being is brought about by the careful balancing of the five flavours – sweet, salty, bitter, sour, and pungent – with the texture and colour of the food. Yin herbs such as mint and parsley slow down the metabolism, whereas yang spices such as chilli and ginger activate it. Similar principles are followed in Iran, where the cook strives to maintain a balance between ingredients classed as hot or cold. In the West, herbs and spices add flavour to low-salt and low-fat foods, and some evidence suggests that garlic may help lower cholesterol.

Flavourings rooted in tradition

In the past herbs and spices were also important for their preservative properties: before the arrival of refrigeration their volatile oils and other compounds prolonged the useful life of many foodstuffs. Pickled or salted meat, fish, and vegetables would last through the winter months, and aromatics were used to improve their flavour. Although we no longer need these methods of preserving, we still use many of them simply because we have come to like the taste they impart to foods.

All round the world, traditional flavour combinations, using local ingredients, have come to characterize the foods of those regions. Saffron, pimentón, garlic, and nuts dominate in Spain; wine and herbs in France; basil, garlic, olive oil, anchovy in Italy. In Britain, it is parsley, thyme, sage, and mustard; in eastern Europe soured cream, dill, and caraway. The Middle East uses lemon, parsley, and cinnamon. In northern India ginger, garlic, and cumin are the most important spices; in the south it is mustard seed, coconut, chilli, and tamarind. Thailand has fish sauce, lemon grass, galangal, and chilli; China uses soy sauce, ginger, and Sichuan pepper. Mexico remains faithful to its chillies, coriander, and cinnamon.

Herbs and spices stimulate all the senses through their aroma, flavour, texture and visual appeal, but don't use them to excess. Too much can ruin a dish. Experiment with combinations that appeal to you, and you will find that herbs and spices bring subtlety, harmony, and complexity to your cooking.

Jill Norman

Herbs

Introducing
herbs

Scented geranium

Fresh herbs are now so widely available from supermarkets, garden centres, as well as specialist nurseries that the most common ones often form part of the weekly shopping. Herb specialists usually sell several varieties of basil, mint, thyme, or marjoram, and herbs like rau ram and Chinese chives have been adopted. There are still some – perilla, mitsuba, Vietnamese balm, rice paddy herb, epazote – that remain hard to find, though it is possible to order seeds online.

New markets for fresh herbs

Today international trade brings herbs grown in Turkey, Cyprus, and Israel to supermarket shelves as a matter of course. Frequent deliveries from Japan, Thailand, and Singapore bring tropical herbs and fresh spices to specialist shops and some supermarkets. Demand from immigrant communities and restaurants may still account for the biggest sales, but many more local enthusiasts now buy regularly. Fresh spices like makrut lime leaves, lemon grass, and chillies can also be found in freezer cabinets. These plants will not grow in northern Europe, but in parts of the US, and in other countries with sufficiently warm climates, several tropical herbs are cultivated, often by immigrants, to meet the demands of their own communities and a wider public. Perhaps in a few years our shops, too, will sell bunches of fresh culantro, rau ram, and epazote alongside familiar European varieties.

Garlic

The European tradition

European herbs remain essential to our present-day cooking: tarragon, thyme, bay, and garlic in France; basil, sage, and rosemary in Italy; oregano in Greece; dill in Scandinavia; parsley, sage, thyme, and bay in Britain. The traditional uses of these herbs are still reflected in daily meals, as travels in Europe or visits to a French, Italian, or Greek restaurant confirm, but uses beyond the traditional are increasingly common, as cooks explore different flavour combinations and try new interpretations of standard dishes, partly thanks to the availability of fresh herbs year round. If you are a novice in cooking with herbs, start with classics such as chicken with tarragon, guacamole with coriander and chilli, grilled cod or tuna with salsa verde, roast potatoes with rosemary and garlic, or a beef stew with a bouquet garni and red wine. Once you begin to appreciate how the blending of flavours affects a dish, you will be drawn to experiment and adapt or devise combinations to your own taste.

We are rediscovering many herbs that once were in common use but have long been forgotten or neglected as weeds. In 17th-century Europe, salad herbs were grown and used widely. In 1699 John Evelyn's *Acetaria* recorded more than 30 salad herbs, including basil, balm, chicory, corn salad, clary sage, various cresses, dandelion,

Chives

Rosemary   Flat-leaf parsley

fennel, hyssop, mallow, mint, orach, purslane, rocket, and sorrel. In 1731 Philip Miller's *Gardener's Dictionary* instructed gentleman gardeners in herb cultivation. Some have become easily available once more, in season and even all year round, but others – such as sweet cicely, clary sage, and hyssop – you will have to grow yourself. Specialist nurseries are constantly extending their stocks to meet the demand for a wider range of herbs. But there is also a trend to overuse certain herbs – rocket and chervil are currently the worst affected – which I hope will not lead to their disappearance once the fashion changes.

Tarragon

Choosing and using herbs

Generally herbs are used to add fragrance and flavour rather than to provide the dominant taste. The light flavours of dill, parsley, and chervil are good with fish and seafood; the more pungent rosemary, oregano, and garlic will flavour braised or baked lamb or roast pork beautifully. Root vegetables respond well to thyme and rosemary, aubergines to Provençal herbs, green peas to chives, tomatoes to basil and parsley. It is important always to balance delicate and hearty flavours, and to use herbs judiciously.

The wealth of fresh herbs now available has had the beneficial effect of banishing from many kitchens a lot of small packets of stale dried herbs. Some herbs that are sold dried, such as basil and parsley, are never worth having; their aroma is musty at best, and their taste insipid. Such herbs are meant to be eaten fresh. The clean, herbaceous notes of fresh parsley, and the complex, sweet scent of anise and clove wafting from a bunch of basil, beguile first the sense of smell and later also the tastebuds. Unlike many herbs, these two are not overwhelming if used in large quantities – as they are in the basil sauce pesto and the parsley salad tabbouleh. Robust herbs, such as oregano, thyme, sage, savory, mint, and rosemary, respond well to drying, which preserves and often concentrates

Mountain mint

Pounding leaves
Herbs intended for sauces or pastes may be pounded in a mortar and pestle. Other ingredients may be worked into the crushed herbs.

Chopping herbs
Chop herbs just before they are needed – freshly chopped herbs have the best aroma and flavour.

Drying herbs
Some herbs can be dried at home and their leaves stripped and kept in an airtight jar.

their flavour. Whether fresh or dried, these herbs should be used sparingly or they will overwhelm other flavours in the food instead of complementing them.

Herbs added early on in cooking will release their flavours into the dish. Dried herbs should always be put in at the beginning, and herbs with tough leaves, such as rosemary, lavender, winter savory, thyme, and bay, will withstand long cooking. If you add sprigs of herbs to a dish, remove them before serving. To restore the aroma of herbs used in a slow-cooked dish, stir a few finely chopped leaves into the pan towards the end of the cooking process. Strongly flavoured herbs, such as mint, tarragon, fennel, marjoram, and lovage, can be added at any stage during cooking. The essential oils of delicate herbs, like basil, chervil, chives, dill, coriander, perilla, and lemon balm, soon dissipate when heated. To keep them fresh in taste, texture, and colour, add them just before a dish is served.

TASTING NOTES

Parsley has a lightly spicy aroma with hints of anise and lemon; its taste is tangy, herbaceous, and has a light, peppery note. Flat-leaf parsley has a more persistent and finer flavour than curly parsley, and a finer texture. Both bring out the flavours of other seasonings.

PARTS USED

Fresh leaves are the most used, but stalks are good for flavouring stocks; Hamburg parsley is grown for its roots.

BUYING / STORING

Buy a pot of parsley for your windowsill; or buy a bunch, wrap it in plastic and store in the refrigerator. Discard any sprigs that look slimy and it should keep for 4–5 days. Parsley can be chopped and frozen in small containers or in ice-cube trays with a little water. Don't buy dried parsley.

GROW YOUR OWN

Parsley seeds take some weeks to germinate, but soaking them overnight in hot water helps to speed up the process. Sow in the ground, and thin seedlings when they are big enough. Sow seeds every year, so that when one batch runs to seed in its second year a new batch is ready to use. Harvest from late spring.

Parsley
Petroselinum crispum

Probably the only herb considered indispensable by most western cooks, parsley is a versatile hardy biennial, native to the eastern Mediterranean region. Today it is cultivated throughout most of the temperate world. Hamburg parsley, which is valued for its root rather than its leaves, was first grown in Germany in the 16th century.

Culinary uses

Parsley is liked for its clean, fresh taste and is rich in iron and vitamins A and C. It is used in sauces, salads, stuffings, and omelettes in many parts of the world. In Anglo-Saxon cultures its use as a flavouring ingredient (except for parsley sauce) rather than simply as a garnish is quite recent. Add chopped parsley at the end of cooking time for a fresh flavour. Sprigs of dark green, deep-fried curly parsley make an excellent garnish for fried fish. Hamburg parsley is used in soups and stews, but it can also be blanched and roasted or cooked in other ways as a root vegetable. It mashes well with potato.

Curly parsley *P. crispum*
Good for garnishes, curly parsley also gives a light, herbaceous flavour and attractive green colour to mayonnaise and other sauces.

Flat-leaf parsley

P. c. var. 'Neapolitanum'

Also called French or Italian parsley, flat-leaf parsley has the best flavour for cooking and is most widely used throughout Europe and the Middle East.

Stalks

Parsley stalks are coarser in flavour than the leaves. Tie them in a bundle and use in long-cooked stocks and stews; discard the stalks when the cooking is finished.

FLAVOUR PAIRINGS

Essential to a number of traditional flavouring mixtures: French bouquets garnis, fines herbes, and persillade; Italian gremolata and salsa verde; Lebanese tabbouleh.

Good with eggs, fish, lemon, lentils, rice, tomatoes, most vegetables.

Combines well with basil, bay, capers, chervil, chillies, chives, garlic, lemon balm, marjoram and oregano, mint, pepper, rosemary, sorrel, sumac, tarragon.

Hamburg parsley

P. c. var. tuberosum

Mostly cultivated in central and northern Europe, Hamburg parsley is no more difficult to grow than leaf parsley. The root is rather like a small parsnip, or occasionally round, like celeriac. Its flavour is between those of parsley and celeriac, combined with a light nuttiness. The leaves have a coarse flavour and texture.

TASTING NOTES

Purslane has little aroma; the fleshy leaves and stems have a refreshing, lightly piquant, astringent, lemony taste, and a crunchy, juicy texture.

 PARTS USED

Leaves and young shoots. The flowers can be added to salads. Purslane is always eaten fresh.

 BUYING / STORING

Fresh purslane will keep for 2–3 days in a plastic bag in the vegetable drawer of the refrigerator. In summer, Greek and Turkish shops usually have large bunches of purslane. In Mexico you find it readily in markets.

 GROW YOUR OWN

Purslane does best on moist, light soil in a sunny position. Seeds can be sown outdoors from early summer and the leaves are ready to harvest about 60 days later. In hot, dry weather it will need more watering than other herbs. Cut purslane a little above the ground, leaving two leaves for regrowth. For salad, harvest young leaves regularly because older leaves become tough. Yellow flowers appear in summer, but only open for a short time around midday.

 FLAVOUR PAIRINGS

Good with beetroot, broad beans, cucumber, eggs, feta cheese, new potatoes, spinach, tomatoes, yogurt.
Combines well with borage, chervil, cresses, rocket, salad burnet, sorrel.

Purslane

Portulaca oleracea

Purslane is a sprawling annual that grows wild through much of the world. It has been used as a food plant for centuries in southern Europe and the Middle East. An important source of iron and vitamin C, purslane is also one of the best plant sources for Omega-3, one of the fatty acids that help to maintain a healthy heart.

Culinary uses

Young leaves make an agreeable addition to a salad. In the Middle East, chopped purslane with a garlicky yogurt dressing is served as an accompaniment to grilled meats. The herb is also a standard ingredient of fattoush, the Lebanese salad.

Blanch older leaves to use as a vegetable. Cooking emphasizes their mucilaginous content, which provides a good thickening for soups and stews. In Turkey large bunches of purslane are used in a traditional lamb and bean stew, and all around the Mediterranean it turns up in soups. The Mexicans cook it with pork, tomatillos, and chillies, especially their smoky chipotle chillies (*p.245*). Purslane combines well with spinach tossed in olive oil and lemon juice.

Fresh sprigs and flowers

Green purslane has oblong, thick, succulent leaves and a round stem tinged with red. Golden purslane (*P. sativa*) is a smaller plant and is less hardy.

Claytonia
Claytonia perfoliata

Claytonia, also called winter purslane and miner's lettuce, is a hardy, delicate-looking annual that makes an excellent winter salad herb. It received the name miner's lettuce because miners in the California gold rush ate the wild plant to avoid scurvy – like the unrelated purslane *Portulaca oleracea* (*p.20*), claytonia is high in vitamin C.

Culinary uses

Leaves, young stems, and flowers make a useful and pretty contribution to the salad bowl. I particularly like claytonia for its winter hardiness, when other salad greens can be dreary. The leaves and stems can be cooked – try them alone, or combined with other greens, stir-fried with a little oyster sauce.

Fresh sprigs and flowers

Claytonia leaves totally encircle the smooth stems. The tiny, white flowers are borne on thin stalks from early summer.

TASTING NOTES

Claytonia is not aromatic. It is mild, with a clean, fresh flavour.

PARTS USED

Leaves, young stems, and flowers.

BUYING / STORING

Claytonia can be gathered from the wild in shady grasslands in North America, its native habitat, but it is less commonly found in Europe. It is best picked and used at once, but it can be kept in a plastic bag in the vegetable drawer of the refrigerator for 1–2 days.

GROW YOUR OWN

A few herb nurseries now stock claytonia, but it is also easy to grow from seed. Seeds sown in spring will produce plants for summer use; summer sowing will produce plants for winter picking. Claytonia survives in the garden through the winter unless there is a very severe frost. It prefers a light soil, but is adaptable. Claytonia makes a pretty garden edging plant.

FLAVOUR PAIRINGS

Combines well with cresses, chives, rocket, sorrel.

TASTING NOTES

Borage has a gentle aroma and a somewhat stronger flavour of cucumber. It is cool and fresh-tasting, with a slight saltiness.

PARTS USED

Leaves and flowers. Avoid the bristly stalks.

BUYING / STORING

Borage is best used fresh. Leaves can be kept for a day or two in the vegetable drawer of the refrigerator, either wrapped in damp kitchen paper or placed inside a plastic bag. Flowers are best used soon after picking or they will wilt. Freeze them in ice cubes and serve in drinks.

GROW YOUR OWN

Grow borage in well-drained soil in a sunny spot. It is a large, untidy plant and will self-seed easily. Plant borage only where you intend it to grow because it has a long taproot and does not like to be moved. Harvest young leaves in spring and summer, and pick the flowers as soon as they open.

FLAVOUR PAIRINGS

Good with cucumber, eel, and other fatty fish, potato salad, white cheeses, yogurt; Pimm's and other long summer drinks.

Combines well with chervil, cresses, dill, garlic, mint, rocket, salad burnet.

Borage
Borago officinalis

This robust, annual herb, native to southern Europe and western Asia, is now naturalized throughout Europe and North America. It is worth growing just for its dazzling, blue, star-like flowers. The old herbalists held that borage made people cheerful and courageous; it is now known to stimulate the adrenal glands and have mild sedative and anti-depressant effects.

Culinary uses

Borage is essentially a salad herb. Shred the young leaves because their hairy texture is disagreeable if they are left whole. Combine the shredded leaves with cucumber tossed in yogurt or soured cream, and add them to dressings and salsas. Tough older leaves can be sautéed, or cooked in water and treated like spinach. The Italians use borage with spinach or with breadcrumbs, egg, and Parmesan to stuff ravioli and cannelloni. The Turks add the leaves to green pea soup. The flowers will impart a delicate cucumber note to salads, and they look wonderful floating on a creamy soup or flavouring a jug of Pimm's. They can also be candied to decorate cakes and desserts. Use borage sparingly.

Fresh leaves and flowers
Of borage species, only *B. officinalis* is edible. The white-flowered cultivated variety *B. o.* 'Alba' can be used in the same way as the blue or purple-flowered varieties.

Salad burnet

Sanguisorba minor

Salad burnet is a graceful, bushy, perennial plant with sharply toothed, deep-green leaves. Delicate in appearance, it is actually sturdy and hardy, its evergreen leaves often pushing up through a light covering of snow. Native to Europe and western Asia, salad burnet was taken to North America by early European colonists and is now naturalized there.

Culinary uses

The subtle flavour of young, feathery leaves is best appreciated by eating them raw. Add them to salads – they are particularly good in autumn and winter, when interesting salad leaves can be in short supply. Chop as a garnish for vegetables or egg dishes; combine with tarragon, chives, and chervil for fines herbes. The leaves are good scattered over soups and casseroles and made into sauces and herb butters. Burnet is often recommended to flavour vinegar, but I have found this disappointing.

Fresh sprigs

The tender, young leaves have the best flavour. The pretty, red flowers have no taste.

TASTING NOTES

Salad burnet is not aromatic and has a mild, lightly astringent flavour reminiscent of cucumber with a hint of nuttiness. Old leaves become bitter and are best cooked.

PARTS USED

Leaves and young stems.

BUYING / STORING

Burnet will keep for a day or two in a plastic bag in the vegetable drawer of the refrigerator. In some parts of Europe you can buy bunches of burnet in the market, alongside other herbs and salad leaves.

GROW YOUR OWN

Easy to grow from seed, burnet flourishes in light, well-drained soil in sun or light shade. Remove the flower heads and cut leaves regularly to encourage new growth. Divide after the second year to maintain tender growth.

FLAVOUR PAIRINGS

Good with broad beans, cream cheese, cucumber, eggs, fish, salad leaves, tomatoes.
Combines well with chervil, chives, claytonia, mint, parsley, rosemary, tarragon.

TASTING NOTES

Green perilla is sweetly yet strongly aromatic, with notes of cinnamon, cumin, citrus, and anise basil, and a pleasant warmth on the palate. Red perilla is less aromatic and has a more subdued flavour. It is faintly musty and woody with cumin, coriander leaf, and cinnamon overtones.

PARTS USED

Leaves, flowers, and growing sprouts. Seeds are harvested commercially for their oil.

BUYING / STORING

Fresh perilla leaves are sold in oriental shops. They keep for 3–4 days in a plastic bag in the vegetable drawer of the refrigerator. Growing sprouts are sold by some greengrocers and supermarkets. Red leaves are sold pickled in vacuum packs. Dried perilla is available from Japanese shops.

GROW YOUR OWN

Perilla is not demanding about soil or situation, but does not like to be waterlogged and is not frost-hardy. Well-drained, light soil is best and a sheltered spot in sun or partial shade. Pinch out the tops to produce bushy plants. Perilla self-seeds easily, especially the red variety.

FLAVOUR PAIRINGS

Good with beef, chicken, courgettes, fish, mooli, noodles, rice, tomatoes.
Combines well with basil, chives, fresh and pickled ginger, lemon grass, mitsuba, parsley, sansho, wasabi.

Perilla
Perilla frutescens

The aromatic leaves of perilla – or shiso, to give the plant its Japanese name – are widely used in Japan, Korea, and Vietnam. More recently they have been discovered by cooks in Australia, the US, and Europe. An annual herb, related to mint and basil, perilla is native to China. The flavour of dried perilla only palely reflects that of the fresh.

Culinary uses

In Japan red perilla is mostly used for colouring and pickling umeboshi (salted and dried "plums"). Green perilla is served with sushi and sashimi – it is said to counteract parasites in raw fish. The leaves are also used in soups and salads and to wrap rice cakes. Coated with batter on one side only, they are deep-fried for tempura. The Vietnamese shred green perilla and add to noodles; they serve meats, prawns, and fish wrapped in leaves with a dipping sauce.

Chopped green perilla gives a wonderful flavour to cooked rice; substitute dried if necessary. I grow perilla (seeds are readily available online), and while I mostly use the red in salads and as a garnish, I increasingly extend my use of the green. I add it to slices of lemon or lime in the cavity of fish to be roasted or steamed, to sauces for fish and chicken, and to salsa verde instead of basil. Sometimes I use it instead of basil with tomatoes, or with pasta or noodles.

Oil extracted from the seeds is a rich source of Omega-3 fatty acids.

Green perilla *P. frutescens*

Green perilla has soft, downy leaves with a crinkly edge. They look somewhat like nettle leaves.

Mitsuba
Cryptotaenia japonica

Mitsuba is also known as Japanese parsley, Japanese chervil, and trefoil. This cool-climate, elegant perennial grows wild in Japan and is used extensively in Japanese cooking. It is now cultivated in Australia, North America, and Europe, initially to supply to Japanese restaurants but increasingly to sell to herb enthusiasts.

Culinary uses

In Japan, mitsuba is used to season soups, simmered dishes (nabemono), and savoury custards, in salads, and with fried or vinegared foods. It adds its highly individual, delicate flavour to matsutake no dobinmushi, a dish made only for a few weeks when the much prized pine mushrooms are in season. The mushrooms are simmered in a broth and the mitsuba is added for a few seconds at the end. Small bundles of stalks may be tied in a knot below the leaves and fried for tempura. Mitsuba is often blanched quickly to tenderize the leaves, or added to stir-fried foods at the last moment; overcooking destroys the flavour of the leaves. The cress-like sprouted seedlings are good in salads.

Fresh leaves

Mitsuba means "three leaves" in Japanese, from the three leaflets that make up the leaf. The meaning is echoed in the English name trefoil.

TASTING NOTES
Mitsuba has little aroma but a distinctive, mild, restrained, and agreeable taste, showing elements of chervil, angelica, and celery, with something of the astringency of sorrel and a hint of clove.

PARTS USED
Leaves and stalks.

BUYING / STORING
You may find mitsuba in a Japanese or oriental shop, otherwise buy a plant from a herb nursery. Leaves keep for 5–6 days if wrapped in damp kitchen paper or placed in a plastic bag in the vegetable drawer of the refrigerator.

GROW YOUR OWN
Mitsuba is a woodland plant and is easy to grow in light shade. It seeds itself readily. In summer mitsuba bears insignificant white flowers above the leaves. Leaves and slender stalks are harvested from spring through to autumn or winter. Mitsuba is not long-lived; I have found it necessary to replace mine after 4–5 years.

FLAVOUR PAIRINGS
Good with eggs, fish and seafood, mushrooms, poultry, rice, and as a garnish for most vegetables, especially sweet roots such as carrots and parsnips.
Combines well with basil, chives, ginger, lemon balm, lemon grass, marjoram, sesame.

TASTING NOTES

Orach is not aromatic; the leaves have a mild, agreeable, spinach-like flavour, which contrasts well with more pungent salad herbs.

PARTS USED

Young leaves.

BUYING / STORING

Seeds and plants are available from specialist nurseries. It is best to use leaves straight after picking but they will keep for a day or two in a plastic bag in the refrigerator vegetable drawer. Orach is sometimes included in up-market bags of salad leaves.

GROW YOUR OWN

Orach produces bigger leaves if planted in rich, well-drained soil. Red orach benefits from partial shade, where the leaves will not scorch in hot sun. It grows fast, and it is best to sow seeds in late spring and again in summer for a continuous supply of young leaves. Orach has a tendency to grow tall and straggly, but the plants should remain bushy if you harvest leaves regularly and remove the flower spikes as they begin to form. Orach is a self-seeding annual.

FLAVOUR PAIRINGS

Good with catalogna (puntarelle), corn salad, lettuce, mizuna, mustard greens, and other salad leaves.

Combines well with borage, chicory, the cresses, dill, fennel, purslane, rocket, salad burnet, and sorrel.

Orach
Atriplex hortensis

Orach belongs to the goosefoot family, as does epazote (*p.116*). It grows wild in Europe and much of temperate Asia and was formerly gathered and also cultivated for use as a vegetable. Its old popular name was mountain spinach. Out of fashion for a long time, orach has been rediscovered as an attractive salad herb.

Culinary uses

Orach is best used as a salad herb, but it can also be cooked with spinach or sorrel (it alleviates the acidity of the latter). The triangular leaves, particularly of red orach, make an attractive addition to the salad bowl, and an ornamental asset in the garden.

Fresh leaves
Green orach may have red-tinged stems; red orach has deep plum-coloured leaves and stems.

Sweet cicely
Myrrhis odorata

Sweet cicely is an under-rated herb, a natural sweetener with a fine flavour, and its leaves remain green and edible from early spring to late autumn. A hardy perennial indigenous to upland pastures from the far west of Europe to the Caucasus, it is long naturalized in northern Europe and is now cultivated in other temperate zones.

Culinary uses

The leaves and green seeds reduce the tartness of fruits such as gooseberries and rhubarb when cooked together, although the flavour of the herb itself is dissipated. Leaves and seeds add an anise note to fruit salads and cream cheese desserts, and sweetness and a hint of spice to cakes, breads, and fruit pies. Sweet cicely is a useful herb for savoury dishes too, but to retain the flavour it is best to add it at the end of the cooking time. Young leaf tips give a subtle flavour to green salads and cucumber, and to cream and yogurt sauces made to accompany fish or seafood. Chop leaves into omelettes and clear soups, and stir them into a purée of carrot, parsnip, or pumpkin to enhance the sweetness. Use leaves as a garnish for cheese, and flowers to decorate salads.

Fresh sprigs
By late spring the large, feathery plant bears sweetly scented, lacy, white flowers, followed by large, attractive seed heads.

TASTING NOTES
Sweet cicely has an attractive, musky aroma with notes of lovage and anise; the flavour tends more to anise with a hint of celery and a pleasing sweetness. The whole plant is aromatic. The unripe seeds have the strongest flavour and a nutty texture. The glossy, black, ripe seeds have less flavour and are fibrous and chewy.

PARTS USED
Fresh leaves, flowers, and green seeds. In the past, raw roots were added to salads or boiled and eaten as a vegetable.

BUYING / STORING
Plants are available from herb nurseries, and can also be grown from seed. The leaves will keep for 2–3 days in damp kitchen paper or a plastic bag in the refrigerator.

GROW YOUR OWN
Sweet cicely is easy to grow and prefers semi-shade. Cut back the whole plant after flowering to encourage new growth. Cut leaves between spring and autumn, flowers in spring, and green seeds in summer.

FLAVOUR PAIRINGS
Good with apricots, gooseberries, nectarines, peaches, rhubarb, strawberries, root vegetables; chicken, prawns, and scallops.
Combines well with chervil, chives, lemon balm, lemon verbena, mint, and vanilla.

TASTING NOTES

Pot marigolds have a sweet, resin-like aroma, French marigolds a distinctive muskiness with light citrus notes that reminds me of coriander seeds. Fresh marigold petals have a delicate, aromatic bitterness and earthy taste. The leaves are slightly peppery.

PARTS USED

Fresh and dried petals, fresh young leaves.

BUYING / STORING

Marigold petals can be dried in a low oven and then ground. Dried pot marigold petals can be bought from some herb and spice suppliers; dried marigold powder is less easily found. Store dried marigold petals and powder in airtight containers. The leaves of Mexican mint marigold will keep for a day or two in a plastic bag in the refrigerator.

GROW YOUR OWN

Marigolds thrive in any soil, but do best in a sunny position. Picking the flowers prolongs flowering, but if a plant goes to seed it will readily self-seed. Common and French marigolds are annuals. Mexican mint marigold is a perennial but should be taken indoors to overwinter in cool climates.

Marigold
Calendula officinalis and *Tagetes species*

Marigolds are used in many different ways. The dried, ground petals of pot marigold (*C. officinalis*) and French marigold (*T. patula*) are prized in the Georgian republic; in Mexico and the southern US, Mexican mint marigold (*T. lucida*) is used as a tarragon substitute; in Peru huacatay (*T. minuta*) is an essential flavouring; in Europe fresh petals are used as a garnish and in salads.

Pot marigold C. officinalis

This marigold is a long-lived annual with pale green, lance-shaped leaves and single or double flowers. The petals and young leaves should be used immediately after picking.

Dried petals
Dried pot marigold petals from Georgia have a sweet, musky aroma with hints of citrus peel.

Culinary uses

Apart from adding a lively note to salads, marigold petals have long been used to colour food and give it a slightly pungent flavour. Fresh petals can be added to cookies and small cakes, to custards, savoury butters, and soups. Dried petals were often used to adulterate saffron; they can be used as an inexpensive substitute for colouring rice.

In Georgia powdered petals are an essential flavouring, used in spice mixtures and with other aromatic staples – chillies, garlic, walnuts. Georgians prefer the French marigold, and the flavour blends particularly well with cinnamon and cloves. They call it Imeretian saffron after the province of Imereti, where the dried petals are highly appreciated.

Mint marigold leaves are used with other indigenous American foods – avocado, corn, squash, tomatoes – as well as with fish, chicken, and other foods that marry well with tarragon. They also combine well with melon, summer berries, and stone fruits.

Huacatay, also called black mint, is strongly aromatic with citrus and eucalypt notes and a bitter aftertaste. Black mint is hard to find fresh outside South America, though jars of black mint paste are available online. Widely used in Peruvian cuisine, often combined with ají amarillo (*p.247*), it flavours sauces, meats, and stews.

Mexican mint marigold *T. lucida*

The long, narrow leaves of Mexican mint marigold smell more of anise than mint, with light notes of hay and some spicy warmth. The plant's other English names, winter or Mexican tarragon, refer to its tarragon-like taste.

French marigold
T. patula

This marigold species is a bushy annual with divided, toothed leaves and flat single or frilly double flowers that vary in colour from yellow to deep orange.

TASTING NOTES

Sweet basil has a complex sweet, spicy aroma with notes of clove and anise. The flavour is warm, peppery, and clove-like with underlying mint and anise tones. Purple (opal) basil, bush basil, lettuce basil, and 'Ruffles' basils have rather similar flavours (*pp.31–33*).

PARTS USED

Fresh leaves; add buds from flower spikes to salads or use as a garnish.

BUYING / STORING

Most basil leaves bruise and wilt easily, so avoid bunches with drooping or blackened leaves. Store for 2–3 days in damp kitchen paper or a plastic bag in the refrigerator vegetable drawer. Thai basil (*p.35*) is more sturdy and will keep for 5–6 days. Sweet basil and Thai basil plants are sold in many supermarkets. Basil leaves will freeze well for up to 3 months; one of the best ways is to purée them with a little water or olive oil and freeze in ice-cube trays.

GROW YOUR OWN

Most basils are tender annuals. Basil grows easily from seed, and needs a sheltered, sunny position in rich, well-drained soil. In cool climates it prefers a greenhouse or a window sill. Delay flowering and encourage bushiness by pinching out the tops. Harvest until the first frost.

Basil

Ocimum species

Lightly brushing basil leaves releases an aroma that promises warmth and sunlight – in every Greek village the intoxicating fragrance of basil fills the air. Basil belongs to the mint family, as is clear from the minty, anise notes that accompany its sweetness. Native to tropical Asia, where it has been cultivated for 3,000 years, it is now grown almost everywhere where the climate is warm enough.

Sweet basil O. basilicum

Also called Genoese basil, this plant has large, bright green, silky leaves and small, white flowers. Good for all western cooking, it is the best basil for pesto, pistou, and tomato salads. It combines very well with garlic. One way to preserve the leaves is to put them in a jar with an airtight lid, layer lightly with salt, and cover with olive oil. Kept in the refrigerator, the leaves eventually blacken, but they flavour the oil beautifully.

Culinary uses

In western cooking basil is the natural companion of tomatoes, whether in salad, sauce, or soup. It is a good flavouring for poultry stuffings – combine softened butter with chopped basil, garlic, grated lemon rind, and a few breadcrumbs, then work the mixture under the skin of a chicken or chicken pieces before baking or pot-roasting. Use basil with fish and seafood, especially lobster and scallops, and with roast veal and lamb. It also has an affinity with raspberries. Opal basil makes a pretty, pale pink vinegar.

Sweet basil turns black when cooked in a tomato sauce or other acid medium, but retains its flavour. It quickly loses its aroma when cooked, so use it in a dish for depth of flavour, then stir in a little more to add fragrance when the cooking is finished. Basil leaves can be torn, or chopped or shredded with a knife, but cutting bruises them and they darken quickly.

FLAVOUR PAIRINGS

Essential to pesto and pistou.

Good with aubergines, haricot beans, beetroot, fresh white cheeses, courgettes, eggs, lemon, olives, pasta, peas, pizza, potatoes, rice, sweetcorn, tomatoes.

Combines well with capers, chives, coriander, garlic, marjoram, oregano, mint, parsley, rosemary, thyme.

Purple basil

O.b. var. *purpurascens*

This handsome plant, also called opal basil, has purple or almost black leaves and pink flowers. It is highly aromatic, with clear notes of mint and clove. Use with rice and grains and to add a splash of colour to salads.

Other basil varieties

There are many varieties of basil, some of them with names that indicate their aroma or appearance. All have the underlying sweet, warm, clove-anise aroma of sweet basil, but different aspects are dominant: a pungent warmth in 'Ruffles', a peppery note in bush basil, anise in lettuce basil. In Mediterranean cooking, basil's natural partners are garlic, olive oil, lemon, and tomato. The herb is best known as the key ingredient of Genoese pesto and the related pistou of the south of France.

O. b. 'Purple Ruffles'

'Purple Ruffles' is an ornamental plant with large, shiny, purple-maroon leaves with a ruffled edge and pink flowers. Its flavour is warm and liquorice-like. 'Green Ruffles' has big, lime-green leaves with a frilly edge and white flowers. Use both as sweet basil (p.30).

Bush basil O. b. var. *minimum*

Also called Greek basil, this makes a compact bush with small leaves, white flowers, and a peppery aroma. It is easy to grow in a pot. Use as sweet basil; add whole leaves to salads.

O. b. 'Cinnamon'

This variety is native to Mexico. The leaves are flushed purple and the flowers pink. It has a pronounced, sweet scent with clear cinnamon notes rising above hints of camphor. Serve it with bean and pulse dishes and with spicy, stir-fried vegetables.

O. 'African Blue'

This variety has become one of my favourite basils for its striking appearance and excellent flavour. The leaves are mottled green-purple, the flowers purple. It is strongly scented with peppery, clove, and mint notes and a hint of camphor in the background. Use it with rice, vegetables, and meats; it is very good in potato salad and makes an outstanding pesto. Unlike most basils, it is a perennial as long as it is kept frost free.

Lettuce basil

O. b. var. *crispum*

This basil has large, floppy, wrinkled leaves with a soft texture. It is excellent in salads, or chopped and mixed with diced tomato and extra virgin olive oil to make a pasta dressing. Lettuce basil is much prized in southern Italy.

Asian basils

Asian basils (many are *Ocimum basilicum* varieties) are as numerous as European basils, and herb nurseries now supply some of the common ones. Their flavours differ from those of western basils because of the different chemical constituents of the essential oils. The dominant aroma constituent of sweet basil (*p.30*) is linalool (floral) with some methyl chavicol (anise) and a little eugenol (clove), but in Asian basils methyl chavicol is dominant with some eugenol and a little camphor.

Culinary uses

Basil flavours Southeast Asian salads, stir-fried dishes, soups, and curries. It is added at the end of cooking so that the aromatic leaves balance the spices in the dish. It is also used in Thai green curry paste.

Good with beef, chicken, coconut milk, fish and seafood, noodles, pork, rice.

Combines well with chillies, coriander leaf and root, galangal, garlic, ginger, makrut lime, krachai, lemon grass, tamarind, turmeric.

Lemon basil *O. b. citriodorum*

This bushy, compact basil has a clean, lemon fragrance. In Indonesia, where it is called kemangie, it is fried with fish and seafood. Add it to salads, and scatter over poached scallops, grilled fish, or pork kebabs.

Holy basil *O. sanctum*

Holy basil, or bai gaprow, is intensely aromatic with a spicy, sweet pungency, hints of mint and camphor, and a touch of muskiness. If you can't find it, use sweet basil and a few mint leaves. The flavour is enhanced by cooking; when raw, the taste is slightly bitter. It is the essential ingredient in a Thai dish of stir-fried chicken with chillies and basil, and is extensively used in meat curries.

Lime basil *O. americanum*

This basil is similar to *O. b. citriodorum*, but the leaves are slightly darker and the aroma is decidedly of lime, not lemon. Use in salads and with fish and seafood.

Thai basil *O. b. horapa*

Thai bai horapa has a heady, sweet, peppery aroma backed by pronounced anise notes, and a warm, lingering, anise-liquorice flavour.

Liquorice basil *O. b. Anise*

This decorative plant, also called anise basil, has purple-veined leaves, reddish stalks, pink flower spikes, and an agreeable, anise-liquorice aroma. Use as Thai basil.

Thai lemon basil *O. canum*

Also called hairy basil, or bai manglak, this plant has an attractive lemon-camphor aroma and a peppery, lemony flavour. Thai cooks stir it into noodles or fish curry just before serving. The seeds are soaked and used in a coconut milk dessert and in cooling drinks. Sometimes sold as green holy basil.

TASTING NOTES

Bay has a sweet, balsamic aroma with notes of nutmeg and camphor and a cooling astringency. Fresh leaves are slightly bitter, but the bitterness fades if you keep them for a day or two. Fully dried leaves have a potent flavour and are best when recently dried.

PARTS USED

Fresh and dried leaves.

BUYING / STORING

Fresh leaves can be used from a tree, but are less bitter if kept until wilted. To dry fully, lay leaves flat in a dark, well-aired place until brittle. If stored in an airtight container, dried leaves keep their aroma and flavour for at least a year, but stale leaves have no flavour.

GROW YOUR OWN

Although bay does best in warm regions, it will survive in a sheltered, sunny position in cooler climates. It is a good container plant, which has the advantage that it can be moved indoors in very cold spells. In warm climates it produces small, yellow flowers in spring, followed by purple berries (which are not edible). Leaves can be picked throughout the year.

Bay
Laurus nobilis

The bay tree is native to the eastern Mediterranean, but has long been cultivated in northern Europe and the Americas. It came to symbolize wisdom and glory to the Greeks and Romans, who crowned kings, poets, Olympic champions, and victorious generals with wreaths of its glossy, leathery leaves. Although there are several varieties of bay, only *L. nobilis* is used in the kitchen.

Culinary uses

Bay leaves yield their flavour slowly, so they are useful in stocks, soups, stews, sauces, marinades, and pickles. Put a leaf or two on top of a homemade pâté or terrine before baking it; add bay to any fish stew or combine with lemon and fennel when filling the cavity of a fish to be baked; thread leaves onto kebabs (soak dried leaves in water first), or add them to a pilaf. Bay is always included in a bouquet garni, and to flavour the milk for béchamel sauce. It goes well with beans, lentils, and tomatoes, especially to flavour a tomato sauce.

The Turks use bay in steamed and slow-cooked lamb dishes; the Moroccans in chicken and

Fresh leaves
Fresh leaves need to be crushed or rubbed to release their aromatic compounds. Bay is indispensable in French and Mediterranean cooking.

lamb tagines; the French partner it with beef in Provençal daubes. Bay also gives a pleasant, unusual, spicy fragrance to custards and rice pudding and to poached fruit dishes. In Turkish spice bazaars, boxes of dried figs are often lined with bay leaves.

Two or three bay leaves flavour a dish for four to six people; if you put in too many, the flavour is too strong. Remove the leaves before serving. Note also that in India, parts of the Caribbean, and South America, leaves of other species may be called bay leaves.

FLAVOUR PAIRINGS

Essential to bouquets garnis, béchamel sauce.

Good with beef, chestnuts, chicken, citrus fruits, fish, game, haricot beans, lamb, lentils, rice, tomatoes.

Combines well with allspice, garlic, juniper, marjoram and oregano, parsley, sage, savory, thyme.

Bouquet garni

A bouquet garni is a bundle of herbs used to flavour slowly-cooked dishes. This one includes a few sprigs of thyme and parsley and a bay leaf (*recipes, p.266*).

Dried leaves

Dried bay leaves should remain a matt, sage green, and not turn yellow or brown. Crumble or grind the leaves only when you need them.

TASTING NOTES

All parts of the plant are aromatic. The leaves are slightly resinous with a sweet, orange-blossom note; they taste juniper-like and astringent. The berries are sweet with notes of juniper, allspice, and rosemary. The flowers are more delicately scented.

PARTS USED

Leaves, flowers, berries. Leaves, flowerbuds, and berries may be dried.

BUYING / STORING

Myrtle plants can be bought from specialist nurseries. Use leaves fresh from the plant or dry them in a dark, well-ventilated place until brittle, then keep in an airtight container. Dry buds and berries in the same way, and then store.

GROW YOUR OWN

Myrtle is a half-hardy, evergreen shrub with small, shiny, oval leaves, bearing scented, white flowers with pretty, yellow stamens in summer and purple-black fruits in autumn. In cool climates, a young myrtle plant is best grown in a container and taken indoors in winter. Once established it can be planted out in a sunny, sheltered site. If frost threatens, the plant may be protected with fleece. Myrtle leaves can be harvested throughout the year.

Myrtle

Myrtus communis

Myrtle is native to the hilly regions of the Mediterranean basin and the Middle East, where for centuries it has been used as a flavouring. Although mainland Europe came to prefer imported oriental spices, myrtle continued to be an important flavouring on the Mediterranean islands of Crete, Corsica, and Sardinia.

Culinary uses

Use myrtle flowers picked straight from the plant in salads or as a garnish. The leaves make a good flavouring for pork and wild boar, and for venison, hare, and pigeon. Use very sparingly and add towards the end of cooking if you are making a stew. Combine with thyme or savory to flavour meat and game, or with fennel to flavour fish. When barbecuing meat, add a few sprigs to the charcoal to impart a juniper-like flavour. Place myrtle berries and a clove of garlic in the cavity of pigeon or quail to be roasted or fried, or use them as you would juniper berries. Crush dried buds and berries and use as a spice.

Myrtle leaves are still used in southern Italy as a wrapping for small, newly made cheeses; as the cheeses cure, the leaves absorb their moisture, at the same time giving them a subtle flavour.

Fresh sprigs
Common myrtle is most frequently used, but the compact *M. c.* subsp. *tarentina*, native to Corsica and Sardinia where it is used with chicken and pork, has the same aromatic qualities.

Angelica
Angelica archangelica

A statuesque biennial – flower stalks may be over 2m (6½ft) high – angelica does best in cool climates and is hardy enough to grow in northern parts of Scandinavia and Russia. Although it needs a lot of space it is worth growing for its showy clump of bright green, serrated leaves and large domes of tiny, yellow-green flowers.

Culinary uses

Young stalks are candied. Young leaves and stalks may be used in marinades and poaching liquids for fish and seafood, or cooked as a vegetable – boiled or steamed angelica is very popular in Iceland and northerly parts of Scandinavia. Leaves may be added to salads, stuffings, sauces, and salsas.

Angelica's musky sweetness has a natural affinity with rhubarb for compotes, pies, and jams – use a handful of sliced young stalks or chopped leaves to 1kg (2¼lb) of rhubarb. Angelica can also be infused in milk or cream to make ice cream or custard.

Fresh leaves and stalks
Young stalks and leaves are best cut during the first summer or early the following spring.

TASTING NOTES

The whole plant is aromatic. When rubbed, young stalks and leaves have a sweet, musky scent; the taste is musky and bittersweet, slightly earthy, and warm, with notes of celery, anise, and juniper. The flowers have a honeyed fragrance.

PARTS USED

Young leaves and stalks. Essential oil, distilled from the seeds and roots, is used to flavour drinks such as vermouths and liqueurs.

BUYING / STORING

Fresh angelica is not available commercially, so it is necessary to grow your own. Young plants are available from some herb nurseries; it can also be grown from seed. Young stalks will keep in a plastic bag in the refrigerator for up to a week; leaves will wilt after 2–3 days.

GROW YOUR OWN

Angelica grows best in rich soil and partial shade. It produces long, tubular stalks in the first year, dies down in the winter, then comes back vigorously the following spring. Purple-tinged flower stalks rise up and open spectacular flower heads. These set to seed, after which the plant dies. The plant will self-seed easily.

FLAVOUR PAIRINGS

Good with almonds, apricots, hazelnuts, plums, rhubarb, strawberries; fish and seafood.
Combines well with anise, juniper, lavender, lemon balm, nutmeg, pepper, perilla.

TASTING NOTES

There are hundreds of varieties of scented geraniums, smelling of apple or citrus fruits, cinnamon, clove, nutmeg or mint, roses or pine. The best for cooking are rose- and lemon-scented plants.

 PARTS USED

Fresh leaves. Flowers have little fragrance, but make a pretty garnish for desserts. Although leaves retain their aroma when they die on the plant or are dried, they are not good for cooking.

 BUYING / STORING

Nurseries have a good supply of scented geraniums each spring. Cut leaves are quite sturdy and will keep in a plastic bag in the refrigerator vegetable drawer for 4–5 days. Flowers are best picked just before they are to be used.

 GROW YOUR OWN

Scented geraniums are tender perennials that will wither at the first frost, but they grow well in pots and can be taken indoors or put in a sheltered spot through the winter. You can also grow them indoors, in a conservatory or on a windowsill. Leaves can be cut throughout the summer and cuttings for propagation in early autumn.

Scented geranium
Pelargonium species

Scented geraniums offer a profusion of perfumes that echo the scents of other plants. The plants were carried to Europe from South Africa in the 17th century and had reached America by the 18th. Their commercial potential was realized in the mid-19th century when the French perfume industry found a way to use oil from rose-scented geraniums in place of imported and costly attar of roses.

Lemon geranium
P. crispum

This variety is a stiff plant with small, rough, crinkly leaves, lavender flowers, and a fresh, lemon scent.

Fresh leaves
Geranium leaves release their fragrance when they are brushed against or rubbed.

Culinary uses

Sugar scented with rose geranium leaves can be used for desserts and cakes. Bury a handful of the leaves in a jar of caster sugar and leave for two weeks. Remove the leaves before use.

Geranium leaf syrup can be used to make sorbets, to poach fruits, or diluted for a refreshing drink. Bring 250ml (9fl oz) water and 150g (5½oz) sugar to the boil, add 10–12 lightly crushed geranium leaves, remove from the heat, and leave to cool.

Strain and add 2 tbsp lemon juice for lemon-scented leaves, or 1 tbsp rose water for rose-scented ones. Store in an airtight jar in the refrigerator for a week or so. Use scented sugar when cooking blackberries or mixed berries for a summer pudding, or add a couple of leaves to the pan.

Macerate summer fruits in wine or syrup that contains a few geranium leaves. When making jam or jelly, add leaves for the last few minutes; rose geranium goes well with apples, blackberries, and raspberries; lemon geranium with peach, apricot, and plum. For ice creams, custards, and sauces, infuse 10–12 lightly crushed leaves in 500ml (16fl oz) heated cream or milk, cool, strain, and use.

Rose geranium leaves may be used to line the bottom of a cake tin before pouring in the batter; this gives a subtle flavour to a sponge cake or pound cake. Remove the leaves when the cake has cooled.

Rose geranium
P. graveolens

This variety is an upright plant with triangular, deep-cut leaves and small, pink flowers. The scent is a blend of rose and spice, reminiscent of Turkish delight.

P. 'Lady Plymouth'

This variegated variety has triangular, deep-cut leaves edged with cream, pink flowers, and a lemon-mint-rose scent.

TASTING NOTES

Lavender has a penetrating, sweetly floral, and spicy aroma with lemon and mint notes; the taste echoes the aroma with undertones of camphor and a touch of bitterness in the aftertaste. The flowers have the strongest fragrance, but leaves can also be used.

PARTS USED

Fresh and dried flowers; leaves.

BUYING / STORING

Lavender plants are widely available. Fresh lavender flowers and leaves will keep in a plastic bag in the refrigerator for up to a week. Dried lavender will keep for a year or more. To dry flowers, hang stalks in small bunches or spread on trays; when fully dry, rub the flowers from the stalks and store in an airtight container.

GROW YOUR OWN

Lavender needs an open, sunny position and well-drained soil, whether in the garden or a container. The flowers are best harvested just before they are fully open, when their essential oils are most potent. Harvest leaves at any time during the growing season.

FLAVOUR PAIRINGS

Good with blackberries, blueberries, cherries, damsons, mulberries, plums, rhubarb, strawberries; chicken, lamb, pheasant, rabbit.
Combines well with marjoram, oregano, parsley, perilla, savory, rosemary, thyme.

Lavender
Lavandula species

The sight of the deep purple-blue lavender fields shimmering in the heat as you travel down the Rhône valley is, for me, the first real indication of reaching the warm south. Native to the Mediterranean region, lavender became a popular garden plant in Tudor England. Today lavender is grown in many parts of the world for display, for the kitchen, and for its aromatic oils.

English lavender *L. angustifolia*

The grey-green foliage and lilac, purple, or white flowers of this hardy evergreen perennial make it one of the most attractive garden plants. Also called common lavender, it is the best lavender for the cook because of its lower camphor content.

Fresh leaves
Like rosemary, lavender has tough leaves that must be chopped finely; flowers also have a firm base, but petals can be plucked out.

Dried flowers

Soft, floral-scented, English lavender is no less prized for its oils than the intensely aromatic original lavender from the Mediterranean.

Culinary uses

Lavender is very potent and must be used sparingly. A few dried lavender flowers immersed in a jar of caster sugar for a week or so will give it a fine, sweet aroma. Alternatively grind fresh lavender flowers and sugar to a powder – this gives a stronger flavour since grinding breaks down the buds and the sugar absorbs the aromatic oils. Use the sugar for baking and desserts. Fresh flowers may be chopped and added to a cake, shortbread, or sweet pastry mixture before baking. Scatter petals over a cake or dessert to decorate it. Add flowers to a jam or jelly towards the end of the cooking time, or to fruit compotes for a sweetly spiced note. Infuse them in cream, milk, syrup, or wine to flavour sorbets and other desserts. Lavender ice cream is very good, or try adding lavender to chocolate ice cream or mousse. Lavender is successful with savoury dishes, too. Chop leaves for a salad or scatter flowers over the top. Add chopped flowers to rice. Use chopped flowers and leaves to flavour a leg of lamb, roast or casseroled rabbit, chicken, or pheasant. Add lavender to marinades and rubs. Lavender also makes an excellent vinegar. Around the Mediterranean lavender is used in herb mixtures. In Provence it is blended with thyme, savory, and rosemary; in Morocco it is sometimes used in ras el hanout.

French lavender *L. stoechas*

Also called Spanish lavender, this bushy shrub has narrow, green leaves and purple flowers topped by purple bracts. Some varieties are hardy, others are half-hardy and may survive the winter in a sheltered spot. *L. stoechas* has a more pungent camphor note than *L. angustifolia*.

Lavender *is grown commercially on a large scale, mainly to be distilled for its aromatic oils. Long neglected in the*

kitchen, the herb is slowly making a comeback as a versatile, unexpected flavouring in savoury and sweet dishes.

Woodruff

Galium odoratum

As its name suggests, woodlands are the natural habitat of this low, creeping, perennial herb. Native to Europe and western Asia, woodruff is now also found in temperate North America. Its pretty, star-like, white flowers and neat ruffs of narrow, shiny leaves make it a most attractive garden plant in spring.

Culinary uses

The pleasant aroma of woodruff is at its best when the herb has wilted. The principal traditional use of the herb is in the Waldmeisterbowle (Waldmeister is the German name for woodruff) or Maibowle. These are both names for a punch made to celebrate May Day (and other occasions too) using white wine, Sekt, sugar, mint, and lemon balm. Woodruff can also be infused in marinades for chicken and rabbit, in dressings for salads, in wine to make a sabayon or sorbet. Use only one or two stems and remove before serving or using the liquid. Woodruff flowers are decorative on salads.

Fresh leaves and flowers
Since woodruff contains coumarin, a substance that may cause liver damage if used in excess and is now thought to be carcinogenic, it should be used in very small amounts. Luckily just one or two stems will impart the herb's heady aroma.

 TASTING NOTES

The fresh plant has a faint scent, but cutting releases the smell of new-mown hay and vanillin. Flowers are more lightly scented than leaves; the flavour echoes the scent.

 PARTS USED

Leaves and flowers, whole stems.

 BUYING / STORING

Plants are available from garden centres and herb nurseries. Woodruff sprigs are best picked and kept for a day or two before using. The aroma strengthens when the leaves are wilted or dried, and the leaves keep their aroma when frozen. To freeze, spread the woodruff on a tray, and once frozen, store in a plastic bag in the freezer.

 GROW YOUR OWN

Woodruff can be grown from seed, although it is slow to germinate. Once established it spreads readily in shady areas. Leaves and flowers can be picked in spring and early summer; later in the year the fragrance is less pronounced.

 FLAVOUR PAIRINGS

Good with apples, melon, pears, strawberries.

Pandan

Pandanus amaryllifolius, P. tectorius

Pandan or screwpine species grow in the tropics from India to Southeast Asia, northern Australia, and the Pacific islands. The leaves of *P. amaryllifolius* are used as a flavouring and a wrapping for food. Kewra essence, a favourite flavouring of the Moghul emperors of India, is extracted from *P. tectorius* flowers.

Culinary uses

To use pandan leaves, pound or scrape them with the tines of a fork to release their flavour, then tie in a loose knot so that the fibres do not come loose.

Add a leaf or two to rice before cooking to give it a light fragrance, as they do in Malaysia and Singapore. Cooks there also use pandan leaf as a flavouring for pancakes, cakes, and creamy desserts made with sticky rice or tapioca. A knotted leaf is sometimes added to a soup or curry, and in Sri Lanka it adds its flavour to curry powder. Leaves are also used to wrap food. Thai cooks steam or fry parcels of pandan-wrapped chicken or weave leaves as containers for desserts.

Kewra essence is used in India to flavour pilafs and meat dishes as well as sweets and kulfi. It can be diluted with a little water and sprinkled into a dish just before serving. It also gives a special flavour to homemade lemonade.

Fresh leaves

Juice from the leaves is used for colouring food; to extract the juice, put 4–5 coarsely chopped leaves into a blender with a little water.

TASTING NOTES

Pandan leaf smells sweetly fresh and floral, lightly musky, with notes of new-mown grass. The taste is pleasantly grassy and floral. Leaves have to be bruised or cooked to release their flavour. Kewra essence has a sweet, delicate musk and rose aroma.

PARTS USED

Leaves, flowers.

BUYING / STORING

Fresh pandan leaves may be found in oriental shops. They keep well in a plastic bag in the refrigerator for 2–3 weeks. Neither frozen nor dried pandan can match fresh leaves for fragrance. Bottled leaf extract has an unnaturally bright colour and quickly loses what aroma it has. Pandan powder has a light grassiness that fades after a few months. Kewra essence or kewra water (essence mixed with water) will keep for 2–3 years if tightly closed and stored away from strong light.

HARVESTING

Pandan trees, with their shiny, sword-like leaves growing spirally around the trunk, can be seen in gardens throughout southern Asia. They grow easily, especially in damp areas. Leaves are harvested at any time; flowers are at their best soon after they open.

FLAVOUR PAIRINGS

Good with chicken, coconut, curried dishes, palm sugar, rice.
Combines well with chilli, coriander, galangal, ginger, makrut lime, lemon grass.

TASTING NOTES

The whole plant has a distinctive citrus aroma. The flavour is citrus with an added warm, spicy note. Flowers are more delicately flavoured than the leaves.

PARTS USED

Fresh and dried leaves; flowers. Dried leaves are used for infusions.

BUYING /STORING

Plants are available from herb nurseries and garden centres. Flowers and leaves wilt quickly and are best used soon after picking. They can be chopped and frozen. Spread leaves and flowers on trays to dry, or hang bunches of stalks in a dark, well-ventilated place. Store when dry in an airtight container. In North America dried bergamot can be bought as a herbal tea.

GROW YOUR OWN

A perennial of the mint family, bergamot thrives in most situations, but does best in a fertile, moisture-retaining soil, in sun or partial shade. Every 3 years, dig up the plant, discard the centre, and replant the young outer parts. Pick flowers when fully open, and leaves throughout the summer.

Bergamot

Monarda didyma

Native to North America, the *Monarda* genus is named for the 16th-century Spanish physician, Nicolas Monardes, whose *Joyfull Newes Out of the Newe Founde Worlde* was the first American herbal. The name bergamot probably derives from the similarity of the plant's aroma to that of the bergamot orange. Another name is bee balm, because the flowers attract bees.

Fresh leaves

All the cultivated varieties of bergamot, with their showy whorls of different coloured flowers and slightly different scents, can be used in the same way.

Culinary uses

Use only fresh, young leaves and flowers for cooking. Add shredded leaves and petals to green and fruit salads. Bergamot goes well with duck, chicken, and pork; it can be chopped into yogurt or cream for a sauce, or added to a salsa. Flowers are good in sandwiches with cream cheese and cucumber.

Bergamot is also known as Oswego tea – named for the Oswego valley near Lake Ontario, where Native Indian tribes made an infusion from it, a practice that was adopted by early European settlers. Try adding a few fresh or dried flowers or leaves to a pot of Indian tea, to jugs of home-made lemonade, or summer coolers for a lightly scented taste.

Bergamot salsa

A salsa of chopped bergamot leaves, parsley, and orange is delicious with pork kebabs or barbecued fish.

FLAVOUR PAIRINGS

Good with apples, chicken, citrus fruits, duck, kiwi fruit, melon, papaya, pork, strawberries, tomatoes.

Combines well with chives, cresses, dill, fennel, garlic, lemon balm, mint, parsley, rosemary, thyme.

OTHER BERGAMOTS

Wild bergamot *M. fistulosa*, also known as horsemint, is less handsome and has a stronger and coarser fragrance than cultivated varieties. Use sparingly. Another variety, *M. f.* var. *menthifolia*, resembles oregano in aroma and flavour and is sometimes used as a substitute for oregano in the southwest US.

TASTING NOTES

When crushed the young leaves have a fresh, lingering, lemon scent and a mild lemon-mint flavour. The aroma is subtle and pleasant, and not as penetrating as that of lemon verbena or lemon grass.

PARTS USED

Leaves, fresh and dried.

BUYING / STORING

Seeds and plants may be bought from herb nurseries. Fresh leaves will keep for 3–4 days in a plastic bag in the refrigerator vegetable drawer. To dry leaves, hang small bunches of stalks in a dark, airy place. Crumble the leaves when completely dry and store in an airtight container. Dried leaves should keep their flavour for 5–6 months.

GROW YOUR OWN

Lemon balm is easy to grow from seed or by dividing the root stock in spring or autumn. Cut back after flowering to encourage new growth. Balm grows vigorously and will spread unless kept in check: in a small garden it is best grown in a pot. Harvest leaves early in the season before they become rank.

FLAVOUR PAIRINGS

Good with apples, apricots, carrots, soft white cheeses, chicken, courgettes, eggs, figs, fish, melon, mushrooms, nectarines.

Combines well with bergamot, chervil, chives, dill, fennel, ginger, mint, nasturtium, parsley, sweet cicely.

Lemon balm
Melissa officinalis

Lemon balm is a perennial of the mint family, native to southern Europe and western Asia, and now cultivated widely in all temperate regions. With its crinkled, serrated leaves and tiny white or yellowish flowers, it is not a showy plant, but earns its place in the garden by attracting bees and by its agreeable lemon scent.

Culinary uses

Balm's principal use is as a soothing, calming tea, made from fresh or dried leaves. Fresh leaves can be infused in summer coolers or blended in smoothies. For cooking, the lemon-mint flavour of fresh leaves complements fish and poultry beautifully in sauces, stuffings, marinades, and salsas. Tear young leaves for green or tomato salads, or chop them to scatter over steamed or sautéed vegetables or into rice or cracked wheat. Balm makes a delicate herb butter and fragrant vinegar. The fresh flavour is good in fruit desserts and in creams and cakes. A strong balm tea, well sweetened, makes the basis for a good sorbet.

Fresh leaves
Always cook with fresh leaves, and use generous amounts because the aroma is delicate. The variegated form, *M. o.* 'Aurea', can also be used.

Vietnamese balm

Elsholtzia ciliata

Native to temperate eastern and central Asia, Vietnamese balm, or rau kinh gio'i, is a bushy plant with light green, serrated leaves and lavender flower spikes. It somewhat resembles lemon balm in aroma, but the plants are unrelated. It is cultivated in Germany more than in other regions of Europe, and in those parts of the US where there are large Vietnamese population centres. Stray plants also grow wild in parts of Europe and North America.

Culinary uses

Vietnamese balm is used to flavour vegetable, egg, and fish dishes, in soups and with noodles and rice. It may be added to the platter of herbs that accompanies many Vietnamese meals. In Thailand it is most frequently cooked and served as a vegetable.

Fresh leaves
Vietnamese balm has been used as a culinary and medicinal plant for many years in Southeast Asia, but as yet is little known to western cooks.

TASTING NOTES
Vietnamese balm has a clear, lemon aroma with floral undertones; the flavour is reminiscent of lemon balm, but is more concentrated, somewhat like lemon grass. If none is available, lemon balm and lemon grass can be combined as a substitute.

PARTS USED
Fresh leaves and young sprigs.

BUYING / STORING
Vietnamese balm is grown mostly by nurseries that supply herbs to Southeast Asian restaurants, and is sold by oriental shops, but it is not yet widely available in Europe or North America. Leaves keep for 3–4 days in a plastic bag in the refrigerator vegetable drawer.

GROW YOUR OWN
Vietnamese balm is a perennial, often grown as an annual. It can be grown from seed outdoors when the frosts are over, and is likely to become invasive in warm, moist conditions. Sprigs from an oriental shop can be encouraged to root by standing them in water. Cuttings taken in autumn will root and survive if kept in a warm place. Harvest leaves from spring to early autumn.

FLAVOUR PAIRINGS
Good with aubergines, lettuce, cucumber, mushrooms, spring onions, starfruit, fish, seafood.
Combines well with coriander, chillies, Asian basils, galangal, garlic, mint, perilla, tamarind.

TASTING NOTES

Lemon verbena has an intense, fresh lemon aroma. The taste echoes the aroma but is less strong; it is more lemony than a lemon, but lacks the tartness. Leaves keep their fragrance quite well when cooked. The aroma of dried leaves is retained for up to a year.

PARTS USED

Leaves, fresh and dried.

BUYING / STORING

Many herb nurseries stock plants. Cut leaves may be kept for a day or two in the refrigerator. Sprigs can also be put in a glass of water for 24 hours. Leaves can be chopped and frozen in small pots or in ice cubes. To dry, hang stalks in a dark, well-ventilated place. Dried leaves make an excellent tisane, often sold as verveine.

GROW YOUR OWN

Lemon verbena needs sun and well-drained soil. Leaves can be harvested throughout the growing season. Regular trimming will make the plant bushier, and it should be cut back in autumn to remove weak branches. It is not frost-hardy, so is best grown in a container and taken indoors in winter, when it will shed its leaves.

FLAVOUR PAIRINGS

Good with apricots, carrots, chicken, courgettes, fish, mushrooms, rice.

Combines well with basil, chillies, chives, coriander, lemon thyme, mint, garlic.

Lemon verbena
Aloysia citriodora

Lemon verbena is native to Chile and Argentina and was taken to Europe by the Spaniards and to North America by a New England sea captain in the 18th century. In France it was taken up by toilet-water manufacturers for its aromatic oils. Until 100 years ago it was widely grown as an ornamental garden plant; it certainly merits a place in any scented garden for its intoxicating, pure lemon fragrance.

Culinary uses

Lemon verbena is a natural companion to fish and poultry; put some sprigs into the cavity or chop and use in a stuffing or marinade. The vibrant, clean taste is also good with fatty meats such as pork and duck, in vegetable soup, and in a rice pilaf. Lemon verbena is used as a flavouring for desserts and drinks. Add sprigs to a syrup for poaching fruit, chop finely for a fruit salad or tart, or infuse in cream to make a fresh-scented ice cream. Koseret, *Lippia adoensis*, is similar to lemon verbena and widely used as a herb in Ethiopia.

Fresh sprigs

Add sprigs to iced tea or summer coolers, or make an infusion of fresh leaves. Lemon verbena makes one of the best and most refreshing of all tisanes.

Sassafras

Sassafras albidum

Sassafras is an aromatic, ornamental tree native to the eastern US, from Maine to Florida. Native Americans showed early settlers how to make tea from the bark, roots, or leaves. The French-speaking Canadians who went to Louisiana adopted a Choctaw method of using dried, ground sassafras leaves to flavour and thicken stews. The roots used to be one of the essential ingredients of root beer.

Culinary uses

Filé powder, or gumbo filé, made from dried, ground sassafras leaves, is only used in the cooking of Louisiana, but it is the key to the texture and flavour of many Cajun and Creole soups and stews. In particular, it is used in gumbo, a substantial, spicy soup made with a variety of vegetables, seafood, or meat and served with rice. The mucilaginous quality of filé helps thicken the dish, provided it is stirred in when the pan is removed from the heat; cooking makes filé tough and stringy, and ruins its texture. Some brands of filé powder contain other ground herbs, such as bay, oregano, sage, or thyme, in addition to ground sassafras leaf.

TASTING NOTES

Young leaves have an astringent, citrus-fennel aroma; the roots smell camphorous. Filé powder tastes sourish, rather like lemony sorrel with woody notes. Its flavour can be brought out by brief heating.

PARTS USED

Leaves and roots.

BUYING / STORING

It is best not to use fresh sassafras because in its natural form it contains safrole, a carcinogen. Root bark and leaves are now treated to remove safrole before they are sold or used commercially. Buy prepared filé powder, sassafras tea, or tea concentrate only if marked "safrole free". Filé powder will keep for 6 months, and sassafras tea for a year or more.

GROW YOUR OWN

Sassafras trees are mostly found in the wild. Only young specimens can be transplanted because established trees have long taproots, and so they are seldom offered for sale. Leaves for making commercial filé powder are harvested in spring, then dried and ground.

Dried leaves

The large leaves, which provide dramatic autumn colours, may have one, two, or three lobes, even on the same branch.

Filé powder

Filé powder is essential in creating the rich texture of Louisiana dishes. It also serves as a condiment to accompany them.

TASTING NOTES

Crushed leaves have a coriander and citrus aroma, sometimes with distinctive fishy notes. The flavour is sourish and astringent with similarities to rau ram and coriander but with fishy undertones; it is aptly known as fish plant and Vietnamese fish mint. Some plants smell rank, while others are pungent but pleasing. People either love or hate this herb.

PARTS USED

Fresh leaves.

BUYING / STORING

Plants are available from nurseries and garden centres. Crush leaves to smell them before buying. Leaves will keep for 2–3 days in a plastic bag in the vegetable drawer of the refrigerator.

GROW YOUR OWN

Houttuynia can be grown in damp soil or in shallow water at the edge of a pond or stream, but it is invasive. If you grow the variegated variety, plant it in a sunny spot to get the most vivid foliage. Harvest leaves from spring to autumn. With its heart-shaped leaves and small, white flowers it makes a pretty ground-cover plant.

FLAVOUR PAIRINGS

Combines well with chillies, cresses, galangal, garlic, ginger, lemon grass, mint.

Houttuynia
Houttuynia cordata

This perennial, water-loving plant is not appreciated as a herb by western cooks, but it is widely used in Southeast Asia. Native to Japan, houttuynia now grows wild across much of eastern Asia. The dark green-leaved variety is most commonly used for cooking, but you can use the striking cultivated variety *H. c.* 'Chameleon', which has green, red, pink, and yellow foliage. In Vietnam houttuynia is called rau diep ca; the name is anglicized to vap ca in the West.

Culinary uses

In Japan, houttuynia is used as a vegetable rather than a herb, and simmered with fish and pork dishes. In Vietnam, where it is very popular, it is chopped and steamed with fish and chicken. Leaves can also be shredded into a clear oriental soup. More often it is eaten raw, to accompany beef and duck, with raw vegetables to dip in fiery nam prik, or as a salad. Combine it with lettuce, mint, young nasturtium leaves and flowers. I have shredded it into stir-fried vegetable and seafood dishes and into fish soups. Coriander, rau ram, or culantro could be used instead.

Fresh leaves
Japanese houttuynia shows clear orange and coriander aromas, whereas Chinese houttuynia smells more rank. *H. c.* 'Chameleon' has multi-coloured leaves (right).

Rice paddy herb
Limnophilia aromatica

Rice paddy herb is native to tropical Asia. It is now available from nurseries in the US, but has yet to catch on in Europe. Brought to the US by Southeast Asian immigrants in the 1970s and 1980s, it is also known by its Vietnamese names, rau om and ngo om. It is readily available in Vietnamese neighbourhoods of US cities and deserves to be more widely known; its agreeable aroma should encourage experimentation.

Culinary uses

The Vietnamese are enthusiastic users of rice paddy herb. They chop it into vegetable and sour soups just before serving them, include it in fish dishes, and frequently add it to the platter of herbs provided with many Vietnamese meals. Rice paddy herb is often eaten with freshwater fish. In northern Thailand it is served with fermented fish and chilli sauce, and in curries made with coconut milk. Chop and use in a dressing for a bean or lentil dish, with grilled fish, or add to stir-fries at the last minute. Use fresh or heat briefly.

Fresh sprigs
This small, trailing herb is easily recognized by the whorls of three long leaves along the thick stem.

TASTING NOTES
Rice paddy herb has an attractive floral-citrus, musky aroma and flavour with a hint of the pungent earthiness of cumin. It is a fragrant, delicate herb.

PARTS USED
Fresh young shoots and leaves.

BUYING / STORING
Buy plants from nurseries. Keep stems for a few days in a plastic bag in the refrigerator vegetable drawer.

GROW YOUR OWN
A rather straggly plant, with long, mid-green leaves and lilac flowers, rau om grows wild in ponds throughout Southeast Asia, and is cultivated in flooded rice fields. It will grow in or at the edge of ponds, covered by just a few centimetres of water, and does well in sun or partial shade. It is a perennial but needs protection from frost. Leaves can be harvested throughout the growing season.

FLAVOUR PAIRINGS
Good with coconut milk, fish and seafood, lime juice, noodles, rice, shallots, green and root vegetables.
Combines well with chillies, coriander, lemon grass, galangal, tamarind.

TASTING NOTES

Sorrel has no aroma; the taste of garden sorrel ranges from refreshingly tangy and sharp to astringent, and large leaves may be slightly bitter. The texture is spinach-like. Buckler leaf sorrel has a milder, more lemony, and more succulent flavour.

PARTS USED

Fresh leaves.

BUYING / STORING

Sorrel is seldom seen in food stores because it wilts quickly and is best used within a day or two of picking. To freeze, remove stalks, steam leaves until wilted, or cook in a little butter and freeze in small pots. Using butter helps soften the drab colour of cooked sorrel.

GROW YOUR OWN

Garden sorrel grows best in rich, moist soil with partial, light shade. Buckler leaf prefers a drier, warmer spot. Both are hardy perennials that grow well from seed. Plants grow to sizeable clumps and can be divided in autumn. Sorrel runs to seed quickly, so remove the flower stalks to encourage leaf growth.

FLAVOUR PAIRINGS

Good with chicken, cucumber, eggs, fish (especially salmon), leeks, lentils, lettuce, mussels, pork, spinach, tomatoes, veal, watercress.

Combines well with borage, chervil, chives, dill, lovage, parsley, tarragon.

Sorrel

Rumex acetosa, R. scutatus

This member of the dock family grows wild in Europe and western Asia and is worth growing in the garden. Garden sorrel, *R. acetosa,* is the common variety; French or buckler leaf is more delicate; astringent *R. sanguineus* has slender leaves with striking veins. Sorrel has been appreciated for the tartness it imparts to rich foods since ancient times.

Culinary uses

Sorrel is high in vitamins A and C, and also in oxalic acid, which gives the herb its sour taste. It is best served in combination with other foods. It makes a good soup with potato or combined with spinach in green Ukrainian borscht, and a rich sauce for fish with butter, stock, and cream.

Garden sorrel R. acetosa

Sorrel leaves can be harvested from spring until the plant dies down in winter. The more you pick, the more prolifically they grow.

Agastache
Agastache species

The agastaches are handsome, hardy perennials of the mint family. Anise hyssop, *A. foeniculum*, native to North America and Korean mint, *A. rugosa*, native to east Asia are worth the cook's attention. Mexican giant hyssop, *A. mexicana*, grows wild in Mexico and is used to make an infusion.

Culinary uses

Anise hyssop and Korean mint can be used interchangeably in the kitchen. Widely used in teas or summer drinks, they can also be used in similar ways to anise. Use in marinades for fish and seafood, chop them into rice, or add to chicken or pork dishes. Their natural sweetness complements the sweetness in beetroot, carrots, squash, and sweet potatoes; they combine well with green beans, courgettes, and tomatoes. Use as a garnish, or stir in chopped leaves just before serving. A few leaves in a salad will add an elusive anise note; mix with other summery herbs to add to pancake batter or an omelette, or to make a herb sauce for pasta with olive oil, sautéed fresh breadcrumbs, and garlic. Agastaches are also good with summer fruits – apricots, blueberries, peaches, pears, plums, raspberries. To make agastache honey, fill a small jar with leaves and flowers, pour in warmed runny honey, cover, and leave for a month.

Anise hyssop
A. foeniculum

Anise hyssop, also called liquorice mint, is an upright, branched plant with grey-green, oval leaves tinged with purple. The showy, lilac flower spikes appear in late summer and attract bees.

Flowers
Anise hyssop smells of anise and its flowers resemble those of hyssop, but it is not related to either plant.

TASTING NOTES
Anise hyssop has a sweet, anise aroma and flavour; its natural sweetness underpins the anise elements. Korean mint smells of eucalypt and mint, but the taste resembles that of anise hyssop, with a lingering anise aftertaste.

PARTS USED
Fresh leaves; flowers for garnishes.

BUYING / STORING
Some specialist nurseries stock plants. Leaves are sturdy and keep in a plastic bag in the refrigerator vegetable drawer for 4–5 days. Leaves can be frozen, but are best used fresh. Dry leaves only to make infusions – otherwise don't bother.

GROW YOUR OWN
Anise hyssop and Korean mint prefer a sheltered, well-drained spot in full sun. Both can be grown from seed. After 2–3 years plants can be divided and replanted. If you leave some flowers to seed, agastaches will self-seed but the new plants come up quite late in the year. Harvest young leaves throughout the growing season. They are most aromatic just before the plant flowers.

FLAVOUR PAIRINGS
Good with green beans, root vegetables, courgettes, pumpkin, squash, tomatoes, berries, and stone fruits.
Combines well with basil, bergamot, chervil, marjoram, mint marigold, parsley, salad burnet, tarragon.

TASTING NOTES

Chervil is sweetly aromatic. The taste is subtle and soothing, with light anise notes and hints of parsley, caraway, and pepper.

 PARTS USED

Fresh leaves; flowers for garnish.

 BUYING / STORING

Chervil is not a herb for long keeping; in a plastic bag or in damp kitchen paper it will keep for 2–3 days in the vegetable drawer of the refrigerator. You may find a pot of chervil in the supermarket in spring. Chopped and frozen in small containers it will keep for 3–4 months. Chervil butter can be frozen. Dried chervil has almost no flavour and is not worth buying.

 GROW YOUR OWN

Chervil is easy to grow from seed and prefers rich, moist soil in semi-shade. Sow seeds where you want it to grow because chervil doesn't like to be transplanted. It does best in cool temperatures; in summer, plant it between taller plants that will provide shade. Old leaves turn pink or yellow and no longer have a fresh flavour. Sow the first batch of seeds towards the end of winter, and sow every 3–4 weeks to ensure a continuing supply.

Chervil
Anthriscus cerefolium

Native to southern Russia, the Caucasus, and southeastern Europe, chervil was probably introduced to northern Europe by the Romans. A traditional symbol of new life, the arrival of chervil in markets signals springtime, when chervil sauces and soups appear on menus in France, Germany, and Holland. Often seen in restaurants as a garnish, chervil deserves to be more widely used in domestic cooking.

Fresh leaves
Chervil grows quickly and can be harvested 6–8 weeks after sowing, but its lifespan is short – once it flowers it is of no use in the kitchen. Be rigorous about cutting out flower stems and harvest frequently, cutting outer leaves first to encourage new growth at the centre of the plant.

Culinary uses

Chervil is one of the indispensable herbs of French cooking: in classic fines herbes it is combined with chives, parsley, and tarragon. Fines herbes, or chervil alone, stirred into eggs make an excellent omelette or scrambled egg dish. In Holland and Belgium there is a long tradition of making chervil soup, either based on potato and shallot or in a richer version that uses cream and egg yolks.

Chervil is delicious in consommés, and gives a delicate flavour to vinaigrettes and butter or cream sauces to serve with fish, poultry, and vegetables. It is a great addition to salads; try it in a warm potato salad or a beetroot salad with shallots or chives. Chervil is sometimes used with tarragon in béarnaise sauce, and its flavour can usually be detected in Frankfurt green sauce. A small amount of chervil brings out the flavour of other herbs, but you can use it lavishly on its own. Scatter it prolifically over vegetables, and if you are using it in a hot dish, stir it in when the cooking is at an end, because the aroma and flavour quickly dissipate with heat.

Curly chervil, *A. c. crispum*, has the same properties as the flat-leafed variety.

FLAVOUR PAIRINGS

Essential to fines herbes.

Good with asparagus, broad beans, green beans, beetroot, carrots, cream cheese, eggs, fennel, fish and seafood, lettuce, mushrooms, peas, potatoes, poultry, tomatoes, veal.

Combines well with basil, chives, cresses, dill, hyssop, lemon thyme, mint, mustard, parsley, salad burnet, tarragon.

Fines herbes

This classic French flavouring for egg, fish, and poultry dishes is a combination of chervil, chives, parsley, and tarragon (*recipe, p.266*).

TASTING NOTES

The leaves are sweetly aromatic, with hints of pine, anise, or liquorice; the flavour is strong yet subtle, with spicy anise and basil notes and a sweetish aftertaste. Long-cooking diminishes the aroma but the flavour is not lost.

PARTS USED

Fresh leaves and sprigs.

BUYING / STORING

Supermarkets sometimes have pots of tarragon, but otherwise sell sprigs in minute quantities, so it is a good idea to grow your own. Avoid the Russian variety when buying plants. Young sprigs keep for 4–5 days in a plastic bag in the vegetable drawer of the refrigerator. To dry stalks, hang in bundles in an airy, dark space, but they lose much of their aroma; freezing the leaves, whole or chopped, retains more of the flavour.

GROW YOUR OWN

French tarragon can be propagated by cuttings or in spring by division of the brittle, white rhizomes – do this every 3 years to preserve the flavour of the plant. The more vigorous Russian tarragon will grow from seed. Tarragon needs a rich, dry soil and much sun. Until well established, the roots of French tarragon may need some protection from hard frost.

Tarragon
Artemisia dracunculus

Native to Siberia and western Asia, tarragon was unknown to Europe until the Arabs introduced it when they ruled Spain. During the 16th and 17th centuries, the development of classic French cooking extended its use in the kitchen. Indeed, the best cultivated variety is usually called French tarragon (or, in Germany, German tarragon) to distinguish it from the inferior Russian variety.

French tarragon A. d. var. *sativa*

This tarragon has mid-green leaves and is the preferred culinary variety. The leaves can be harvested when required, and whole stalks removed for drying in mid summer.

Culinary uses

Tarragon is an essential ingredient in French cooking, with fish, poultry, and egg dishes. Used discreetly, it lends a pleasant, deep note to green salads. It is very good in marinades for meat and game, or to flavour goat's cheeses and feta preserved in olive oil. Whole stalks can be used under fish or with roast chicken and rabbit – "tarragon chicken" appears in nearly every cook's repertoire.

Tarragon makes one of the most versatile of herb vinegars and is often used in mustards and butters. It adds a fresh, herbal fragrance to mushrooms, artichokes, and ragouts of summer vegetables; with tomatoes it is almost as good as basil. Use tarragon in moderation and it will enhance the flavour of other herbs.

Bouquet garni for fish

Intended to be added to the liquid of slowly-cooked fish dishes, this bouquet garni comprises tarragon, thyme, parsley, and a strip of lemon peel (*recipes, p.266*).

FLAVOUR PAIRINGS

Essential to fines herbes and similar herb mixtures, to béarnaise, ravigote, and tartare sauces.

Good with artichokes, asparagus, courgettes, eggs, fish and seafood, potatoes, poultry, salsify, tomatoes.

Combines well with basil, bay, capers, chervil, chives, dill, parsley, salad herbs.

OTHER TARRAGONS

Russian tarragon, *A. d.* var. *inodora*, or sometimes *A. dracunculoides*, is lighter in colour, more coarse in appearance, and has a bitter taste. It is best avoided. When buying a tarragon plant, check that the label says French tarragon; if the type of tarragon is not specified, it may be the Russian variety.

Mexican tarragon, *Tagetes lucida*, is actually a species of marigold (*p.29*); its flavour is similar to that of tarragon but with a more pronounced liquorice note.

TASTING NOTES

Dill leaves have a clean, fragrant aroma of anise and lemon. The taste is of anise and parsley, mild but sustained. The seeds smell like a sweet caraway due to carvone in the essential oil; the taste is of anise with a touch of sharpness and a lingering warmth.

PARTS USED

Fresh and dried leaves; seeds.

BUYING / STORING

Choose a bunch that looks crisp and fresh. If you have a large quantity, use it quickly; after 2–3 days, kept in a plastic bag in the refrigerator, it will droop. You may be able to buy a plant in a supermarket or from a greengrocer. Dried dill stored in an airtight container will keep its flavour for up to a year. Similarly stored seed has a shelf life of 2 years. Ground dill seed does not keep.

GROW YOUR OWN

Dill is easy to grow from seed. Sow in a sheltered, sunny spot with well-drained soil in spring, and water well. Successive sowings provide plants throughout the season. Dill seedlings are frail, so make sure the ground is weed-free. Flower heads left to ripen will readily self-seed. Do not transplant; the long tap root is easily damaged. Avoid planting dill and fennel close to each other or they will cross pollinate and create hybrids.

Dill

Anethum graveolens

An annual plant, native to southern Russia, western Asia, and the eastern Mediterranean, dill is widely grown for its feathery leaves (often called dill weed) and its seed. Indian dill, *A. g.* subsp. *sowa*, is grown primarily for its seed, which is lighter in colour, longer, and narrower than European dill seed and has a more pungent taste. It is preferred for curry mixtures.

Culinary uses

Fresh dill is an excellent partner for fish and seafood. Scandinavian dishes include herrings marinated with dill, gravad lax (salmon cured with salt and dill and served with a mustard and dill sauce), and crab, scallops, or prawns with a creamy dill sauce.

In northern and central Europe, dill is used with root vegetables, cabbage, cauliflower, and cucumber. Some Russian cooks use it in borscht, their classic beetroot soup, and dill combined with soured cream or yogurt and a little mustard also makes a good

Fronds
The feathery fronds of *A. graveolens* resemble fennel, although the dill plant is much smaller.

Fresh leaves
Freezing preserves the flavour of dill better than drying. Freeze the stems whole in a plastic bag and cut off sprigs when needed. Add dill leaves at the end of cooking because they lose their flavour if overheated.

sauce for beetroot. German cooks make a similar sauce, but replace the mustard with horseradish and serve it with braised beef. In Greece, dill is added to stuffed vine leaves. In Turkey and Iran, dill flavours rice, broad beans, courgettes, and celeriac. Spinach with dill and shallots is a standard Iranian dish, echoed in a lentil and spinach dish of northern India that uses both dill leaves and seeds. Don't forget dill for salads and salad dressings, especially for potato salad.

Both leaves and seeds are used in pickling, as in the crunchy dill-pickled cucumbers of a New York deli and the garlicky version popular in Poland, Russia, and Iran. Seeds are added to breads and cakes in Scandinavia, where they are also used to flavour vinegar. In India, seeds and leaves are used in curry powders and masalas.

FLAVOUR PAIRINGS

Leaves good with beetroot, broad beans, carrots, celeriac, courgettes, cucumber, eggs, fish and seafood, potatoes, rice, spinach.

Leaves combine well with basil, capers, garlic, mustard, horseradish, paprika, parsley.

Seeds good with cabbage, onion, potatoes, pumpkin, vinegar.

Seeds combine well with chilli, coriander seed, cumin, garlic, ginger, mustard seed, turmeric.

Drying leaves
Dill leaves can be dried, either by spreading them on a cloth and leaving in a dark, warm, well-ventilated place for a few days, or in the microwave. Dried leaves retain some of the aroma and flavour of the fresh plant.

Seeds
The seeds are oval and flattish with five ribs, two of which form a broader rim. They are extremely light: 10,000 weigh only about 25g (scant 1oz). Harvest seeds when they are light brown and fully formed; put seed heads in a large paper bag and leave in a warm place until dry. When they have dried, rub the seed heads between the hands to separate seeds from husks. Use the seeds for slow-cooked foods.

TASTING NOTES

The whole plant has a warm, anise-liquorice aroma. The taste is similar: pleasantly fresh, slightly sweet, with a hint of camphor. Fennel seed is less pungent than dill, and more astringent than anise.

 PARTS USED

Young leaves, flowers, pollen, stalks, seeds.

 BUYING / STORING

Leaves will keep in a plastic bag in the refrigerator for 2–3 days. Stalks can be used fresh or tied in bundles and hung up to dry; store in an airtight container and use within 6 months. Seeds will keep for up to 2 years when stored in an airtight container. Wild fennel pollen, an intensely flavoured, golden-green dust, can be bought via the internet.

🌿 GROW YOUR OWN

Fennel will grow in most conditions, but prefers a well-drained, sunny site. It grows to 1.5m (5ft) or more. Plants will self-seed very prolifically. Don't grow fennel near dill or they will cross-pollinate and produce hybrids. When the seed is yellowy green, cut off the seed heads, place them in a large paper bag, and keep in an airy, warm place until quite dry; then shake the seeds loose. Fennel plants should be replaced every 3–4 years.

Fennel

Foeniculum vulgare

This tall, hardy, graceful perennial, indigenous to the Mediterranean and now naturalized in many parts of the world, is one of the oldest cultivated plants. The Romans enjoyed fennel shoots as a vegetable; the Chinese and Indians valued fennel as a condiment and digestive aid. Today in India fennel water is used to treat colic in babies. The herb should not be confused with the bulbous sweet or Florence fennel, *F. v.* var. *dulce*, which is eaten as a vegetable.

Green fennel *F. vulgare*

Green fennel is a tall, stately plant with tangled, feathery foliage. All parts of the fennel plant are edible; the roots are no longer eaten, but the leaves, stalks, and fruits (seed) are esteemed as flavourings. Fennel's anise character derives from anethole, the main constituent of its essential oil, which is most concentrated in the seed.

Stalks

Stalks have a mild flavour that keeps well when they are dried.

Culinary uses

In spring, fennel gives a fresh, lively note to salads and sauces. Later in the season a garnish of flowers or a sprinkling of pollen gives an anise fragrance to cold soups, chowders, and grilled fish.

Fennel is an excellent foil for oily fish. The Sicilians use it liberally in their pasta with sardines. In Provence whole red mullet, bass, and bream are baked or grilled on a bed of fresh or dried fennel stalks, which imparts a delicate flavour.

Pollen gives a more heady flavour to fish, seafood, grilled vegetables, pork chops, and Italian breads.

Fennel seed can be added to pickles, soups, and breads; try combining ground fennel and nigella to flavour bread, as is done in Iraq. In Greece, leaves or seeds are combined with feta cheese and olives to make a well flavoured bread. Fennel seeds flavour sauerkraut in Alsace and Germany, and Italians use them with roast pork and in finocchiona, the renowned salami of Florence.

Fennel seed is one of the constituents of five spice powder, the principal Chinese spice blend used mostly with meat and poultry. Bengal in northeast India also has a five spice mixture, panch phoron, with fennel as an ingredient; the mixture is used with vegetables, beans, and lentils. Elsewhere in the Indian subcontinent fennel appears in garam masala, in spiced gravies for vegetables or lamb, and in some sweet dishes. Indians also chew fennel after a meal as a breath freshener and digestive aid.

FLAVOUR PAIRINGS

Essential to Chinese five spice powder and panch phoron.

Good with beans, beetroot, cabbage, cucumber, duck, fish and seafood, leeks, lentils, pork, potatoes, rice, tomatoes.

Combines well with chervil, cinnamon, cumin, fenugreek, lemon balm, mint, nigella, parsley, Sichuan pepper, thyme.

Bronze fennel *F. v. 'Purpureum'*

This is a less vigorous plant than green fennel and has a milder aroma and flavour.

Seeds

Fennel seed has a stronger flavour than the leaves and a bittersweet aftertaste. Dry-roasting the seed brings out the sweetness. Seed colour varies from light brown to greenish-yellow – the latter is the best quality. Store seeds and grind them as needed.

Leaves

Only young fennel leaves are suitable for use in the kitchen. They have a mild taste and are best used soon after picking.

TASTING NOTES

Spearmint is mellow and refreshing, with a sweet-sharp, pleasantly pungent flavour backed by hints of lemon. Peppermint has pronounced menthol notes and a fiery bite, yet is also slightly sweet, tangy, and spicy with a fresh, cool aftertaste.

 PARTS USED

Leaves, fresh and dried; flowers for salads and garnishes.

 BUYING / STORING

Supermarkets sell pots of spearmint and bunches will keep for 2 days in a glass of water in the kitchen, or in the refrigerator. Leaves can be chopped and frozen in small containers or mixed with a little water or oil and frozen in ice-cube trays. Mint dries well; pick before flowering and hang bunches in a dry, airy place, or dry stalks in a low oven or microwave. Store dried mint in an airtight container.

 GROW YOUR OWN

Mints are perennial plants and are easy to grow. They prefer a temperate climate, partial shade or full sun, and need plenty of water. They have a spreading habit, so unless you have space for mint to run wild it is best to grow it in a pot. Otherwise, plant in a large, bottomless pot or bucket.

Mint

Mentha species

One of the most popular flavours in the world, mint is at once cooling and warming, with a sweet fragrance. Native to southern Europe and the Mediterranean, mints have long naturalized throughout the temperate world. They hybridize easily, leading to some confusion in their naming, but for the cook they broadly divide into two groups: spearmint and peppermint (*pp.68–69*).

Fresh leaves

The most widely grown mint, spearmint or garden mint (*M. spicata*), has pointed leaves and bears lilac flowers in late summer. This mint and its cultivated varieties suit all recipes calling for mint. Leaves can be picked thoughout the growing season but are best harvested shortly before flowering, when the essential oils are at their strongest. The aroma of mints is due to menthol, which also leaves cooling and mild numbing sensations in the mouth.

Culinary uses

Mint has many uses worldwide. Fresh and dried mints are not usually used interchangeably in recipes.

FRESH MINT

Western cooks use mint to flavour aubergines, carrots, courgettes, peas, potatoes, and tomatoes. Mint goes well with chicken, pork, veal, and the traditional spring lamb, whether as a marinade, mint jelly, mint sauce, or a salsa. Sauce paloise (a béarnaise sauce made with mint instead of tarragon) is a good accompaniment to grilled fish and chicken.

In the Middle East, mint is essential to tabbouleh and is part of the bowl of fresh herbs and salad vegetables that accompanies mezze. In Vietnam, it is added to salads and to platters of herbs that accompany spring rolls. Mint also finds its way into Southeast Asian dipping sauces, sambals, and curries. The cooling notes of mint make it the perfect herb for chilled Iranian yogurt and cucumber soup, and the Indians emphasize its refreshing qualities in chutneys and raitas. Indian cooks also use the freshness of mint to counter the warmth of spices in vegetable and meat dishes. In much of South America, mint is combined with chillies, parsley, and oregano as a flavouring for slow-cooked dishes; Mexicans use a little with meatballs and chicken.

Mint's refreshing effect enhances fruit salads, fruit punches, and, of course, Pimm's and mint julep. It makes a surprisingly good iced parfait, and minty notes are a welcome addition to several kinds of chocolate desserts and cakes.

DRIED MINT

Around the eastern Mediterranean and in the Arab countries, dried mint is often preferred to fresh. In Greece, dried mint, sometimes with oregano and cinnamon, seasons keftedes (meatballs) and the filling for vine leaves; the Cypriots use it for their Easter cheesecakes, called flaounes. Cacik, the Turkish cucumber and yogurt salad, is best with dried mint. A teaspoon of dried mint, quickly fried in a little olive oil or clarified butter and added just before serving, imparts a fine, lively aroma to some Turkish and Iranian dishes. Try it with lentil and bean soups, and lamb or vegetable stews.

DRIED LEAVES
Spearmint is the dried mint most commonly found commercially. The aroma is pungent and concentrated but lacks the sweetness of fresh.

FLAVOUR PAIRINGS

Essential to sauce paloise and mint sauce.
Good with root vegetables, tomatoes, aubergines, lamb, courgettes, cucumber, yogurt, dark chocolate.
Combines well with basil, cardamom, cloves, cumin, dill, fenugreek, ginger, marjoram and oregano, paprika, parsley, pepper, sumac, thyme.

Other mint varieties

Spearmint and its relatives are the most important mints for the cook. Peppermint and its related varieties are too pungent for most culinary uses and are used primarily to flavour confectionery and toothpaste. Fresh or dried, mint has long been prized for its digestive properties, which helps explain its popularity in the yogurt drinks of Turkey, Iran, and India; sweet Moroccan mint tea served in small glasses; or French infusions of mint, or lime flowers and mint (tilleul-menthe).

Moroccan mint *M. s. 'Moroccan'*

This mint has bright green leaves and white flowers. It is prized for its fine, spicy aroma and is less sweet than spearmint. It is used in tea and for all minted dishes.

Bowles' mint

M. x villosa f. *alopecuroides*

This mint has soft, furry, round leaves and spikes of lilac flowers. It wilts rapidly after cutting. It has a fine flavour but the leaves should be chopped finely to eliminate the furry texture. Use for all dishes requiring mint.

Apple mint *M. suaveolens*

Apple mint has wrinkled leaves, and the whole plant is downy. Dense flower spikes are pale pink. The plant smells subtly of mint combined with ripe apple and has a good flavour. The leaves have an unattractive texture and are best shredded.

OTHER MINTS

Peppermint *M. x piperita* This mint is a hybrid of spearmint and water mint. A vigorous plant with tall stems and long, green, slightly hairy leaves. Rather strident and pungent. Use sparingly for desserts, cooling drinks, and fresh or dried for teas. Grown commercially for its oil.

Tashkent mint *M. s.* 'Tashkent' This cultivated variety has large leaves and deep pink flowers. It has an intense aroma and flavour. Use as spearmint.

Pineapple mint *M. s.* 'Variegata' Smaller than apple mint, this mint has light green leaves edged with cream. Young leaves have a tropical fruit aroma; older leaves are more minty. Use young leaves to flavour salads, cool drinks, and fruit desserts.

Basil mint *M. x piperita citrata* 'Basil' The leaves of this mint are dark green with a purple tinge; they have a spicy scent with light notes of basil. Good for aubergines, courgettes, and tomatoes.

Field mint, corn mint *M. arvensis* This mint has downy, grey-green leaves and whorls of pink flowers on the stem. Pungently aromatic but fairly mild in flavour, it is often used in Southeast Asian cooking. It has a high menthol content.

Pennyroyal *M. pulegium* There are upright and creeping varieties of this plant. It smells very strongly of peppermint and has an intense, bitter flavour. I recommend using it with caution.

Chocolate mint *M. x piperita citrata* 'Chocolate'

This mint has dark green to purple leaves and a scent of after-dinner chocolate mints. Good for chocolate desserts and as a garnish for ice creams and sorbets.

Black peppermint *M. x piperita piperita*

This hybrid mint has deep purple stalks, dark green leaves tinged with purple, and a fine if pungent aroma. Use as peppermint.

Mountain mint *Pycnanthemum pilosa*

This graceful plant is not a true mint, but young leaves and buds can be used as a mint substitute. Native to the eastern US, it smells and tastes of mint but is more bitter.

TASTING NOTES
The whole plant smells warm and minty with notes of thyme and camphor; the taste is pleasantly pungent, warm, minty, and peppery with a light bitterness in the aftertaste. Lesser calamint has a stronger odour and flavour than large-flowered calamint.

 PARTS USED

Leaves and sprigs; flowers for garnishes and salads.

 BUYING / STORING

Calamint is not available as a cut herb, but specialist nurseries stock plants. In North America calamint is often available under the name nepitella. Sprigs will be good for 1–2 days if kept in a plastic bag in the refrigerator. Tie stalks in bundles to dry and hang in a well-ventilated place.

 GROW YOUR OWN

Calamint prefers a chalky, well-drained soil and full sun, although it will tolerate partial shade. It can be propagated by division or grown from seed. Large-flowered calamint makes a handsome garden plant; all are attractive to bees. Leaves may be harvested from spring to late summer.

 FLAVOUR PAIRINGS

Good with aubergines, beans, fish, green vegetables, lentils, mushrooms, pork, potatoes, rabbit.
Combines well with bay, chilli, garlic, mint, myrtle, oregano, parsley, pepper, sage, thyme.

Calamint
Calamintha species

These aromatic, perennial plants deserve to be better known. For the cook, lesser calamint, *C. nepeta*, also called nepitella or mountain balm, is the most rewarding. Common calamint, *C. sylvatica*, is less fragrant but can be used in the same way. Large-flowered calamint, *C. grandiflora*, is a showy garden plant and the leaves are used for infusions. The calamints are related to savory.

Culinary uses

Lesser calamint is a favourite flavouring in Sicily and Sardinia; also in Tuscany, where it is popular with vegetables and especially in mushroom dishes. The Turks use it as a mild form of mint. It is good with roasts, stews, game, and grilled fish; in stuffings for vegetables and meat; and in marinades and sauces. Fresh leaves are best for cooking; dried are used for infusions. Large-flowered calamint has big, slightly floppy leaves.

Fresh sprigs
Lesser calamint is a bushy plant with downy, greyish foliage. It bears small, lilac or white flowers throughout the summer.

Catnip
Nepeta cataria

The names catnip and catmint are used interchangeably, and catmint is also used for some of the ornamental species of Nepeta. Native to the Caucasus and southern Europe, this attractive plant is now widely cultivated in many temperate regions, as well as being found in the wild. The mint-like odour induces a state of bliss in cats, but only if the leaves have been bruised and the aroma released.

Culinary uses

Catnip was a more important culinary herb in the past than it is today, although it is still used in Italy in salads, soups, egg dishes, and stuffings for vegetables. A few of the sharply flavoured leaves certainly give zest to a green or mixed herb salad. The robust flavour also goes well with fatty meats like duck and pork. It is widely used as a herbal tea.

Fresh sprigs
Catnip's grey-green, heart-shaped leaves are covered by a white down; the flowers are white to lavender, dotted with red spots.

TASTING NOTES
When bruised, catnip leaves release a sweet, minty, camphorous aroma; the taste is also pungently mint-like with an acrid, bitter note. Use sparingly.

PARTS USED
Leaves and sprigs.

BUYING / STORING
Plants are available from garden centres and specialist nurseries. Sprigs will keep for a day or two in a plastic bag in the vegetable drawer of the refrigerator.

GROW YOUR OWN
Catnip is a hardy perennial that is easy to grow from seed, and left to seed, it self-seeds readily. It grows best in partial shade and needs very little attention. It is as attractive to bees as it is to cats. Leaves can be harvested throughout the spring and summer.

TASTING NOTES

Raw, dried garlic is pungent and hot; "wet" garlic is milder. The disulphate allicin is formed when raw garlic is cut, and this accounts for the smell that raw garlic leaves on the breath. Cooking garlic degrades the allicin but forms other disulphates that have less odour. Black garlic was first used in Korean cooking and in recent years it has become popular in the West. The heads are gently heated for several weeks to achieve a blackened appearance. The slow-heating caramelizes the garlic, the flesh is soft, almost jellied and the flavour is mellow, balsamic, and slightly nutty. Use as fresh garlic.

 PARTS USED

Bulbs.

 BUYING / STORING

Garlic is available all year round. Choose unbruised, firm heads without signs of mould or sprouting. If your garlic is sprouting, remove the indigestible green shoots. Store garlic in a cool, dry place. Dehydrated garlic flakes, granules, and powder are available. Garlic paste can be had frozen, in tubes. Smoked garlic is chic but not especially useful.

Garlic
Allium sativum

Garlic is native to the steppes of central Asia and spread first to the Middle East. It was one of the earliest cultivated herbs, but its early use was mainly medical and magical – except in ancient Egypt where it was eaten in quantity. When the first English settlers took it to America it was still regarded as a medicinal herb. Today it is recognized for lowering blood pressure and cholesterol, but its culinary use has become vastly more important.

Fresh heads
At the beginning of the growing season, heads of new "wet" garlic are succulent and mild and have a soft, thick, white skin.

Culinary uses

If crushed with the flat blade of a heavy knife, dried garlic cloves are easy to peel. Once peeled, garlic is easily pounded in a mortar. Avoid garlic presses because they can make the taste unpleasantly acrid.

Garlic can be used to enhance the flavour of many foods. Whole cloves cooked slowly have a mellow, nutty taste; cut garlic is more pungent, even when cooked. Similarly, a whole clove gently sautéed in oil and then removed will leave a delicate flavour: a crushed clove leaves a much stronger one. Never let garlic burn or it develops a bitter, acrid taste. Garlic roasted whole can accompany new potatoes or root vegetables. In European cooking, garlic is roasted with chicken or lamb; braised in wine; puréed, blanched, or sautéed. Young, "wet" garlic can be used in summer vegetable stews without peeling. In Spain, young garlic shoots are fried for tapas. Raw garlic flavours salads, is rubbed over bread with tomato and oil, and is pounded with egg yolks and oil to make aïoli or, with nuts and basil, pesto. In Asia, where the per capita consumption of garlic far exceeds that of the Mediterranean countries, its companions are lemon grass, fresh ginger, coriander, chillies, and soy sauce. Garlic is used in stir-fried dishes, curry pastes, sambals, and nam prik. In Cuba, it is combined with cumin and citrus juice to make the ubiquitous table sauces called mojos. Garlic can also be steeped in oil for a few days, and in vinegar for at least two weeks. In Korea and Russia, garlic makes a much-loved pickle.

GROW YOUR OWN

Garlic is propagated by the cloves. It grows best in a rich, moist soil in a sunny position. Perennial or biennial, it is extremely hardy and survives long periods of frost. Harvest when the tops dry out and begin to collapse. Pull up the whole plant and hang in the shade to dry. As harvested garlic dries, the skin becomes papery and the flavour intensifies.

FLAVOUR PAIRINGS

Essential to many sauces (aïoli, allioli, skordalia, rouille, tarator, pesto).

Good with almost anything savoury.

Combines well with most herbs and spices.

Dried cloves
Dried cloves of garlic may have a white, pink, or violet skin, depending on variety.

Garlic *was one of the earliest herbs to be cultivated.*
Although its strong taste and smell were disliked by many,

its medical and magical properties were never in doubt.
Its culinary use is greatest in Southeast Asia and Europe.

Garlic varieties

Several plants have aromatic qualities similar to those of garlic. Slender rocambole is actually related to the leek. European wild garlic, or ramsons, comes closest to garlic in taste and has the advantage that it can be gathered early in spring. The huge cloves of elephant garlic, *A. ampeloprasum*, may be too mild for real garlic aficionados, but they are good roasted with other vegetables. North American wild garlic, *A. canadense*, has a flavour between garlic and leek.

Rocambole *A. s.* var. *ophioscorodon*

The rocambole, or sandleek, is native to the northern UK. The stalks turn into spirals and twirls as they mature, and the mauve flowers give way to purple bulbils. All parts can be used: early in the year the new, slender, pointed leaves as chives; in summer the pea-sized bulbils and the bulbs as garlic. All the parts are milder in flavour than garlic.

Ramsons *A. ursinum*

Ramsons grow wild in much of Europe. The leaves resemble those of lily-of-the-valley, but with the smell of wild garlic; the flavour is milder than the smell. They are easy to cultivate, but invasive. Leaves are picked in late winter and early spring; then come the more strongly scented, white, star-like flowers; the bulbils have the strongest flavour of all. Leaves are best used fresh to enhance winter salads, to garnish potato and egg dishes, in soups, in cream or yogurt sauces, with asparagus or morels in a risotto, cooked briefly with spinach, or wrapped around fish fillets before steaming.

Green onion

Allium fistulosum

Green onions are native to Siberia. Also called Welsh onions, oriental bunching onions, and Japanese leeks, they are Asia's largest onion crop. European cookery books usually refer to them as bunching onions, but in books on oriental cooking they are most often called scallions, a name we have also given to spring onions (*A. cepa*), which do resemble them but have a different taste.

Culinary uses

Green onions are used as a flavouring and as a vegetable. They are essential to oriental cooking, often in combination with garlic and ginger. They are used with meats, fish, seafood, and poultry, finding a place in many soups, stews, and braises. They are usually added at the end of the cooking process, even in stir-frying, to preserve their colour and crunchy texture. Chopped fine, they can be added to western stews or potato and pulse dishes, again shortly before the end of cooking. Raw, they can be used as a substitute for spring onions.

Fresh stems

Asian varieties of the green onion are stronger in flavour than those grown in Europe. While most of them are green, some varieties have red stems.

TASTING NOTES

Green onions have only a faint onion aroma when cut. The onion flavour is pronounced if rather mild.

PARTS USED

White "stems" (the slightly bulbous leaf bases), and green leaves.

BUYING / STORING

Green onions are sold in oriental shops; avoid any that look wilted and yellowed. To grow, buy seeds or plants from a nursery. Keep onions, well wrapped, in the vegetable drawer of the refrigerator for about a week.

GROW YOUR OWN

Green onions are hardy perennials and are grown from seed in well-drained, fertile soil, sometimes in stages for a continuing crop. They are non-bulbing, producing only a slight swelling at the base, but like most alliums multiply in clumps, which should be split occasionally. Harvest plants after 5–6 weeks, when they are about 25cm (10in) high. The true oriental scallion has round and hollow leaves; European varieties have flatter leaves.

FLAVOUR PAIRINGS

Good with eggs, fish and seafood, meat, poultry, most vegetables.

Combines well with chervil, chillies, coriander, galangal, garlic, ginger, lemon grass, parsley, perilla.

TASTING NOTES

All parts of chives have a light, onion aroma and a spicy, onion flavour.

PARTS USED

Stems and flowers.

BUYING / STORING

Buy a clump from a nursery and divide the small bulbs as needed to guarantee a sufficient supply. Drying chives is pointless, but chopped and frozen they retain their flavour tolerably well. Use straight from the freezer.

GROW YOUR OWN

Chives grow as grass-like clumps of hollow, bright green stalks, with small, spherical, pink to purple flower heads. They are hardy perennials, easy to grow in any garden soil, but they must be watered well because the small bulbous roots remain very near the surface. Propagate by division. The plants die back in winter, but reappear very early in spring. They should be cut, preferably the outer ones first to keep the clump tidy. Always leave some top growth on the clumps to preserve the strength of the bulbs.

FLAVOUR PAIRINGS

Essential to fines herbes.

Good with avocados, courgettes, cream cheese, egg dishes, fish and seafood, potatoes, smoked salmon, root vegetables, yogurt.

Combines well with basil, chervil, coriander, fennel, sweet cicely, paprika, parsley, tarragon.

Chives

Allium schoenoprasum

This smallest and most delicately flavoured member of the onion family originated in northern temperate zones. Chives have long grown wild all over Europe and North America, but widespread cultivation in Europe does not seem to have begun until the later Middle Ages. The herb became popular only in the 19th century.

Culinary uses

Chives should never be cooked, since cooking quickly dissipates their taste. Chopped with a knife or with scissors, they can be added in generous measure to many dishes and salads. Their delicate onion flavour, crunchy texture, and fresh green appearance livens up potato salad and many a soup, and lends an equally upbeat note to any herb sauce. It has become traditional to serve chives with butter or sour cream as a dressing for baked potatoes. Stirred into thick yogurt, chives make a fresh relish for grilled fish. The attractive, bright flowers have a pleasant, light, onion taste and look good scattered over herb salads or added to omelettes.

Fresh stems
Chives should be crisp, not floppy. Use quickly after cutting.

Chinese chives
Allium tuberosum

Chinese chives, also known as garlic chives, are native to central and northern Asia but also grow in subtropical China, India, and Indonesia. Records of the use of chives in China go back thousands of years. The plants have flat leaves rather than the hollow stems of western chives, and the star-like flowers are white.

Culinary uses

Cut into short lengths, Chinese chives can be quickly blanched to accompany pork or poultry. They are used in spring rolls and added at the last minute for pungency in stir-fried dishes of beef, prawns, tofu, and many vegetables. Little bundles dipped in batter can be deep-fried. The flower buds, sold separately on their stalks, are a much-prized vegetable. In China and Japan, the flowers are ground and salted to make a spice. Blanched chives are a popular but expensive delicacy; they are stirred into soups, noodle dishes, and steamed vegetables at the last minute. Flower stems and leaves of Chinese chives look good placed inside a bottle of white wine vinegar and soon give it a light garlic flavour.

Leaves and flower stalks
Bright green leaves, pale, blanched leaves, and bud stalks are sold in Chinese shops.

TASTING NOTES
Leaves and flowers have a stronger, more distinct garlic taste than those of ordinary chives; blanched leaves are milder. The taste is stronger in the flowers than in the leaves.

PARTS USED
Leaves and flower buds.

BUYING / STORING
Oriental shops sell the chives in bundles, and blanched chives and the stiff flowerbud stalks in smaller bundles. Once cut, chives wilt quickly – blanched Chinese chives fastest of all. Green chives will keep for a few days in a plastic bag in the refrigerator but the smell is strong.

GROW YOUR OWN
Chinese chives are robust; in warm climates they stay green all winter. The plants are taller than western chives but tend to form neater and smaller clumps. They do not produce real bulbs and propagation is by the rhizome. Leaves can be cut for use at any time. Sometimes the plants are cut back and kept in the dark: the pale yellow shoots produced by this blanching are a prized delicacy. Flowers are harvested as buds, on the stalks.

Celery
Apium graveolens

Wild celery, or smallage, is an ancient European plant from which garden celery and celeriac were bred in the 17th century. Cutting or leaf celery resembles the original wild celery. Chinese celery is mid-green with leaves similar to those of garden celery. The unrelated water or Vietnamese celery, *Oenanthe javanica*, has upright stalks with small, serrated leaves; do not confuse it with the poisonous European water dropwort, *O. crocata*.

Cutting celery A. *graveolens*
Cutting celery looks like a dark green, glossy version of flat-leaf parsley. It produces an abundance of leaves on erect stems to form a bushy plant.

Seeds
Celery seed has an aroma and taste that is much more pronounced than that of the parent plant. It is penetrating, spicy, with hints of nutmeg, citrus, and parsley and it leaves a somewhat bitter, burning aftertaste.

TASTING NOTES
Cutting celery leaves have a herbaceous, parsley-like aroma and taste combined with warmth and a bitter note. Chinese celery is similar in flavour. Water celery has a fresh taste; parsley notes are more dominant than celery's warm bitterness.

PARTS USED
Leaves, stalks, and fruits (seeds).

BUYING / STORING
Cutting celery will keep for 4–5 days. Leaves of garden celery will last for about the same time. Chinese celery is often sold with its roots and will last for a week if kept whole. Water celery keeps for 1–2 days. Store them all in plastic bags in the refrigerator. Seeds in an airtight container will remain aromatic for up to 2 years.

GROW YOUR OWN
Celery's natural habitat is marshland, but it is easily grown from seed in the garden in moisture-retentive soil; as yet few British herb nurseries stock cutting celery plants. Harvest leaves throughout the growing season. Water celery grows wild in Southeast Asia; if you can find a plant, keep it in a pot because it spreads quickly. Water frequently.

FLAVOUR PAIRINGS
Good with cabbage, chicken, cucumber, fish, potatoes, rice, soy sauce, tomatoes, tofu.

Combines well with cloves, coriander leaves, cumin, ginger, mustard, parsley, pepper, turmeric.

Culinary uses

Cutting celery is used in Holland, Belgium, and Germany as a garnish or stirred into dishes before serving. It is one of the herbs used for the traditional dish of eel in green sauce. In northern France it is sold as a soup herb; in Greece it is popular in fish and meat casseroles. Cutting celery is useful because you can pick leaves to add to bouquets garnis, soups, and stews, instead of having to use a celery stick.

Chinese celery is used as a flavouring and as a vegetable. It is rarely eaten raw. Stems are sliced and used in stir-fried dishes; leaves and stems flavour soups, braised dishes, rice, and noodles throughout Southeast Asia. I have also enjoyed a very good Thai dish of fish steamed with Chinese celery.

Garden celery and celeriac are eaten raw or cooked as vegetables, but you can also use the leaves as a flavouring. Cooking tempers the bitterness of all types of celery, but they retain their other aromatic properties. Water celery, with its mild taste, is very popular in Vietnam as a salad herb, or lightly cooked, when it is added to soups, fish, and chicken dishes. Thais use it in a similar way and serve it raw with larp or blanched with nam prik.

The Japanese use it for sukiyaki. It also flavours tomato salad.

The Russians and Scandinavians add the seeds to soups, and a few lightly crushed seeds give a pleasant warmth to dressings for winter vegetable salads. Indian cooks also pair celery seed with tomato in curries. Try seeds in potato salad, in cabbage dishes, in stews, and in breads. Because they are so small, celery seeds are usually used whole. The flavour is strong: use sparingly. Celery salt is a mixture of ground seed and salt, usually about 75 per cent salt and 25 per cent seed.

Chinese celery

A. graveolens

Chinese celery (kun choi) looks like a small head of green garden celery. The stalks are thin and hollow.

TASTING NOTES

Lovage is strongly aromatic, somewhat similar to celery (in French it is called *céleri bâtard*, or false celery) but more pungent, with musky overtones and notes of anise, lemon, and yeast. The aroma and taste are distinct and tenacious.

PARTS USED

Leaves, stems, roots, seeds.

BUYING / STORING

Seeds and ground, dried roots can be bought from some spice merchants. Cut lovage is seldom sold, but it is easy to grow your own; buy seeds or plants from a herb nursery. Pick leaves at any time; in a plastic bag they will keep for 3–4 days in the refrigerator. Cut stalks off at their base, the outer ones first. As the seeds turn brown, pick fruiting stalks and hang them upside down to dry, with a paper bag over the seed heads. These will keep for a year or two.

GROW YOUR OWN

This perennial herb can be grown from seed or by division. It does equally well in shade or sun, but its deep roots need moist, fertile, well-drained soil. The plant dies down in winter but is extremely hardy, surviving in several centimetres of frozen topsoil.

Lovage
Levisticum officinale

Lovage is native to western Asia and southern Europe, where it has been used since Roman times; outside Europe its use has never become popular. Wild and cultivated forms are indistinguishable, and the herb has long been naturalized elsewhere – even in Australia. In Italy it is chiefly associated with Liguria – the name *levisticum* may be a corruption of *ligusticum*, or Ligurian. The Pilgrim Fathers are believed to have taken lovage to North America.

Fresh stalks
Lovage is a tall, stately umbellifer with rather large, dark-green, toothed leaves and ridged, hollow stems. The small but attractive yellow flowers bloom in late summer, then give way to huge heads of seeds.

Culinary uses

Lovage can be used as celery or parsley in almost any dish, but is much stronger than either of these and should be used with caution. Its pungency diminishes in cooking.

Leaves, chopped stalks, and roots do well in casseroles, soups, and stews. In some diets it may be an advantage that lovage can be used as a salt substitute. Young leaves make a good simple soup, on their own or with potato, carrot, or Jerusalem artichoke, and are often used in seafood chowders. They are good in green salads; older leaves liven up bean or potato dishes and are good in stuffings for poultry.

Lovage-flavoured potato and swede gratin is worth trying, as are potato cakes with lovage and Cheddar or Gruyère, and creamy baked vegetable dishes with lovage. Whole or ground seeds can be used in pickles, sauces, marinades, breads, and biscuits. The hollow stems can be blanched and used as a vegetable.

Seeds

The tiny, ridged seeds (fruits) are aromatic and have a taste similar to that of the leaves, but with added warmth and a hint of clove.

FLAVOUR PAIRINGS

Good with apples, carrots, courgettes, cream cheese, egg dishes, ham, lamb, mushrooms, onions, pork, potatoes and other root vegetables, pulses, rice, smoked fish, sweetcorn, tomatoes, tuna.

Combines well with bay, caraway, chilli, chives, dill, garlic, juniper, oregano, parsley, thyme.

OTHER LOVAGES

Scots lovage *Ligusticum scoticum*, is native to the northern temperate region. It does not grow as tall as *L. officinale* and is less pungent; it has white rather than yellow flowers. Use in the same ways as lovage.

Black lovage *Smyrnium olusatrum*, or alexanders, is another tall umbellifer grown in southern and western Europe from antiquity and was cultivated in monastery gardens from the Middle Ages. Much loved in Elizabethan fish and seafood dishes, it was taken to North America in the 16th century. It is almost as easy to grow as lovage, looks much like it, and all parts can be used in the same way. Crushed seeds are now often added to vodka as a flavouring.

Dried leaves
Whether dried or frozen, the leaves retain most of their strength; dried leaves are more yeasty and celery-like than fresh ones.

TASTING NOTES

Hyssop has a strong and pleasant aroma of camphor and mint. The taste of the dark green leaves is refreshing but potent, hot, minty, and bitterish – reminiscent of rosemary, savory, and thyme.

PARTS USED

Leaves and young shoots; flowers.

BUYING / STORING

In a plastic bag in the vegetable drawer of the refrigerator hyssop will keep for about a week.

GROW YOUR OWN

Hyssop grows well from seed but can also be divided or propagated by cuttings. It likes dry, rocky, well-drained soils, needs sun but tolerates shade, and is hardy enough for northern temperate zones. Every 3 years or so, hyssop plants should be divided or they will become too woody. As hyssop is virtually evergreen, its leaves can be picked even in winter. The long, dense flower spikes that appear in late summer are attractive to bees. Their colour depends on the variety grown: *H. o. albus* has white flowers; *H .o.* subsp. *aristatus*, dark blue ones; *H. o. roseus*, pink.

FLAVOUR PAIRINGS

Good with apricots, beetroot, cabbage, carrots, egg dishes, game, mushrooms, peaches, pulses, pumpkin, squashes.

Combines well with bay, chervil, mint, parsley, thyme.

Hyssop
Hyssopus officinalis

Hyssop is a low, perennial shrub, semi-woody and semi-evergreen, that is native to northern Africa, southern Europe, and western Asia. It is a handsome, compact plant that has long been naturalized in central and western Europe. The Romans used it as a base for a herbal wine, and it was cultivated as a condiment and a strewing herb in monastic gardens during the early Middle Ages.

Culinary uses

Hyssop leaves and young shoots can be used in salads (to which the flowers can make a robust garnish) or added to soups. The herb is particularly good in rabbit, kid, and game stews; rubbing it on to fatty meats such as lamb can make them easier to digest. It has long been used to flavour non-alcoholic summer drinks, digestives, and liqueurs. It is very good in fruit pies and compotes, and with sherbets and desserts made using assertively flavoured fruits such as apricots, morello cherries, peaches, and raspberries. A sugar syrup made for a fruit dish will benefit from boiling with a sprig of hyssop.

Fresh sprigs
Hyssop should be used sparingly or it will overwhelm other flavours.

Leaves
Both leaves and flowers retain much of their strength when dried. The tiny flowers have a more delicate flavour than the leaves.

Chicory
Cichorium intybus

Chicory is a tall herbaceous perennial, native to the Mediterranean basin and Asia Minor. The modern cultivated forms originated in 16th-century Europe. In time they gave rise to two very different forced forms: in the late 18th century the Dutch grew the roots for use as a cheaper substitute for coffee – as an additive without caffeine it remains popular in Belgium, France, Germany, and the US; in 1845 the Belgians developed the blanched form grown under soil or sawdust that we still know as French endive, or witloof.

Culinary uses

Young leaves are used in salads; the edible flowers may also be added to salads as cheerful decoration. Older leaves benefit from quick blanching and are then used in cooked dishes – they are not appetizing in salads.

Fresh leaves

Chicory grows wild in much of Europe and North America. In the garden it can reach 1m (3ft) or more by flowering time.

TASTING NOTES

Chicory has no smell. It has a milky white juice containing inulin, which accounts for the bitter taste – quite pleasant in the crisp, young leaves but harsh in old ones. The flowers are not at all bitter.

PARTS USED

Young green leaves; flowers.

BUYING / STORING

Seeds and plants can usually be bought from a herb nursery. Leaves will keep in a plastic bag in the vegetable drawer of the refrigerator for 2–3 days. Flowers need to be used immediately.

GROW YOUR OWN

Chicory is easily grown from seed in almost any water-retentive but reasonably well-drained soil that allows penetration by the very long taproots. The light green leaves are large at the base, smaller on the upper, branching stalks. The large, light blue, daisy-like flowers, which last only a day or so and close in the midday sun, appear all through the summer and early autumn. Suppressing the flower-stalks early encourages leaf growth.

FLAVOUR PAIRINGS

Good with fresh cheeses, lettuce and other salad greens, nuts.

Combines well with chervil, coriander, cresses, parsley, purslane, salad burnet, sweet cicely.

TASTING NOTES

The basic taste is warm, slightly sharp, and bitterish with a note of camphor. To this marjoram adds a sweet, subtle spiciness, even in temperate climates. Oregano is more robust and peppery, with a bite and often a lemony note. These qualities diminish in colder climates.

 PARTS USED

Leaves, flower knots.

 BUYING / STORING

Marjoram and oregano plants can be bought from herb nurseries and supermarkets. To dry the herbs, pick stalks after the flower buds form and hang bunches in a well-ventilated, dry place. Rub the leaves off and store them in an airtight container. In supermarkets oregano is more easily available dried than fresh. Dried oregano keeps for a year.

 GROW YOUR OWN

Most varieties are upright bushes with woody stems. They can be grown from seed or propagated by division. They need well-drained soil and much sun. Cutting back plants before winter prevents them from growing straggly. Leaves can be picked freely at any time; harvest for drying just after the flower buds form. Although perennial, marjoram is often grown as an annual in cool climates.

Oregano and marjoram
Origanum species

Low, bushy perennials of the mint family, the marjorams and oreganos are native to the Mediterranean and western Asia. The plants are often confused, partly because marjoram used to have its own genus, *Majorana*, but also because the word "oregano" is often used simply as a term for a certain type of flavour and aroma. Thus, unrelated plants with a similar aromatic profile may also be called oregano.

Common oregano
O. vulgare

This plant has reddish stalks that are slightly woody; the leaves are mid-green and hairy underneath; the flowers deep pink, white, or mauve.

Dried leaves
Dried marjoram and oregano are more intensely aromatic than fresh and have a stronger flavour. Several varieties of oregano are sold dried under the Greek name *rígani*.

Culinary uses

Oregano has become an essential ingredient in much Italian cooking, especially pasta sauces, pizza, and roasted vegetables. For the Greeks it is the favourite herb for souvlaki, baked fish, and Greek salad. In Mexico it is a key flavouring for bean dishes, burritos, taco fillings, and salsas. Throughout Spain and Latin America it is used for meat stews and roasts, soups, and baked vegetables. Combined with paprika, cumin, and chilli it flavours Tex-Mex chilli con carne and other meat stews. Its strong flavour works well with grills and in stuffings, hearty soups, marinades,

vegetable stews, even hamburgers. It will also flavour oils and vinegars.

The more delicate flavour of marjoram is easily lost in cooking: it should be added only at the last moment. It is good in salads, egg dishes, and mushroom sauces, with fish and poultry. It makes more delicate stuffings than oregano. Fresh, it makes a great sorbet. Use leaves and flower knots in salads, and with mozzarella and other young cheeses.

Stalks of either marjoram or oregano placed on the coals of a barbecue give a fine flavour to whatever is cooked on top.

FLAVOUR PAIRINGS

Good with anchovies, artichokes, aubergines, beans, cabbage, carrots, cauliflower, cheese dishes, chicken, courgettes, duck, eggs, fish and shellfish, lamb, mushrooms, onions, peppers, pork, potatoes, poultry, spinach, squashes, sweetcorn, tomatoes, veal, venison.

Combines well with basil, bay, chilli, cumin, garlic, paprika, parsley, rosemary, sage, sumac, (lemon) thyme.

Sweet marjoram *O. majorana*

This pretty plant, also called knotted marjoram, has grey-green, slightly hairy leaves and clusters of white flowers. Its taste is more delicate and somewhat sweeter than that of common oregano and it does not lend itself to long-cooking.

Oregano and marjoram varieties

In addition to common oregano and sweet marjoram, there are many other varieties and plants of other species with similar characteristics. The flavour of oregano depends on the relative concentration of the phenols carvacrol and thymol in the volatile oil of the plants. Carvacrol is primarily responsible for the typical oregano flavour; its level is generally highest in Greek and some Mexican oreganos.

Cretan dittany *O. dictamnus*

Also called hop marjoram and native only to Crete and southern Greece, this plant grows less tall than most other varieties and has thick, silvery foliage and deep pink flowers. Its flavour is very similar to that of sweet marjoram. It goes well with grilled fish.

Pot marjoram *O. onites*

Sometimes called Sicilian marjoram but native to Greece and Asia Minor, this is a dwarf shrub with light green, downy leaves and white or pink flowers. A close relative of sweet marjoram, it is less sweet and more piquant.

Greek or Turkish oregano
O. heracleoticum (O. v. hirtum)

Also called winter marjoram, this plant is native to southeastern Europe and western Asia. In Turkey it is sometimes labelled black oregano because of its dark green, almost black colour. It has small, white flowers and a more peppery note than most oreganos. It is the species most widely cultivated in Greece and Turkey and the most important economically, being the source for much of the dried oregano sold in Europe and North America.

OTHER OREGANOS

There are a number of unrelated plants used and sold as oregano.

Cuban oregano, *Plectranthus amboinicus,* is a tender perennial with an intense flavour, native to southern Africa, now widely cultivated in the tropics. Its pungent, thick leaves are good to eat raw; they are much used in the Philippines and in Cuba, especially for black beans. Use in marinades for fish or meat or add towards the end when braising. Also marketed as

oregano are *Poliomintha longiflora* and *Monarda fistulosa* var. *menthifolia.* These grow in the southwestern US and Mexico, where they are prized for their pungent flavours. Cumin and coriander (cilantro) are their natural partners in the kitchen.

Golpar, an Iranian spice described erroneously as marjoram or angelica seed, is in fact the seed of a hogweed, *Heracleum persicum.* Whole seeds, yellow-green with brown markings in

the centre (*p.176*), can be bought from Iranian shops, as can the powdered spice. Golpar has a herbaceous, balsam aroma with yeasty overtones. The taste is mellow at first but has a persistent bitter note. When cooked, mellowness dominates. It is used in soups, particularly lentil and bean, in pickles, over broad beans or potatoes, and eaten as a snack on pomegranate seeds.

Golden-leaved oregano
O. v. 'Aureum'

This oregano is a handsome ground-cover plant with dense foliage. It can be used in the same way as ordinary oregano but has a much milder flavour.

Mexican oregano
Lippia graveolens

This is an attractive plant with grey-green, oval leaves and creamy-white flowers. Related to lemon verbena, it has a high volatile oil content.

Syrian oregano *O. syriacum*

This oregano is cultivated for culinary use in the Middle East. Its flavour is pungent, reminiscent of thyme, marjoram, and oregano but sharper. Sometimes used in za'atar (*p.98*).

Strongly aromatic, warm and peppery, resinous and slightly bitter, with notes of pine and camphor. Nutmeg and camphor are present in the taste; the aftertaste is woody, balsamic, and astringent. The flavour dissipates after leaves are cut. Flowers have a milder flavour than leaves.

PARTS USED

The small needle-like leaves, sprigs, stalks, flowers.

BUYING / STORING

Buy plants from a nursery, or grow from cuttings. Pots of rosemary are available all year round from supermarkets and greengrocers. This means there is little demand for dried rosemary, although this retains most of its flavour and the leaves can easily be crumbled for use.

GROW YOUR OWN

Rosemary is hard to grow from seed but easy to propagate by cutting or layering. It needs light, well-drained soil and ample sun, preferably in a sheltered space. There are creeping varieties as well as upright ones. Fairly harsh spring pruning will keep plants bushy. The attractive, small flowers are usually blue, sometimes pink or white. Leaves and sprigs can be cut at any time of the year.

Rosemary

Rosmarinus officinalis

Rosemary is a dense, woody, evergreen perennial, native to the Mediterranean but long cultivated in temperate zones throughout Europe and America. It has been grown in England since Roman times and is hardy enough for all but the most northern zones. In the early 9th century, Charlemagne, in his *Capitulaire de Villes*, included it in the list of essential plants to be grown on the imperial estates; in the later Middle Ages it was still used as a strewing or incense herb.

Fresh leaves

Rosemary leaves can be tough, so they are best chopped before being added to any dish in which they will be eaten.

Culinary uses

The flavour of rosemary is strong and unsubtle; it is not diminished by long-cooking, so use rosemary judiciously, even in slow-stews. In Mediterranean cuisines it is much used with vegetables fried in olive oil; in Italy it is popular with veal. Whole sprigs are good in marinades, especially for lamb, and will give a subtle, smoky flavour when placed under meat or poultry being barbecued or roasted. Older, stronger stalks can be used as skewers for kebabs, or as basting brushes. Rosemary is very good in biscuits, both sweet and savoury, and in focaccia and other breads. Young sprigs can be used to flavour olive oil, infused in milk, cream, or syrup for desserts, or steeped for summer drinks such as lemonade. Flowers frozen in ice cubes make a pretty garnish for such drinks. Crystallized rosemary flowers are pretty, but quite fiddly to make.

FLAVOUR PAIRINGS

Essential to Herbes de Provence.

Good with apricots, aubergines, cabbage, cream cheese, eggs, fish, lamb, lentils, mushrooms, onions, oranges, parsnips, pork, potatoes, poultry, rabbit, squash, tomatoes, veal.

Combines well with bay, chives, garlic, lavender, lovage, mint, oregano, parsley, sage, savory, thyme.

Herbes de Provence

Used with meat, game, vegetable, and tomato dishes, this herb blend can be fresh or dried. This version includes rosemary, thyme, marjoram, savory, and bay (*recipe, p.267*).

TASTING NOTES

 TASTING NOTES

Sage can be mild, musky, and balsamic, or strongly camphorous with astringent notes and a warm spiciness. Generally, variegated species are milder than common sage. Dried sage is more potent than fresh and can be acrid and musty; it is best avoided, except for tea.

 PARTS USED

Leaves, fresh or dried. All sages have attractive, hooded flowers that make pretty garnishes.

 BUYING / STORING

Pots of sage are now sold in many supermarkets. Fresh sage leaves, ideally, are picked and used as soon as possible. If you buy them, wrap in kitchen paper and keep in the salad drawer of the refrigerator for no more than a few days. Dried sage will keep for up to 6 months when stored away from light in an airtight container.

 GROW YOUR OWN

Sage does best on warm, dry soils. Its aromatic strength varies according to soil and climate. Leaves can be harvested from spring to autumn. Plants are best cut back after flowering. Purple, variegated, and 'Tricolor' sages (pp.93–95) are less hardy than common sage, and pineapple sage (p.95) needs protection from freezing temperatures.

Sage
Salvia species

The sages are native to the north Mediterranean and are mostly perennial, shrubby plants that thrive on warm, dry soils. The great variety of their textured, velvety foliage – from pale grey-green to green splashed with silver or gold, as well as the dark leaves of purple sage – makes them attractive garden plants as well as an invaluable addition to the cook's repertoire of seasonings.

Common sage S. *officinalis*

There are broad and narrow-leaved varieties of common sage. Young, green leaves are less pungent than the older, grey ones. Narrow-leaved sage has pretty, lilac, blue, or white flowers. Broad-leaved sage seldom flowers.

Culinary uses

Sage aids the digestion of fatty and oily foods and is traditionally used as a partner for them. In Britain sage is associated with pork, goose, and duck, and may be used in stuffings for these meats. In America sage and onion stuffing is often used for the Thanksgiving turkey. Sage also makes an excellent flavouring for pork sausages, and in Germany it accompanies eel. The Greeks use it in meat stews and with poultry, and also in a tea. Italians use sage with liver and veal (saltimbocca alla romana is the classic dish), and to flavour focaccia and polenta; they make a well-flavoured pasta sauce by gently heating a few leaves in butter. Sage is not a subtle herb, so use sparingly.

FLAVOUR PAIRINGS

Good with apples, dried beans, cheese, onions, tomatoes.

Combines well with bay, caraway, celery leaf, garlic, dried ginger, lovage, marjoram, paprika, parsley, savory, thyme.

Purple sage

S. o. Purpurascens Group

This sage has musky, spicy tones and is slightly less pungent than common sage. It rarely flowers, but when it does the blue flowers look stunning against the foliage.

Bouquet garni for meats

Little bundles of herbs such as this can be varied to suit the dish to be cooked. Sprigs of thyme, sage, cutting celery, and parsley make a fine flavouring for stews (*recipes, p.266*).

Other sage varieties

Pungent common sage, *Salvia officinalis*, has many cultivated varieties grown mainly for the colour of their foliage or flowers; all may be used for cooking, and each has its own flavour. Others have milder tastes and distinctly fruity fragrances; pineapple sage and blackcurrant sage smell like their eponymous fruits; clary sage, a statuesque biennial with large, wrinkled leaves, has a delicate scent of muscat grapes.

S. o. 'Tricolor'

Perhaps the most striking of all the sages, this has mottled green, cream, and pink leaves, and blue flowers. The flavour is quite gentle.

Blackcurrant sage *S. microphylla*

Rub the leaves in your hands for a rich scent of blackcurrant; the flavour is less pronounced, however. Deep purple-pink flowers appear in late summer. Half-hardy except if very sheltered.

Greek sage *S. fruticosa*

The large, grey-green, downy leaves of this species are intensely aromatic, with dominant resinous notes. Use very sparingly in cooking, or as a tisane.

Clary sage *S. sclarea*

This aromatic biennial has a scent reminiscent of muscat grapes; the taste is slightly bitter and balsam-like. The leaves can be used for fritters, while the flowers make a beautiful, edible garnish.

S. o. 'Icterina'

This cultivated variety has pretty gold-and-green variegated foliage, but rarely flowers. The flavour is considerably milder than that of common sage.

Pineapple sage *S. elegans*

Overwintered indoors, this sage grows into a large shrub. The long leaves have a clear, pineapple scent but the flavour is less marked. Striking red flowers appear in autumn. Leaves can be placed in a cake tin to scent a sponge cake.

TASTING NOTES

The whole plant has a warm, earthy, and peppery fragrance when lightly brushed. The taste is spicy, with notes of cloves and mint, a hint of camphor, and a mouth-cleansing aftertaste.

PARTS USED

Leaves and sprigs; flowers for garnishes.

BUYING / STORING

Many varieties of thyme are sold by nurseries, but make sure they smell when brushed lightly by hand. Common and lemon thyme are available as growing plants or fresh sprigs from supermarkets. Fresh leaves will keep for up to a week stored in a plastic bag in the refrigerator. Dried thyme will retain its flavour through the winter.

GROW YOUR OWN

All thymes need very well-drained, sandy soil and as much sun as they can get. They benefit from the heat reflected off patio stone paving and the rocks in rock gardens. Propagation is easiest by division. Pick leaves when needed – the more often the better, or the plant may become straggly and woody. Harvest thyme for drying just before it flowers.

Thyme

Thymus species

Thyme is a small, hardy, evergreen shrub with small, aromatic leaves, indigenous to the Mediterranean basin. It grows wild on the hot, arid hillsides of its native region, where it has infinitely more flavour than it ever achieves in cooler regions. Wild thyme tends to be woody and straggly. Cultivated varieties have more tender stalks and a bushy form; there are hundreds of them, each with a slightly different aroma, and they have a tendency to cross-breed as well.

Common thyme *T. vulgaris*

The basic thyme for cooking, also called garden thyme, is a cultivated variety of wild Mediterranean thyme. It forms a sturdy, upright shrub with grey-green leaves and white or pale lilac flowers. There are a number of garden thymes, including English "broad-leaved" and French "narrow-leaved" varieties.

Culinary uses

Thyme is an essential flavouring in much western and Middle Eastern cooking. Unlike most herbs, it withstands long, slow-cooking; used with discretion, it enhances other herbs without overpowering them, and in stews and casseroles combines well with onions, beer, or red wine. Thyme has become indispensable in every French stew, from pot-au-feu to cassoulet, but equally in Spanish ones and, by extension, those of Mexico and Latin America, where it is often used in combination with chillies. It is widely used to flavour pâtés and terrines, thick vegetable soups, tomato and wine-based sauces, and in marinades for pork and game. In Britain it is used in stuffings, pies, and jugged hare. The dried herb is essential in the Creole and Cajun cooking of Louisiana, where it appears in gumbos and jambalayas; in New England fresh thyme is used as a traditional ingredient of clam chowder.

FLAVOUR PAIRINGS

Essential to most bouquets garnis.

Good with aubergines, beef, cabbage, carrots, lamb, leeks, wild mushrooms, onions, potatoes, pulses, rabbit, sweetcorn, tomatoes.

Combines well with allspice, basil, bay, chillies, clove, garlic, lavender, marjoram, nutmeg, oregano, paprika, parsley, rosemary, savory.

Lemon thyme *T. citriodorus*

This is a compact, upright shrub with mauve-pink flowers that gives a fresh lemony note to fish and seafood, roast chicken, or veal; it can be used in biscuits, bread, and fruit salads. For the cook, lemon thyme is the most important variety after garden thyme.

Other thyme varieties

Cultivated varieties of common thyme (*T. vulgaris*) and lemon thyme
(*T. citriodorus*) as well as other species offer different flavours to the cook.
In the Middle East the Arab name za'atar is given to thyme, to *Thymbra
spicata*, and to other herbs with a thyme-savory-oregano aroma: Syrian
oregano (*p.89*), conehead thyme (*p.99*), and thymbra (*p.102*). Any of these
can be combined with sesame (*p.132*) and sumac (*p.158*) to make the
spice mixture also called za'atar.

Caraway thyme

T. herba-barona

This is a trailing plant native to Corsica and Sardinia
with red stems, narrow glossy leaves, and pink flowers.
Its taste has a light caraway note that goes well in root
vegetable and cheese dishes, and cream sauces.

Creeping thyme *T. serpyllum*

This thyme grows throughout the Mediterranean region
and also in central and northern Europe. It is milder than
common thyme and should only be used fresh. Scatter
the tiny leaves over salads or grilled vegetables. It
combines well with hyssop.

Za'atar *Thymbra spicata*

This is a dark-leaved, woody shrub, rather like savory. Its showy
clusters of purple flowers make it a great rock-garden plant, but
outside the Middle East, its native region, it is not really hardy.

Conehead thyme *T. capitatus*

The Arabic for this variety is za'atar farsi, or Persian thyme; in the Middle East it is the most widely used thyme.

Variegated thyme

T.citriodora. 'Golden Queen'

This variegated thyme has a mild flavour. The aromatic properties of thyme varieties vary according to the composition of their essential oils, and in particular the amount of thymol contained in the essential oils.

Orange-scented thyme

T. citriodora. 'Fragrantissimus'

Leaves of this cultivated variety of thyme can be used as a flavouring instead of a piece of orange peel.

Lemon-scented thyme

T. sp. 'Lemon Mist'

This lemon-scented thyme has narrow leaves and a mounding growth habit. It is used in salads and as a flavouring for tea. A few chopped leaves added in the last few minutes of cooking will add zest to soups.

TASTING NOTES

Savories have a peppery bite. Summer savory has a subtle, herbaceous scent and flavour, is agreeably piquant, slightly resinous, and reminiscent of thyme, mint, and marjoram. Winter savory has a more assertive, penetrating aroma and flavour, with notes of sage and pine.

 PARTS USED

Leaves and sprigs; flowers for garnishes and salads.

 BUYING / STORING

Savory is not available as a cut herb, but plants are available from nurseries. Summer savory will keep for 5–6 days, winter savory for up to 10 days, in a plastic bag in the refrigerator. Savory keeps its flavour well if frozen, chopped, or as sprigs. To dry summer savory, hang the stalks in an airy, dark place.

 GROW YOUR OWN

Summer savory is an annual, winter savory an evergreen perennial. Both can be grown from seed, and winter savory can be propagated by division in spring. Both prefer light, well-drained soils and full sun. Summer savory does best in a rich soil; cut back on flowering to encourage new growth. Winter savory will grow in poorer soils.

Savory
Satureja species

Highly aromatic, as the name suggests, savory was one of the strongest flavourings available before spices reached Europe. Summer savory (*S. hortensis*) is native to the eastern Mediterranean and the Caucasus; winter savory (*S. montana*) to southern Europe, Turkey, and North Africa. Both were taken to northern Europe by the Romans and to America by early settlers.

Summer savory *S. hortensis*

This savory is a slender plant with soft, greyish leaves and white or pinkish flowers. Summer savory leaves are tender, whereas those of winter savory are tough.

Fresh sprigs
The leaves have the most intense aroma if harvested just before flowering.

Culinary uses

Because they are pungent, both savories are good flavourings for long-cooked meat and vegetable dishes and stuffings. Savory is frequently associated with beans, as its German name Bohnenkraut (bean herb) indicates.

Summer savory is best with green and broad beans, whereas either may be used with haricot beans and other pulses. Savory is also good with cabbage, root vegetables, and onions, and reduces their strong cooking smells. Summer savory is often added to bouquets garnis for lamb, pork, and game dishes. It is also good with oil-rich fish such as eel and mackerel. Chopped finely, it can be added to salads; it is especially good with potato, bean, and lentil salads.

Winter savory (called poivre d'âne or pebre d'aï – donkey pepper – in Provence) tends to be more widely used around the Mediterranean. Chopped leaves and flowers are added to soups, fish stews, frittate, pizza, rabbit, and lamb dishes.

FLAVOUR PAIRINGS

Good with beans, beetroot, cabbage, cheese, eggs, fish, peppers, potatoes, pulses, rabbit, tomatoes.

Combines well with basil, bay, cumin, garlic, lavender, marjoram, mint, oregano, parsley, rosemary, thyme.

Winter savory *S. montana*

This is a woody, compact shrub with stiff, glossy, dark green leaves and lavender or white flowers. Although the savories may be used interchangeably to some extent, both should be used judiciously, and winter savory in much smaller amounts than summer savory.

Fresh sprigs
Winter savory leaves can be harvested year round.

Other savory varieties

The genus *Satureja* encompasses many plants with pungent, spicy aromas in the mint-thyme-oregano spectrum; they have a variety of common names. Many are used as flavourings in their native habitat. There is also some confusion with the Micromeria species in the naming of certain plants.

Indian mint, *S. douglasii,* is a pretty, trailing plant with small, heart shaped, toothed leaves and tiny, white flowers. It has a rather synthetic, sweet smell with notes of mint (a little like chewing gum) and a minty, bitterish taste. Indian mint is native to western and central America, and probably was given this name because it was used by Native Americans. In California it is called yerba buena (the good herb) and in the past it was used to make a restorative tea: use it sparingly. In Mexico yerba or hierba buena is the common name used for any minty plant, whether it be spearmint or one of the *Satureja* varieties.

Costa Rican or Jamaican mint bush, *S. viminea,* has small, oval, glossy, light leaves and an agreeable, minty smell and flavour. Native to central America and the Caribbean, it grows in the southern and western regions of the US. In Trinidad and Tobago it is used as a meat flavouring; it seems mostly to be used for tea elsewhere.

Thymbra *S. thymbra*

Also called thyme-leaved savory, this is a small, woody perennial found in Sardinia, Crete, and the Aegean islands, and on the western coast of Turkey. Its scent is of thyme, mint, and savory, and the taste has an agreeable bite. Leaves and flower tips are used to flavour meat, game, and vegetable stews, grilled meats, and in cures for olives.

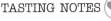

Micromeria
Micromeria species

Micromerias are perennial herbs or dwarf shrubs native to southern Europe, the Caucasus, southwestern China, and western America. In these regions they are regularly used as a culinary herb and to make infusions. In Europe they thrive particularly in the Balkan peninsula; in Croatia one species has appeared on postage stamps. Micromerias are closely related to savories (*Satureja* species, *p.100*), and there is some confusion and duplication in the naming of certain plants.

Culinary uses

Among the micromerias the species *M. thymifolia* has the finest flavour: warmly aromatic with delicate notes of thyme and savory. It is also rich in unsaturated fatty acids. Italian cooks use young leaves with thyme-savory aromas to flavour soups, marinades, and frittate, in stuffings for meat and vegetables, and with roast chicken or pigeon. Finely chopped leaves are added to pasta sauces or sprinkled over meat or poultry before grilling. In Balkan cooking the leaves are used like thyme. Micromeria brings out the flavour of ripe tomatoes and soft, fresh cheeses. A few chopped leaves give a depth of flavour to summer berry desserts.

A minty tea is made from *M. fruticosa*. Pulegone, the main constituent of that herb's essential oil, is known to be toxic, but, taken in normal quantities, the tea is not likely to cause health problems. Emperor's mint is the micromeria most commonly available in Britain; it can be used sparingly in place of garden mint.

Emperor's mint
M. species

Emperor's mint has an assertive, minty aroma, reminiscent of spearmint, and a bitterish minty flavour.

TASTING NOTES
Flavours of some micromerias tend towards mint, others towards thyme and savory. *M. juliana* (also called *Satureja juliana*) resembles savory. *M. fruticosa* resembles pennyroyal (*p.69*).

PARTS USED
Fresh leaves.

BUYING / STORING
Micromerias are not available as cut herbs, but plants are stocked by some specialist nurseries. They can also be picked from the wild. Sprigs will keep for a few days in a plastic bag in the vegetable drawer of the refrigerator.

GROW YOUR OWN
In the wild micromerias thrive on thin soils on dry, exposed cliffs and rocky meadows. They can be grown from seed, or by plant division in loamy, well-drained soil in pots or in the garden. They make attractive ornamental plants for rock gardens, with their bushy habit and thin stalks bearing white, red, or purple flowers above the foliage. Harvest leaves from spring to late summer.

TASTING NOTES

Leaves, roots, and unripe seeds all have the same aroma. Some people are addicted to its refreshing, lemony-ginger aroma with notes of sage; others hate it and find it soapy and disagreeable. The flavour is delicate yet complex, with a suggestion of pepper, mint, and lemon.

PARTS USED

Leaves and sprigs, roots.

BUYING / STORING

Fresh coriander is available in pots or as a cut herb from greengrocers and supermarkets; bunches are sold with roots intact in Southeast Asian shops, or you can grow your own. In a plastic bag, it keeps for 3–4 days in the refrigerator vegetable drawer. Frozen coriander keeps its flavour fairly well; chop and freeze in small pots or in ice-cube trays covered with a little water. Dried coriander is not worthwhile and is never used in Asian cuisines.

GROW YOUR OWN

Coriander is an annual that grows easily from seed in a warm, sunny spot. Leaves can be gathered throughout the growing season. Clusters of small, white, or pinkish flowers produce the seeds. Seeds should be harvested when fully ripe; to dry them, hang bunches of stalks in a warm place and put a paper bag over the seed heads.

Coriander
Coriandrum sativum

Native to the Mediterranean and western Asia, coriander is now grown worldwide. It is both a herb and spice, and a fragrant staple in many cuisines. The fresh leaves are essential to Asian, Latin American, and Portuguese cooking. Thai cooks also use the thin, spindly root. In western cooking the fruit or seed is used as a spice; in the Middle East and India both are common in the kitchen. In North America coriander is often called cilantro, or Chinese parsley.

Fresh sprigs
Coriander was called a "very stinking herbe" by Gerard, the 16th-century herbalist, and is known as the "fragrant plant" by the Chinese. The herb's aroma continues to provoke both dislike and enthusiasm today.

Roots
The roots are more pungent and musky than the leaves, with a light, citrus smell.

Culinary uses

Except when they are used in a curry or similar paste, coriander leaves are always added at the end of cooking; high or prolonged heat reduces their flavour. Coriander leaves are used prolifically throughout most of Asia, in delicately flavoured soups, in stir-fried dishes with ginger and spring onions, in curries and braised dishes. Thai cooks use the roots for curry pastes and combine leaves with basil, mint, and chillies. In India, leaves garnish many savoury dishes and are combined with other herbs and spices in green masala pastes. India and Mexico share a liking for coriander with green chillies in chutneys, relishes, and salsas.

Mexicans also combine coriander with chillies, garlic, and lime juice to make a dressing for vegetables, or for a sauce in which to cook fish. In Bolivia and Peru, coriander, chillies, and huacatay flavour a very assertive table sauce. In the Middle East, coriander is essential to Yemeni zhug and hilbeh, both pungent spice pastes, and is combined with nuts and spices, lemon juice, and olive oil in flavouring mixtures. The Portuguese are the only Europeans who have continued to use coriander to the same extent as it was used in the 16th century. They partner it with potatoes, broad beans, and their excellent clams.

FLAVOUR PAIRINGS

Essential to hilbeh, zhug, chermoula, ceviche, guacamole.

Good with avocados, coconut milk, cucumber, fish and seafood, lemons and limes, pulses, rice, root vegetables, sweetcorn.

Combines well with basil, chillies, chives, dill, galangal, garlic, ginger, lemon grass, mint, parsley.

Yemeni zhug paste

This mixture of chillies, garlic, coriander, cumin, cardamom, and sometimes small peppers is used as a condiment (*recipe, p.282*).

Culantro
Eryngium foetidum

This tender biennial grows wild on many Caribbean islands and is variously called shado beni (Trinidad), chadron benee (Domenica), and recao (Puerto Rico). Also grown in southeast Asia, it is ngo gai in Vietnam, and reaches Europe with names like sawtooth herb, long or spiny coriander, Chinese parsley, as well as its Spanish name culantro, which is most commonly used in English-speaking countries.

Culinary uses

In its indigenous regions, culantro is consumed enthusiastically. It flavours soups, stews and curries, rice and noodle dishes, meat and fish dishes. It is a key ingredient in Trinidadian fish and meat marinades, and in Puerto Rican sofrito, a mixture of garlic, onion, green pepper, chillies, coriander, and culantro that forms the basis of many of the island's dishes.

Mexican cooks use it in salsas. In Asia it is often used to temper the smell of beef, which many people find too pungent. For northern Thai cooks it is common in larp, a fiery dish of lightly cooked or raw beef served with sticky rice. In Vietnam young leaves are always in the bowl of herbs put on the table to accompany the meal.

Fresh leaves
Leaves are leathery and toothed, sometimes spiny. If so, remove spines or cook thoroughly. Can be used instead of coriander, but use less.

 TASTING NOTES

Culantro has an intense aroma with a fetid element, as its Latin name indicates. The taste is earthy, pungent, and quite sharp – a concentrated version of coriander with a bitter note at the finish.

 PARTS USED

Fresh leaves.

 BUYING / STORING

Plants are available at some herb nurseries. Leaves, tied in bundles, sometimes with rootlets attached, are sold in oriental shops. They keep for 3–4 days in the refrigerator. I have not come across culantro as a dried herb, but it freezes well. Remove the thick central rib and purée the leaves with a little water or sunflower oil, then freeze in ice-cube trays.

 GROW YOUR OWN

Culantro grows best in well-drained soil in partial shade. Shade produces plants with bigger, greener, and more pungent leaves, whereas hot sun encourages the plant to go rapidly to seed. Remove flower stalks to encourage more leaf growth. Culantro has long, tough leaves with serrated edges that may be prickly. Leaves can be picked throughout the growing season by cutting off at soil level.

 FLAVOUR PAIRINGS

Combines well with chillies, coriander, galangal, garlic, makrut lime, lemon grass, mint, parsley.

Rau ram

Polygonum odoratum / Persicaria odoratum

Rau ram seems increasingly to be the accepted name for this popular tropical Asian herb, but it is also sold as Vietnamese coriander (cilantro), Vietnamese mint, daun kesom (its Malay name), and laksa leaf. Vietnamese emigrants took it to France in the 1950s and the US in the 1970s, where it now has an enthusiastic and growing following.

Culinary uses

Rau ram is used as flavouring for fish, seafood, poultry, and pork. The Vietnamese make an excellent chicken and cabbage salad, flavoured with rau ram, chillies, and lime juice. Thai cooks also serve the leaves raw with nam prik or shred them and add to larp and curries. One of its most popular uses in Singapore and Malaysia is as an aromatic garnish for laksa, a spicy soup made with fish, seafood, and coconut milk. Use rau ram as you would coriander; add shredded or torn leaves to stir-fries, soups, and noodles.

Fresh leaves

Rau ram withstands cooking better than coriander and will impart a subtle flavour to cooked dishes if added part way through the cooking. The leaves may also be used as a component of a salad platter.

TASTING NOTES

Rau ram smells rather like a more penetrating version of coriander with a clear citrus note; the taste is similar, refreshing with a hot, biting, peppery aftertaste. Some people find the aroma soapy.

PARTS USED

Fresh, young leaves.

BUYING / STORING

Rau ram plants are available from specialist nurseries and bunches of stems are sold in oriental shops. Enclosed in a plastic bag, these will keep in the vegetable drawer of the refrigerator for 4–5 days if bought in good condition.

GROW YOUR OWN

A bushy herb, rau ram grows wild on the banks and streams in its native habitat. Unless there is a hard frost it will overwinter in a sheltered spot outside. Rau ram grows best in partial shade and rapidly becomes invasive in rich, moist soil. In the tropics it bears red or pink flowers. Keep trimming the plant to encourage new growth. It roots easily if stems are left in a glass of water for 2–3 days, after which it can be planted out.

FLAVOUR PAIRINGS

Good with coconut milk, egg dishes, fish and seafood, meat, poultry, noodles, bean sprouts, red and green peppers, water chestnuts.
Combines well with chillies, galangal, garlic, ginger, lemon grass, salad herbs.

Rocket's toothed leaves have a warm, peppery smell that rises from the bed as soon as the first leaf is picked. The taste is pleasantly pungent. The small, white or yellow, edible flowers have a faint orange aroma; they make an attractive garnish.

PARTS USED

Leaves and flowers.

BUYING / STORING

Rocket is now readily available at greengrocers and in supermarkets, either on its own or in bags of mixed leaves. All the same, it is well worth growing from seed, as it needs no looking after and is at its best freshly picked. It can be stored in a plastic bag in the refrigerator drawer for a few days. Drying rocket is a waste of time, nor does it freeze well, but as fresh leaves can be bought or picked at almost any time this matters little.

GROW YOUR OWN

Rocket and wild rocket are both very easy to grow from seed, and staggered sowing will give a useful crop virtually throughout the year. They thrive in partial shade. Rocket is an annual, wild rocket a perennial; both self-seed only too readily. Leaves are ready for picking in 6–8 weeks.

Rocket

Eruca vesicaria subsp. *sativa*

Rocket is native to Asia and southern Europe and naturalized in North America, where it is known as arugula. It was a popular herb in Europe until the 18th century, when it virtually disappeared everywhere but in Italy. After nearly two centuries of neglect it is having a well-deserved revival, and is currently one of the most fashionable salad herbs in both Europe and North America.

Culinary uses

Whole leaves can be added to any salad of mixed leaves or potato salad, or will make a strongly flavoured salad on their own, especially with a nut oil dressing. Rocket leaves can also be used as a fragrant bed on which to present other kinds of salad, poached eggs, or roasted red peppers. Rocket with raw ham makes a good sandwich filling, and with mushrooms or cheese a filling for ravioli. Shredded leaves are good in herb butter for seafood or herb dressings, especially for pasta. Rocket can also be used to make pesto, with or without basil.

Rocket *E. v.* subsp. *sativa*

The leaves become progressively more peppery the longer they stay on the plant, but once the flowers fully develop their taste diminishes.

Wild rocket *Diplotaxis muralis*

Wild rocket has narrower, more sharply
toothed leaves and a more peppery taste
than its cultivated counterpart. It is sold
at greengrocers, and can be bought
as growing plants from
herb nurseries.

FLAVOUR PAIRINGS

Good with goat's cheese,
lettuce, potatoes,
salad herbs, tomato.

Combines well with basil,
borage, coriander, cresses,
dill, lovage, mint, parsley,
salad burnet.

Turkish rocket

Bunias orientalis

Turkish rocket grows wild in parts of Asia. It has a sharp and coarse
flavour, rather like horseradish, and a tinge of sulphur. Called rokka,
it can often be bought in large bunches from Turkish or Cypriot stores.
It is better cooked, for instance in a vegetable frittata, than used raw.

TASTING NOTES

Watercress has little aroma; sprigs and leaves are crisp and have a peppery, slightly bitterish taste.

PARTS USED

Sprigs and leaves.

BUYING / STORING

Cress and nasturtium seeds can be had from nurseries. In greengrocers and supermarkets watercress is available all year round, either sold separately or in bags of mixed greens. Land cress is occasionally available from upmarket greengrocers. In a plastic bag in the refrigerator drawer cresses will keep for 4–5 days. Nasturtium flowers should be used immediately. Seeds can be harvested in autumn to sow the next year.

GROW YOUR OWN

Watercress grows speedily near springs and open running watercourses – conditions that are imitated in its commercial hydroponic cultivation. It can be grown fairly easily from seed in a tub, where its shining, bright green leaves will soon cover the entire surface.

FLAVOUR PAIRINGS

Good with chicken, cucumber, fish, onion, oranges, potatoes, salmon.

Combines well with fennel, ginger, parsley, other salad herbs, sorrel.

Watercress
Nasturtium officinale

Watercress is a hardy perennial native to Europe and Asia, widely naturalized in North America, and has been introduced also into the West Indies and South America. Its use as a salad herb can be traced back to the Persians, Greeks, and Romans. Its cultivation in northern Europe started relatively late – Germany began growing it in the 16th century, and Britain had not started before 1800.

Culinary uses

Watercress is used in an amazing variety of soups, made either with stock, cream, or yogurt. Best known is French potage au cresson, potato and watercress soup, served hot or cold; Italians use cress in minestrone and other vegetable soups; the Chinese in egg-drop and wonton soups and in Cantonese seafood broths. In the American southwest watercress soup may be served with a red pepper rouille. The herb is also served with fish, often with ginger; made into a sauce, much like sorrel, it goes well with salmon. In China watercress is popular blanched, chopped, and tossed in light sesame oil, or stir-fried with salt, sugar, and a little rice wine.

Fresh sprigs

In the West watercress is mostly eaten raw, as a garnish or in sandwiches and salads, either on its own or combined with, for instance, cucumber, fennel, orange segments, papaya, or red onion.

Other cresses

There are many plants resembling or used like watercress but not necessarily related to *N. officinale*. Nasturtium is the common name of a South American genus cultivated widely for its vivid flowers. The transfer of the name came about because the leaves taste similar to watercress, although few people take advantage of nasturtiums in the kitchen.

Land cress *Barbarea verna praecox*

As its other name, winter cress, indicates, this plant is very hardy. Like watercress, its small, tender leaves have a spicy flavour and make a welcome addition to winter's rather limited array of fresh greens. It is biennial and can be grown from seed in the garden.

Garden cress *Lepidium sativum*

This cress has dark green leaves, which may be curled, and a strong, peppery flavour. Quite hardy, it prefers cold and dry conditions, and tolerates almost any soil. In combination with mustard it is grown as a popular cut-and-come-again seedling crop.

Nasturtium or Indian cress

Tropaeolum majus

Neither the leaves nor the flowers of this plant have much aroma, but both have an agreeably peppery, cress-like taste – the flowers are slightly sweeter and more delicate. Young leaves can be used in salads; the flowers look and taste great scattered over a green salad or one of potato or haricot beans, or floated on a bowl of fruit punch. Flower buds and seeds can be pickled and used instead of capers.

TASTING NOTES

Wasabi has a fierce, burning smell that makes the nose prickle, and a bitingly sharp but fresh and cleansing taste. Dried wasabi only develops its penetrating aroma and flavour when mixed with water and left to steep for about 10 minutes.

 PARTS USED

Roots.

 BUYING / STORING

Outside Japan wasabi is seldom available fresh, but you can buy British-grown wasabi on the internet. Otherwise look for wasabi in the refrigerated cabinet or freezer in a Japanese food store. More usually it is sold either in tubes as a paste or in tins as powder. Fresh wasabi will keep for a week wrapped in plastic in the refrigerator. Powdered wasabi has a shelf life of several months but can develop a rather stale aftertaste. Tubes of paste must be refrigerated after opening, and the paste loses its potency more quickly than the powder.

 HARVESTING

Wasabi can only be cultivated in cold, pure, running water; commercial growing is usually done in flooded terraces, usually in partial shade. It is very expensive to produce.

Wasabi

Eutrema wasabi

This herbaceous perennial grows primarily in cold mountain streams in Japan; cultivation is now progressing well in California, New Zealand, and the UK. The name translates as mountain hollyhock. In the West the plant is sometimes called Japanese horseradish, a reference to its pungency and the fact that the gnarled and knobbly root, on average about 10–12cm (4–5in) long, is the edible part.

Fresh root

In Japan fresh wasabi root is sold in tubs of water. The tough, brownish green skin is removed to reveal pale green flesh.

Culinary uses

Wasabi does not retain its flavour when cooked, so it is generally served with or added to cold food. In Japan it accompanies most raw fish dishes. Sashimi and sushi plates always have a tiny mound of grated wasabi or wasabi paste, which is then mixed to individual taste with a soy dipping sauce. In sushi it often appears as an ingredient as well as a garnish, between raw fish and the vinegared rice. With soy sauce and dashi (soup stock), wasabi makes the popular wasabi-joyu sauce. On its own, wasabi can be used to give a sharp piquancy to dressings and marinades. It also makes a good butter that keeps in the refrigerator for weeks; this makes an interesting change served on tournedos or other good beef.

FLAVOUR PAIRINGS

Essential to sashimi, sushi.
Good with avocado, beef, raw fish, rice, seafood.
Combines well with ginger, soy sauce.

Grated root
In Japan peeled wasabi root is grated finely on an oroshigane, a flat grater tightly set with thin spikes. Made of stainless steel, tinned copper, or plastic, these can be bought from Japanese shops.

Wasabi paste
Because wasabi is so expensive, harsher-tasting horseradish mixed with mustard and green colouring is frequently passed off as wasabi paste or powder. Real paste costs more than twice the price of fake wasabi paste and has a shorter "use by" date.

Horseradish

Armoracia rusticana

Horseradish is a hardy perennial native to eastern Europe and western Asia, where it still grows wild in the steppes of Russia and Ukraine. Its culinary use probably originated in Russia and eastern Europe, spreading to central Europe in the early Middle Ages, later to Scandinavia and western Europe. English settlers took it to North America, and cultivation was established by German and eastern European immigrants around 1850. By about 1860 bottled horseradish was available as one of the first convenience condiments.

TASTING NOTES

Horseradish root is very pungent and mustard-like when just grated, enough to make your eyes water and your nose run. The taste is acrid, sharp, and hot. The leaves are also pungent when crushed; the taste is sharp, but much milder than that of the root.

PARTS USED

Fresh young leaves; fresh or dried roots.

BUYING / STORING

Fresh roots can be hard to find except before Passover – horseradish is one of the five bitter herbs of the Seder. Fresh roots taken from the garden will keep for months in dry sand; bought ones remain good for 2–3 weeks in a plastic bag in the refrigerator, even after being cut and part-used. Grated horseradish can be frozen. Dried roots can be bought powdered or flaked.

GROW YOUR OWN

Horseradish is propagated from root cuttings. It grows very easily in sandy loam soil with good drainage but is invasive – the tiniest bit left in the soil will be enough to overrun a patch, so plant in a container, as one does mint. Harvesting usually starts after a frost has killed off the tops; the roots are frost-hardy and can be lifted throughout the winter.

Fresh root
Slicing a long, thick, hairy, yellowish-brown horseradish root reveals white flesh. Grating releases its highly pungent volatile oil, but this dissipates very quickly and does not survive cooking.

Culinary uses

Freshly grated horseradish can be stabilized with a little lemon juice. It is good on salads of potatoes or root vegetables, and aids the digestion of oily fish. A traditional accompaniment to roast beef – and to ox tongue in Germany – it also goes well with boiled beef. Scandinavian cooks add sliced horseradish, with onion, fresh ginger, and other spices, to some of their pickled herrings and make a rich horseradish and mustard sauce to accompany white fish.

Horseradish is easily made into a sauce by blending it with cream and vinegar, or with soured cream alone,

with or without sugar. A popular Austrian condiment is Apfelkren, made by mixing horseradish with grated apples and a little lemon juice. With apricot preserve and a little mustard, horseradish makes a good glaze for ham. Mixed with mustard into butter it is good with corn on the cob or carrots. A few tender, young leaves will give a pleasant, sharp taste to a green salad. Processed horseradish browns as it ages and loses its strength. Many condiments have too much added sugar, which masks the fresh and pungent flavour.

FLAVOUR PAIRINGS

Good with apple, avocado, beef, beetroot, oily or smoked fish, baked gammon or ham, potatoes, sausages, seafood.

Combines well with capers, celery, chives, cream, dill, mustard, tomato purée, vinegar, yogurt.

Grated root

Sprinkle lemon juice on grated horseradish to preserve its white colour and pungency. Vinegar is used to prevent browning and loss of flavour in commercial horseradish condiments.

TASTING NOTES

Not everyone likes epazote. The aroma is described as that of turpentine or putty by those who hate it, while it reminds others of savory, mint, and citrus. I think of it as camphorous, earthy, and minty. The taste is pungent and refreshing, bitterish with lingering citrus notes and a curious, oddly addictive rankness.

PARTS USED

Leaves, fresh or dried.

BUYING / STORING

In Europe it is almost impossible to obtain fresh epazote unless you grow it yourself; dried epazote has much less taste but is still good in cooking. Buy dried leaves, not stalks.

GROW YOUR OWN

Epazote can easily be grown from seed in dry soil. Its flavour depends on the amount of sun it gets – in colder climates it is less aromatic. It is an annual but reseeds readily. Once established, it should be possible to overwinter plants indoors.

FLAVOUR PAIRINGS

Essential to black bean dishes, quesadillas (cheese-filled tortillas), mole verde, salsas.

Good with chorizo, fish and shellfish, lime, mushrooms, onion, peppers, pork, pulses, rice, squash, sweetcorn, tomatillos, green vegetables.

Combines well with chilli, cloves, coriander leaf, cumin, garlic, oregano.

Epazote

Chenopodium ambrosioides

Native to central and southern Mexico, epazote was an essential ingredient of Mayan cuisine in the Yucatán and Guatemala. It is now widely cultivated and used in southern Mexico, the northern countries of South America, and the Caribbean islands. Its use is spreading in North America, where it is often found as a weed along roadsides and in towns; it is grown commercially in the south. It still has to make its mark in Europe, although it grows wild there also.

Culinary uses

The fresh herb is commonly used in Mexican bean dishes, partly for its flavour and partly because it reduces flatulence. Chopped finely, it is used in soups and stews. Although used raw in salsas, its flavour works best in cooking; add for only the last 15 minutes or so to avoid bitterness. It is essential to mole verde, a green cooking sauce of tomatillos and green chillies, thickened with nuts or seeds. Use epazote lightly: it easily overwhelms other flavours, and in larger doses it is somewhat toxic and can cause dizziness.

Fresh leaves
The taste of epazote is too pungent for many people. Its name, deriving from Nahuatl, an Aztec language still spoken around Mexico City, refers to a disagreeable odour – epatl means skunk and tzotl sweat.

Dried leaves
Use dried leaves only when fresh are unavailable.

Mugwort

Artemisia vulgaris

Mugwort is a herbaceous perennial that grows wild in many habitats through most of Europe, Asia, and North and South America. In the Middle Ages it was used instead of hops as a bittering agent in brewing beer. In the 18th century it was one of the most used kitchen herbs in Europe, but it has since gone out of fashion except in Germany, where it remains popular as Gänsekraut, goose herb.

Culinary uses

Mugwort suits fatty fish or meat, and poultry such as duck or goose, and helps in their digestion. It is good in stuffings and marinades, and also flavours stock quite well. Its aroma develops with cooking, so it should be added early. It has no natural partners among herbs, but garlic and pepper go well with it. Called yomogi in Japan, it is used as a vegetable, as a popular ingredient in mochi (rice cakes), and as a seasoning for soba noodles. Young leaves are boiled or stir-fried thoughout Asia. Young leaves can also be shredded over a green salad or stirred into the dressing. Cider vinegar in which mugwort has been steeped for some weeks is good for salads and marinades.

TASTING NOTES

The aroma of mugwort is of juniper and pepper, lightly pungent with a hint of mint and sweetness. The flavour is similar, with a mild, bitter aftertaste.

PARTS USED

Fresh young shoots; leaves and flowerbuds, both fresh and dried.

BUYING / STORING

Buy plants from a nursery. Pick young leaves as needed. Flower-stalks are dried by hanging in a dark, warm place. This can easily take 3 weeks, or 4–6 hours if left in a warm oven. Once dry, buds and leaves can be stored in an airtight container for up to a year. Dried mugwort is available from some Japanese shops.

GROW YOUR OWN

Mugwort is quite adaptable but does prefer full sun and a rich, moist soil. It can be propagated from seed or by division of the rhizomes. It should be kept in check or it will go rampant. Numerous small, reddish-brown florets bloom in late summer and early autumn on panicled spikes. Harvest just before the flower buds open: the flowers can get unpleasantly bitter.

FLAVOUR PAIRINGS

Good with beans, duck, eel, game, goose, onions, pork, rice.

Combines well with garlic, pepper.

Fresh leaves
Leaves are smooth and green on top, downy white underneath.

Dried leaves
In Germany mugwort is available fresh and dried; elsewhere it is necessary to grow your own, or buy dried via the internet.

Preparing
herbs

Stripping, chopping, and pounding herbs

Some herbs – chives, chervil, coriander – have soft stalks, but in most cases leaves must be stripped from the stalks before being used. Small leaves and sprigs are used whole in salads or as a garnish, but most leaves are chopped, sliced, or pounded depending on the dish being prepared. Keep leaves whole until just before you need them or their flavours will dissipate.

Stripping leaves

When stripping herbs you may find that you are not able to go right to the top of the stalk because it is too tender and will break. Such upper stalks are likely to be soft enough to chop with the leaves. Some herbs are easier to strip from the top down, particularly those with large leaves.

◀ **Stripping tough stalks**
Hold the bottom of the stalk firmly in one hand, place the thumb and first finger of the other hand on either side of the stalk, and, using the thumb to guide, pull upwards, stripping the leaves onto a board.

◀ **Stripping tender stalks**
Strip fennel and dill from the bottom of the stalk, pulling the leaf sprays upwards with one hand. Take out any thick stalks that remain and strip off the leaves.

Chopping leaves

Herbs are chopped according to the dish for which they are needed. Finely chopped herbs integrate well with other ingredients. They provide immediate flavour because so much of their surface is exposed, allowing the essential oils to blend into the food quickly, but they may lose their flavour in cooking. Coarsely chopped herbs keep their identity, flavour, and texture longer and survive cooking better than finely chopped herbs, but are less attractive in a smooth-textured dish.

◀ **Using a mezzaluna**
Some cooks prefer to use the curved mezzaluna for large amounts of herbs. This implement is rocked backwards and forwards to great effect. Herbs may also be chopped in the small bowl of a food processor; use the pulse button and chop briefly. Make sure the herbs are completely dry or they will turn out unattractively paste-like. It is more difficult to obtain uniformly chopped leaves in a processor.

1 Choose a large, sharp knife for cutting herbs or you will bruise rather than cut them. Lay the herbs on a board, hold the point of the blade on the board with the flat fingers of your non-cutting hand, and chop up and down briskly in a rocking motion.

2 Scoop the herbs back into a pile from time to time with the flat of the blade. Continue the chopping action until the herbs are cut as finely as you need.

Making a chiffonade

Any finely shredded vegetable used as a garnish is termed a chiffonade. Shredded herb leaves make an attractive garnish and also keep their texture well in a sauce.

1 If using leaves such as sorrel, remove the thick vein from each one beforehand.

2 Stack a few similar-sized leaves one on top of the other and roll them up tightly.

3 Using a sharp knife, cut the roll of leaves into very fine slices.

Pounding herbs

Herbs can be pounded to a paste using a pestle and mortar, and garlic is easily puréed in a mortar with a little salt. A smoother result is achieved more quickly in a food processor.

1 Pesto (recipe, p.289) is the classic pounded herb sauce. Start by pounding some basil and garlic in a large mortar.

2 Gradually work in some pine nuts, grated Parmesan, and olive oil and mix to a paste.

Drying and rubbing herbs

Drying does not suit all herbs. Those with woody stalks and tough leaves, such as thyme, rosemary, oregano, and lemon verbena, dry best and keep their flavour well, while those with soft leaves and stalks, such as basil, parsley, chervil, and marjoram, lose their flavour almost completely. Mint is an exception; although it has soft leaves, it dries well. The traditional way to dry herbs is to hang them in bunches, but they also dry well in a microwave oven. For the best flavour, harvest herbs just before their flowerbuds open, when the essential oils are at their most concentrated, and pick early in the day.

Freezing herbs

Soft herbs that do not dry well can be frozen. Frozen herbs keep their fragrance for 3–4 months. Use for soups, stews, braised dishes, and sauces.

◀ **Freezing chopped herbs**
Wash and dry the herbs well, chop, and freeze in small pots or in ice-cube trays with a little water or oil. Store the cubes in plastic bags.

◀ **Freezing puréed herbs**
Alternatively purée each herb with a little oil in a food processor and freeze in bags or plastic pots.

Drying herbs

Herbs hanging in a well-ventilated place will dry within a few days to a week. Those kept in a steamy kitchen will not dry well. Avoid direct sunlight or too much heat because they will cause the essential oils to evaporate.

1 When preparing herbs for drying, remove any old or discoloured leaves. Tie the herbs in small bunches and hang in a well-ventilated place out of direct sunlight, such as an attic or shed.

2 Drying is complete when the leaves feel brittle. Large leaves or small flowerbuds can be rubbed between the palms of your hands to crumble them. Otherwise, strip the leaves from the stalks. Store in airtight containers.

▲ **Microwaving herbs**
Scatter two handfuls of cleaned leaves and sprigs evenly on a double layer of kitchen paper and microwave at 100 per cent for 2½ minutes. Bay leaves may need a little longer. Microwaving preserves colour well. Store as right.

Making vinegars, oils, and butters

Flavoured vinegars and oils are useful for sauces, dressings, and marinades, and for stirring into soups and stews just before serving. Basil, dill, garlic, lavender, lemon verbena, rosemary, tarragon, and thyme make excellent vinegars; among spices try chillies, peppercorns, dill, fennel, mustard, or coriander seed. For oil try basil, bay, dill, garlic, mint, oregano, rosemary, savory, or thyme, or chillies, cumin, anise, dill, or fennel. Herb and spice butters provide a quick dressing for grilled or fried fish, poultry and meat, and steamed or boiled vegetables, and also make good sandwiches.

Making herb vinegar or oil

Flavoured vinegars keep for several years, becoming mellower as they age. Oils will keep for a year. Keep both in a cool, dark place, or refrigerate.

1 To make a herb or spice vinegar, take about 60g (2oz) of herb sprigs or whole spices and crush to bring out their flavour.

2 Put them into a preserving jar and cover with 500ml (16fl oz) white wine vinegar, cider vinegar, or rice vinegar. Close the jar and infuse for 2–3 weeks. Flavours will develop more quickly if the jar is placed in the sun.

3 Strain into bottles, add a fresh herb sprig to each one for decoration, close with a cork or plastic-lined cap, and label the bottle.

◀ **Making herb oil**
Follow the above method, but instead of vinegar fill up the jar with virgin olive oil, sunflower oil, or grapeseed oil. Oil is best kept out of sunlight. When the flavours have developed, strain and bottle.

Making herb or spice butter

Most fresh herbs make fine flavoured butters; among spices, choose ground cumin, black pepper, cardamom, allspice, paprika, or cayenne – 1½–2 tbsp per 150g (5½oz) butter. If you combine spices with herbs, use less. Butters keep for a week if refrigerated, or can be frozen.

1 Beat 150g (5½oz) softened butter in a bowl with 1–2 tbsp lemon juice and 4–5 tbsp chopped herb, or blend the butter and lemon juice with the same quantity of herb in a food processor.

2 Lay a sheet of clingfilm on a flat surface and spoon the flavoured butter into the centre. Press the butter into an elongated shape. Wrap in another sheet of clingfilm to prevent tearing.

3 Taking care to avoid folding the clingfilm into the butter, roll the butter into the shape of a sausage. Twist the ends of the clingfilm to compact the butter.

▲ **Herb butter**
Wrap in foil and refrigerate or put into a plastic sealable bag and freeze.

Spices

Introducing
spices

Asafoetida

I have long had a passion for spices and a fascination with their origins and production, as well as their culinary possibilities. What people eat in any particular region is, or was, largely determined by what grew and was reared there. The style of cooking originally depended on local conditions, such as the availability of fuels, but what really differentiates the great cuisines of the world is the spices they use and how they blend them.

Produce of tropical Asia

Most of the important spice plants – cinnamon, cloves, galangal, ginger, nutmeg, pepper – are native to the Asian tropics. They have been used and traded for millennia, and much has been written about the history of their trade – the fortunes and empires founded on it, the brutal conquests, piracy, and greed; but our view of these developments has always been a European one. We know about the overland routes from China to Byzantium, we are aware of the role Arab seafarers played in the introduction of spices to the Tigris-Euphrates basin and later to the Mediterranean ports, and we have read about the Portuguese, Dutch, and English monopolies. But we know little about the equally important early Asian trade, dominated at different times by the large merchant fleets, first of the Korean kingdom of Silla (early 7th to mid-9th centuries), then of southern China under the Sung dynasty (960–1276), and of Sri Lanka. We

Curry leaves

know even less of the much earlier Indian traders who, from 600 BCE, established new Hindu or Buddhist states in Sri Lanka, Malaysia, and some of the Indonesian islands, and supplied them with spices from their homeland.

When Columbus "discovered" America the cultures of that continent were already old and highly developed, and the spices of the American tropics and subtropics – allspice, chillies, vanilla – had played their part in those cultures for a very long time. Here Europeans can indeed be said to have been of importance, for the rapid spread of chillies throughout their colonies transformed the diet of half the world.

The spread of spices

Europe itself had already contributed much to the world of spices. Many of the aromatic seeds – coriander, fennel, fenugreek, mustard, poppy – are native to the Mediterranean region, and Europe's colder regions have contributed caraway, dill, and juniper. European trade remained mainly within the continent and with western Asia, but settlers sailing to the New World took many of their familiar spices with them. Not all the spread of spices has been due to trade. Some resulted from the breaking of jealously guarded monopolies; French botanists and explorers were particularly effective in smuggling plants to new destinations, where plantations were established.

Coriander

Poppy   **Lemon grass**   **Ginger**

Vanilla
Cured vanilla pods, containing tiny, sticky seeds, flavour ice cream, cakes, and sweet syrups. Vanilla also goes well with seafoods and chicken.

Turmeric
Grated turmeric rhizome imparts a warm, earthy flavour to many Indian and Caribbean dishes, as well as giving them their rich yellow colour.

Migration has had a more lasting effect than trade on the spread of spices. For example, ships from southern China carried ginger, planted in troughs, as a necessity of life, and so it came to be cultivated throughout the Pacific region. Immigrant communities, whether established by colonial force or economic plight, brought their own traditional ingredients and married them to local produce – hence Cape Malay and Cajun cooking, the "rijsttafel" of Holland, and the use of Colombo powder in the French West Indies.

The desire for authenticity

Today there is a growing awareness of and demand for authentic regional foods. We have learned that there is no such thing as Italian food because every Italian region has something different to offer. We also know that what used to be the standard food in Chinese restaurants is Cantonese, and that the cooking in Beijing, Sichuan, and Hunan is quite different. The contrast between northern and southern Indian cooking is attracting attention, as is the difference between northern and southern Thai food. Moroccan, Peruvian, and Ethiopian restaurants now exist in most cities. What determines their individuality has much to do with how they use herbs and spices.

It has been said that chemistry is like cooking, but now it would be more accurate to say that cooking is becoming like chemistry. Food companies are constantly formulating new flavours and trying to synthesize others. They use electronic noses and tongues and other sophisticated apparatus to produce "aroma-fingerprints". They "collect headspace" – that is, gather aroma molecules from spices, herbs, and fruits or from finished dishes for reproduction in a laboratory, eventually to be unleashed in ready-prepared foods. The results are certainly impressive, but many of the cultural, tactile, and nutritive values of the original foods are lost.

Successfully making your own blend of spices gives a sense of achievement that nothing squeezed out of a tube or poured from a bottle can equal. In countries where such blends are used regularly there is no such thing as an immutably fixed recipe. Regional tradition, family tastes, and individual preference determine the ingredients, and even fairly standard mixtures will be adapted to the dish they are made for –masalas, bumbus, rempahs, and the like are infinitely variable.

Sri Lankan curry powder
This curry powder is made from curry leaves, coriander, cumin, fenugreek, rice, chillies, black peppercorns, cloves, green cardamom, and cinnamon (*recipe, p.278*).

Qalat daqqa
(recipe, p.283)

Grinding spices
Spices are best stored whole and ground only when needed. Many spices start to lose their aroma within hours of grinding.

Frying spices
For some dishes the spices are fried in oil beforehand to impart their flavour. The oil is then used to flavour the dish.

Grating ginger
Fresh ginger rhizome yields a highly aromatic juice. After fine grating, the ginger shavings are wrapped in muslin and the juice squeezed out.

Choosing and using spices

Complex flavours are built up in mixtures by using spices (or herbs) that complement each other. Some are used for their taste, others for their aroma. Some have souring properties; in others, the colour is important. The moment at which spices are added to a dish makes a crucial difference. Whether or not they are dry-roasted beforehand, they will impart their flavour to the dish if added at the beginning of cooking; if sprinkled on towards the end of cooking, it is their aroma that will be emphasized in the finished dish.

Towards the end of the book, I have given recipes for mixtures from many different parts of the world. These should be regarded as basic formulas, the fundamentals of specific styles of cooking, and fully open to improvisation and experiment. By all means try them first as they are written, then adapt them to your taste and the dish you want to make.

TASTING NOTES

Sesame seeds are not very aromatic but they have a mildly nutty, earthy odour. This is more marked in the taste, which develops even greater richness after dry-roasting or grinding to a paste. Black seeds have an earthier taste than white and are not usually ground.

PARTS USED

Seeds, whole and as a paste, and oil.

BUYING / STORING

White seeds are available from supermarkets and Indian, Middle Eastern, and health food shops, as are the pale brown sesame paste (tahini), and Indian sesame oil. Oriental oil and paste can be bought from oriental shops, as can black sesame seeds. Golden seeds, with their richer aroma, are preferred by Japanese cooks, but these are harder to find. Store seeds in airtight containers and toast them as needed.

HARVESTING

Plants are harvested before the seed pods are fully ripe, when they burst open. The pods are dried and hulled, usually mechanically.

Sesame

Sesamum orientale

Sesame is one of the earliest recorded plants grown for its seeds. The Egyptians and Babylonians used ground seeds in their breads, a practice that continues in the Middle East today. Excavations in eastern Turkey have found evidence of oil being extracted from the seeds as early as 900BCE. High in polyunsaturated fatty acids, the oil pressed from raw seeds is excellent for cooking and is highly stable, with the advantage that it does not turn rancid in hot climates.

Whole seeds

Produced by an annual tropical plant, sesame seeds may be pale gold or white, red, brown, or black, depending on the variety. The seeds are small, flat, and oval, shiny and waxy because of their oil content, and fairly soft. The creamy white seeds are the most common.

Culinary uses

Sesame is scattered over breads or ground and added to the dough before baking. It is essential to the Middle Eastern spice blend za'atar, and to Japanese seven spice powder. It is the main ingredient of the Middle Eastern sweetmeat, halva. In India sesame is also used in sweets; til laddoos, balls of sesame and jaggery flavoured with cardamom, are very good. Indian cooks use pale golden sesame oil, called gingili or til oil, for cooking. Tahini and the oil are made from raw seeds.

Deep brown oriental sesame paste and amber-coloured oriental oil are made from dry-roasted seeds; this enhances the nutty flavour and gives the darker colour. These products are used in Chinese, Korean, and Japanese cooking. Oriental oil is a seasoning oil, not a cooking oil, because it burns at low temperatures. Oriental sesame paste has a dense texture and is used in dressings for noodles, rice, and vegetables.

The Chinese like the crunchy texture of sesame seeds to coat prawn balls and prawn toasts. In Japan, white or golden sesame is blended with soy sauce and sugar to dress cold chicken, noodles, and vegetable salads.

Black sesame is used in Chinese and Japanese cooking as a garnish for rice and vegetables, and to coat fish and seafood before cooking. It is often said to be bitter if dry-roasted, but I have not found it so if done lightly, and Japanese cooks frequently use it dry-roasted. Blended with coarse salt it makes the Japanese condiment, goma shio, that is sprinkled over vegetables, salads, and rice. In China, black seeds coat deep-fried toffee apples and bananas.

FLAVOUR PAIRINGS

Essential to za'atar, goma shio, seven spice powder.

Good with aubergines, courgettes, fish, green vegetables, honey, lemon, noodles, pulses, rice, salad greens, sugar.

Combines well with cassia, cardamom, chillies, cinnamon, cloves, coriander, ginger, nutmeg, oregano, pepper, sumac, thyme.

Oriental oil
Oriental oil is usually added to dishes just before serving. Combined with chillies, garlic, and ginger, it is popular in Sichuan cooking.

Tahini
In the Middle East pale brown tahini is blended with garlic and lemon juice to make a paste, used as a basis for dressings for vegetable and fish dishes, and as the flavouring for the chickpea dip, hummus.

TASTING NOTES

Nigella does not have a strong aroma; when rubbed it is herbaceous, somewhat like a mild oregano. The taste is nutty, earthy, peppery, rather bitter, dry, and quite penetrating; the texture is crunchy.

PARTS USED

Seeds.

BUYING / STORING

Buy whole seeds because they keep better; ground seeds may be adulterated. In an airtight container they will keep their flavour for 2 years. Nigella is stocked by spice merchants and by Indian and Middle Eastern shops.

HARVESTING

Nigella seeds are matt black, small, and teardrop-shaped. Their surface is rough. The seed capsules are gathered as they ripen but before they burst, then dried and lightly crushed so that the seeds can be removed easily.

FLAVOUR PAIRINGS

Essential to panch phoron.

Good with breads, pulses, rice, green and root vegetables.

Combines well with allspice, cardamom, cinnamon, coriander, cumin, fennel, ginger, pepper, savory, thyme, turmeric.

Nigella

Nigella sativa

Nigella is the botanical name of love-in-a-mist, the pretty garden plant with pale blue flowers and feathery foliage. The species grown for its seed is a close but less decorative relative, native to western Asia and southern Europe. India is the largest producer of nigella (kalonji) and a large consumer. The small, black seeds are often misnamed and sold as black onion seed.

Culinary uses

Nigella is sprinkled on flatbreads, rolls, and savoury pastries, alone or with sesame or cumin. Cooks in Bengal combine it with mustard seeds, cumin, fennel, and fenugreek in the local spice mixture, panch phoron, which gives a distinctive taste to pulses and vegetable dishes. Elsewhere in India nigella is used in pilafs, kormas, and curries, and in pickles. In Iran it is a popular pickling spice used for fruit and vegetables. It is good with roast potatoes and other root vegetables. Ground with coriander and cumin it adds depth to a Middle Eastern potato or mixed vegetable omelette.

Whole seeds

Indian cooks usually dry-roast or fry the seeds to develop their flavour before sprinkling them over vegetarian dishes and salads.

Poppy
Papaver somniferum

The opium poppy – *Papaver somniferum* means sleep-inducing poppy – is a plant of great antiquity, native from the eastern Mediterranean to central Asia. It has been cultivated since earliest times for opium, a narcotic latex that oozes from the unripe seed pods if they are cut, and for its ripe seeds. Neither the seeds nor the dried pods from which they are harvested have narcotic properties.

Culinary uses

In the West poppy seeds are sprinkled over or incorporated into breads, bagels, pretzels, and cakes. Ground to a paste with honey or sugar, they are used to fill strudels and other pastries. In Turkey roasted, ground seeds are made into halva or desserts with syrup and nuts. In India the roasted seeds are ground and combined with spices to flavour and thicken kormas, curries, and gravies. They are used extensively in Bengali cooking in shuktas (bitter vegetable stews) and to coat crusty, dry-textured vegetables. Use poppy seeds, with or without other spices, in dressings for noodles or to garnish vegetables.

Whole seeds

Poppy seeds do not grind easily, but dry-roasting followed by a whizz in a coffee grinder can help. If they are to be used to thicken a dish, cover them with a little water and soak for several hours, then process them briefly together with the liquid.

TASTING NOTES

The aroma of dark seeds is lightly nutty and sweet; the flavour is stronger and somewhat almond-like. White seeds are lighter and more mellow in flavour. Both the aroma and flavour are enhanced by dry-roasting or baking. Poppy seeds are rich in protein and oil.

PARTS USED

Seeds.

BUYING / STORING

Poppy seeds may be slate blue, creamy-white, or mid-brown. The latter are common in Turkey and the Middle East; the blue-grey seeds are most used in Europe, and the creamy-white seeds in India. Blue poppy seeds are available from supermarkets; the white can be bought from spice merchants or Indian shops; and the brown in Middle Eastern shops. The seeds tend to go rancid quickly because of their high oil content, so buy in small amounts and use quickly. Store in an airtight container, or in the freezer if you intend to keep them longer than a few months.

HARVESTING

Plants are harvested mechanically when the seed heads turn yellow-brown; the capsules are cut off and dried.

FLAVOUR PAIRINGS

Good with aubergines, green beans, breads and pastries, cauliflower, courgettes, potatoes.

TASTING NOTES

Mahlab is sweetly perfumed and floral with hints of almond and cherry. It has a mouthwatering flavour that is nutty with a soft, almond sweetness, but then finishes with a bitter aftertaste.

PARTS USED

The soft interior of the kernels.

BUYING / STORING

Mahlab is best bought whole because once ground it loses its flavour quite quickly. Store in an airtight container. Middle Eastern and Greek shops or online spice merchants are the best sources.

HARVESTING

The soft kernels are extracted from the cherry stones and dried. They are small, oval, and beige or light-tan coloured.

FLAVOUR PAIRINGS

Good with almonds, apricots, dates, pistachio nuts, rose water, walnuts.

Combines well with anise, cinnamon, cloves, mastic, nigella, nutmeg, poppy seed, sesame.

Mahlab

Prunus mahaleb

This agreeable spice, little known outside the Middle East, comes from a sour cherry tree that grows wild throughout the region and in southern Europe. The trees bear small, thin-fleshed, black cherries, the kernels of which are used to flavour breads and pastries. Mahlab is used in Greece, Cyprus, Turkey, and the neighbouring Arab countries, from Syria to Saudi Arabia.

Culinary uses

Ground mahlab is primarily used in baking, especially in breads and pastries for festive occasions. A piquant note of mahlab spices the plaited Greek Easter bread, tsoureki; Armenian sweet rolls called chorek; Arab ma'amool, little pastries stuffed with nuts or dates baked by Lebanese Christians for their Easter celebrations; and Turkish kandil rings, made for the five religious feast nights each year when the mosques are illuminated. It is also used to flavour sweetmeats. Try adding a little to spiced or fruit breads or to pastry to be used with fruit. Mahlab is best ground in a coffee grinder. If that proves difficult, add a little salt or sugar, according to the recipe, to help break down the mahlab.

Ground kernels
Ground mahlab should be pale cream in colour; if it is dark or turning yellow it is too old.

Whole kernels
Beige mahlab kernels are creamy white inside; their texture is soft and chewy.

Wattle
Acacia species

Several hundred acacia species are native to Australia, but only a few have edible seeds. *A. victoriae* and *A. aneura*, the latter locally called the mulga tree, are two of those most regularly harvested for wattle seed. When dried, roasted, and ground the green, unripe seeds are transformed into a rich, deep brown powder that resembles ground coffee. Wattle is gaining popularity with food enthusiasts.

Culinary uses

Wattle seed yields its flavour when infused in a hot liquid. Do not allow the seed to boil or the flavour becomes bitter. The liquid may be strained and used alone, or the ground seed can be left in for its texture. Wattle seed is used to flavour desserts, especially cream- or yogurt-based desserts such as mousses, ice creams, and cheesecakes, and in cream fillings for cakes. I have added it to a sweet bread dough quite successfully, and a sprinkling gives a good flavour to a traditional bread and butter pudding. Wattle liquid is sometimes drunk as an alternative to coffee.

Ground seeds

Highly nutritious wattle seed has long provided food for indigenous Australians. New interest in bush foods has created a demand that at present exceeds supply.

TASTING NOTES

Wattle seed has a rich, toasty aroma that is faintly like coffee. The flavour has notes of coffee and roasted hazelnuts, with a hint of chocolate.

PARTS USED

Roasted, ground seeds.

BUYING / STORING

In Australia wattle seed is sold by spice merchants and good delicatessens. In the northern hemisphere some spice merchants stock it, and it is available online. In an airtight container it should keep for up to 2 years.

HARVESTING

Wattle seed is quite expensive because it is gathered from the wild and its preparation is extremely labour intensive. Green seed pods are steamed open, the whole green seeds are roasted with embers, and once cooled and cleaned of ash they are ground. The preparation is still mostly done in the bush by Aboriginal women.

TASTING NOTES

Cinnamon has a warm, agreeably sweet, woody aroma that is delicate yet intense; the taste is fragrant and warm with hints of clove and citrus. The presence of eugenol in the essential oil distinguishes cinnamon from cassia, giving it the note of clove.

PARTS USED

Quills of dried bark, ground cinnamon.

BUYING / STORING

Ground cinnamon – the paler its colour, the finer its quality – is widely available, but it loses its flavour quite quickly so buy in small amounts. Whole quills are available from spice merchants, delicatessens, and some supermarkets. They keep their aroma for 2–3 years if stored in an airtight container.

HARVESTING

The Sri Lankan cinnamon gardens lie on the coastal plains south of Colombo. Seedlings grow in thick clumps, with shoots about the thickness of a thumb. In the rainy season the shoots are cut off at the base and peeled. The harvesters work with extraordinary dexterity to cut the paper-thin pieces of bark and then roll quills up to 1m (3ft) long by hand. The quills are then gently dried in the shade.

Cinnamon
Cinnamomum verum / C. zelanicum

True cinnamon is indigenous to Sri Lanka. Like cassia, it is the bark of an evergreen tree of the laurel family. For 200 years a highly profitable monopoly of the island's cinnamon was controlled first by the Portuguese, then the Dutch, and finally by the English. By the late 18th century cinnamon had been planted in Java, India, and the Seychelles and the monopoly could no longer be sustained.

Quills

Pale brown or tan strips of dried bark are rolled one into another to form long, slender, smooth quills.

Grades of cinnamon

There are many grades of cinnamon; quills are classified as Continental, Mexican, or Hamburg, according to their thickness; the thin Continental quills have the finest flavour. Quillings are quills broken in handling; featherings the small inner pieces of bark not large enough to use in quills; and chips are shavings, the lowest grade of cinnamon. Featherings and chips are mostly used to produce ground cinnamon.

Culinary uses

Cinnamon's subtle flavour is well suited to all manner of desserts and spiced breads and cakes; it combines particularly well with chocolate and with apples, bananas, and pears. Use it in apple pie or with baked apples, with bananas fried in butter and flavoured with rum, and in red wine used for poaching pears. It also makes an excellent flavouring for many meat and vegetable dishes in Middle Eastern and Indian cooking. Moroccan cooks use it widely in lamb or chicken tagines, in the stew to accompany couscous, and above all to flavour bstilla, a pie of crisp, layered pastry filled with pigeon and almonds. The glorious Arab stew of lamb with apricots, mishmisheya, uses cinnamon and other spices, and it plays a role in many an Iranian khoresh (stews that accompany rice). In India cinnamon is used in many masalas or spice mixtures, in chutneys and condiments, and in spiced pilafs.

Mexico is the main importer of cinnamon, which is used to flavour coffee and chocolate drinks; cinnamon tea is popular throughout Central and South America. Once popular for spicing ale, cinnamon, together with cloves, sugar, and sliced oranges, makes an excellent flavouring for mulled wine.

FLAVOUR PAIRINGS

Good with almonds, apples, apricots, aubergines, bananas, chocolate, coffee, lamb, pears, poultry, rice.

Combines well with cloves, cardamom, coriander seed, cumin, ginger, mastic, nutmeg and mace, tamarind, turmeric.

Ground bark
Ground cinnamon is immediately aromatic; quills tend to hide their aromatic properties until broken or cooked in a liquid.

TASTING NOTES

Cassia shares the warm woody aroma of cinnamon, but it is more intense because it has a higher volatile oil. It is sweetish with a distinct pungency and an astringent edge. Vietnamese cassia has the highest volatile oil content and the strongest flavour.

 PARTS USED

Dried bark and quills, ground bark; dried unripe fruits, called cassia buds; tejpat leaves.

 BUYING / STORING

Cassia is difficult to grind, so it may be better to buy a small amount of ground cassia as well as pieces or quills. The latter will keep their flavour much longer, up to 2 years if stored in an airtight container. Buy bark, buds, and leaves from specialist spice shops and keep in an airtight container.

 HARVESTING

Harvesting starts in the rainy season when the bark can be stripped easily. As it dries it curls to make quills that are graded according to their essential oil content, length, and colour. Quills are reddish-brown and the layers are thicker than in cinnamon quills. Cassia bark is thicker and coarser than cinnamon and the corky outer layer is often left on when it is sold in pieces.

Cassia

Cinnamomum cassia

Cassia is the dried bark of a species of laurel tree native to Assam and northern Burma. It is recorded in a Chinese herbal in 2700BCE and today most cassia is exported from southern China and Vietnam. The finest quality comes from northern Vietnam. Cassia and cinnamon are used interchangeably in many countries. In the US cassia is sold as cinnamon or cassia-cinnamon, and is preferred to true cinnamon because of its more pronounced aroma and flavour.

Culinary uses

Cassia is an essential spice in China, where it is frequently used whole to flavour braised dishes and sauces for cooking meat and poultry; and ground cassia is a constituent of five spice powder. In India it is found in curries and pilafs, and in Germany and Russia it is often used as a flavouring for chocolate. I prefer cinnamon to cassia for delicate desserts, but it is good with apples, plums, dried figs, and prunes.

Whole bark
The colour of the smooth inner bark is reddish-brown, the rough outside is grey-brown.

Quills
Cassia bark is thick and tough and its quills are simple, crude curls, whereas the thinner, softer bark of cinnamon is rolled more tightly.

Cassia is used in spice blends for baking and sweet dishes. The pungency of cassia is better suited than cinnamon to rich meats such as duck or pork, and it goes well with pumpkin and squash, with sweet potatoes, and with lentils and beans. Cassia buds are used in sweet pickles in the Far East, and they can be used, whole, in place of cassia. They are particularly good in fruit compotes.

Tejpat leaves are often called Indian bay leaves because both come from species of laurel and because they are both used in long-cooked dishes and removed before serving. However, tejpat leaves are quite different from bay aromatically and a clove or a small piece of cassia make a better substitute than bay, if you can't find tejpat leaves. The leaves are extensively used in the biryanis and kormas of northern India and in some garam masalas.

Indonesian or Korintje cassia, *C. burmannii*, from Sumatra has a deep colour and a pleasantly spicy flavour but lacks the depth of Vietnamese or Chinese cassia.

FLAVOUR PAIRINGS

Essential to five spice powder.

Good with apples, plums, prunes, meat and poultry, pulses, root vegetables.

Combines well with cloves, cardamom, coriander seed, cumin, fennel, ginger, nutmeg and mace, Sichuan pepper, star anise, turmeric.

Buds

Cassia buds are a bit like small cloves. The hard, red-brown seed is just visible in the wrinkled grey-brown calyx. The buds have a warm, mellow aroma and the flavour is musky, sweet, and pungent, but less concentrated than that of the bark.

Dried tejpat leaves

Leaves of the related *C. tamala* are oval in shape with three long veins. They are used in the cooking of north India. Dried tejpat leaves have an immediate smell of spiced tea. A prolonged sniff reveals a warm, musky aroma of clove and cinnamon with citrus undertones.

TASTING NOTES

Ripe seeds have a sweet, woody, spicy fragrance with peppery and floral notes; the taste is sweet, mellow, and warm with a clear hint of orange peel.

PARTS USED

Dried fruits (seeds).

BUYING / STORING

Coriander is widely available. Buy whole seeds. They are easy to grind as needed, but their aromatic properties diminish quickly after grinding. In some Indian shops you may find a mix of whole or ground spices called dhana-jeera, a blend of coriander and cumin seed that is popular throughout the subcontinent.

HARVESTING

Seeds are harvested when they change colour from green to beige or light brown. Traditionally plants are cut, left to wither for 2–3 days, then threshed and dried in partial shade. If not fully dry they may be put in full sun before being sieved and packed. In some regions the seeds are dried artificially.

Coriander
Coriandrum sativum

A few plants serve cooks as both herb and spice, and of these coriander is undoubtedly the most widely used in both its forms. As a spice crop it is grown in eastern Europe, India, the US, and Central America as well as in its native habitat of western Asia and the Mediterranean. In all of these regions it is used extensively, sometimes in combination with the green herb.

Whole Moroccan seeds

Spherical Moroccan seeds are more commonly available than the oval Indian variety.

Ground seeds

Seeds are brittle and easy to grind; dry-roasting before grinding enhances the flavour.

Culinary uses

Cooks use coriander in larger amounts than they do many other spices because its flavour is mild. After dry-roasting, coriander forms the basis of many curry powders and masalas. North African cooks use it in harissa, tabil, ras el hanout, and other spice mixtures. Georgian khmeli-suneli and Iranian advieh mixtures usually include it, as do Middle Eastern baharat blends, and throughout the region coriander is a popular flavouring for vegetable dishes, stews, and sausages. Crushed green olives that are flavoured with coriander are a speciality of Cyprus.

In Europe and America coriander serves as a pickling spice and gives a pleasant, mild flavour to sweet-sour pickles and chutneys. West Indian cooks use it in masalas, and in Mexico it is often paired with cumin. French vegetable dishes à la grecque are flavoured with coriander. It is a useful spice to add to marinades, to court-bouillon for fish, or to stock for soup. It is also a constituent of English mixed sweet spice and is used in cakes and biscuits. Its flavour combines well with those of autumn fruits – apples, plums, pears, quinces – baked in pies or stewed in compotes.

FLAVOUR PAIRINGS

Essential to harissa, tabil, dukka, most masalas.

Good with apples, chicken, citrus fruits, fish, ham, mushrooms, onions, plums, pork, potatoes, pulses.

Combines well with allspice, chillies, cinnamon, cloves, cumin, fennel, garlic, ginger, mace, nutmeg.

Whole Indian seeds

Although coriander seeds and leaves smell and taste quite different, they complement each other in Indian and Mexican dishes.

Ground seeds
Indian coriander has a sweeter flavour than Moroccan.

TASTING NOTES

The aroma of juniper is pleasantly woody, bittersweet, and unmistakably like gin. The taste is clean and refreshing, sweetish with a slight burning effect, and has a hint of pine and resin.

PARTS USED

Berries, fresh or dried.

BUYING / STORING

Juniper berries are always sold whole and are usually dried. They are quite soft and bruise easily, so make sure those you buy are whole and dry. They will keep for several months in an airtight jar.

HARVESTING

A juniper bush makes a handsome garden plant all year round. The purple-black, smooth berries are about the size of a small pea. They take 2–3 years to ripen, so green and ripe berries occur on the same plant. There is some cultivation of juniper and also berries are gathered in the wild – a hazardous undertaking because of the very sharp, spiky leaves. Berries are picked when ripe, in autumn. Freshly picked berries have a green-blue bloom that disappears during drying.

Juniper
Juniperus communis

Juniper is a prickly, evergreen shrub or small tree that grows throughout much of the northern hemisphere, especially on chalky, hilly sites. It is a member of the large cypress family, the only one with edible fruit. The berries were used by enterprising Romans to adulterate pepper, and were burned in the Middle Ages (and well beyond) to clear the air of pestilence. Juniper's use as a flavouring for gin and other spirits dates back at least to the 17th century.

Whole berries

Berries growing in southerly latitudes have more flavour. If you come across them in the wild, on holiday in Tuscany perhaps, it is well worth picking them. Most of the berries on the market come from eastern Europe.

Culinary uses

In central and northern Europe juniper is a popular spice for meat and game. It is a natural foil for game and for fatty foods. The Scandinavians add it to marinades for pickled beef and elk and to red-wine marinades for roast pork. In northern France juniper appears in venison dishes and pâtés, in Belgium with veal kidneys flamed in gin, in Alsace and Germany with sauerkraut.

Easily crushed in a mortar, the berries impart a mild but pungent flavour that can benefit many dishes, both savoury and sweet. With salt and garlic they can be rubbed on to lamb, pork, game birds, and venison. Crushed berries also go into brines and marinades; chopped finely, just a few liven up stuffings and pâtés.

Crush or grind juniper just before using it, the essential oils are quickly lost once in contact with the air. Juniper is widely used to flavour cordials, spirits, and other drinks, including Finnish rye beer. Gin, which is flavoured with green berries, was first produced in the Netherlands. The name comes from the Dutch name genever. Dutch genever and corenwijn are served chilled in shot glasses and appreciated for their flavour; they are not diluted to make long drinks, as gin often is. Some of the new gins from small distillers have complex aromas of several spices, but juniper remains a constant among them.

A rub for meats

Juniper berries crushed in a mortar with garlic and rock salt make a well-flavoured rub for lamb, pork, and venison.

FLAVOUR PAIRINGS

Good with apples, beef, cabbage, duck, game, goose, pork.

Combines well with bay, caraway, celery, garlic, marjoram, myrtle, pepper, rosemary, savory, thyme.

Only intensely fragrant roses are used; the highly perfumed damask rose, *R. damascena*, is the one preferred in the Balkans, Turkey, and most of the Middle East. In Morocco a musk-scented rose is grown. Dried buds keep their perfume well.

PARTS USED

Buds, petals.

BUYING / STORING

Rosewater and rose oil are available from Middle Eastern, Indian, Iranian, and Turkish shops, as is very sweet but well-flavoured rose petal jam, which may come from Bulgaria, Turkey, or Pakistan. Some shops stock dried rosebuds. Buds may be stored in an airtight container for up to a year. Grind as needed in an electric grinder.

HARVESTING

Rosebuds and petals are harvested in early summer and either dried or distilled to make rose essence (attar of roses), which may be diluted to make rosewater.

Rose
Rosa species

Western cooks seldom think of roses as a flavouring ingredient, but throughout the Arab world, Turkey, and Iran, and as far east as northern India, dried rosebuds or petals and rosewater are consumed in a variety of ways. Turkey and Bulgaria are the main producers of attar of roses (the essential oil) and rosewater, but roses are also grown commercially in Iran and Morocco. The Japanese rose, *Rosa rugosa*, is the rose grown in East Asia for culinary and medicinal use. In China the rose petals are used to flavour tea and sometimes sugar.

Dried rosebuds
Buds and flowers are picked very early in the morning to capture their fragrance before it is lost to the sun.

Culinary uses

In India powdered, dried purple rose petals are used in marinades and in delicately flavoured kormas. In Bengal and Punjab rosewater features prominently in desserts such as gulab jamun (gulab means rose) and rasgulla, in sweet lassi (a cooling yogurt drink), and in kheer (a rich rice pudding). Its flavour can also be detected in much confectionary, including Turkish delight, in Middle Eastern pastries, and in some savoury dishes. Fresh or dried petals are infused in syrups to make desserts and drinks. A delicately flavoured rose sherbet is served at Turkish ceremonial functions. Rose petals can also be put into a jar of sugar to infuse it with a delicate rose scent that will flavour creams and cakes.

Iranian cooks use rosebuds quite extensively; a blend of ground, dried petals and cinnamon, sometimes with cumin or cardamom, makes a heady flavouring for rice. A more complex blend with dried lime powder is used to flavour stews. Crushed rose petals may garnish a yogurt and cucumber salad or cold soup. In Morocco rosewater is used more than buds, although buds are a constituent of ras el hanout.

Tunisian cooks seem to appreciate rosebuds most of all, using them in several spice blends for a wide range of dishes. A simple bharat of finely ground cinnamon and rosebuds is used together with black pepper to flavour roast meats, stews using fruits such as quinces or apricots, and couscous with fish or lamb. In Tunisian Jewish cooking, the same flavourings are used in meatballs to accompany couscous.

FLAVOUR PAIRINGS

Essential to Iranian advieh, ras el hanout, Tunisian bharat.

Good with apples, apricots, chestnuts, lamb, poultry, quinces, rice, desserts, and pastries.

Combines well with chilli, cardamom, cinnamon, cloves, coriander seed, cumin, pepper, saffron, turmeric, yogurt.

Advieh for rice

Rose petals, cinnamon, and cumin seeds are used in this Iranian flavouring for rice (*recipe, p.279*).

TASTING NOTES

Fresh vanilla pods have no aroma or taste. After fermentation they develop a rich, mellow, intensely perfumed aroma with hints of liquorice or tobacco matched by a delicate, sweetly fruity or creamy flavour. There may also be hints of raisin or prune, or smoky, spicy notes.

PARTS USED

Cured pods.

BUYING / STORING

You are more likely to get good-quality pods from a spice merchant than a supermarket. Stored away from the light in an airtight container, vanilla pods will keep for 2 years or more. When buying vanilla extract, look for bottles labelled "natural vanilla extract", with an indication of alcohol content, usually about 35 per cent by volume.

HARVESTING

Vanilla pods are picked when they begin to turn yellow. Further maturation is prevented by plunging them into boiling water, then they are sun dried by day and sweated by night, wrapped in blankets. The pods shrivel and darken, and enzymes cause a chemical change that produces aromatic compounds, notably vanillin. About 5kg (10lb) of fresh pods yields 1kg (2¼lb) of cured vanilla.

Vanilla

Vanilla planifolia

Vanilla is the fruit of a perennial, climbing orchid, native to Central America. It is not known when vanilla was first cured and used as a flavouring, but tribes ruled by the Aztecs had fairly sophisticated methods of fermenting the bean-like fruits to extract vanillin crystals. The Spanish conquistadors drank chocolate flavoured with vanilla at the court of Moctezuma. They took to it and shipped both chocolate and vanilla back to Spain. They also gave the fruit its name: vanilla is the diminutive of *vaina*, meaning pod. Today vanilla is exported from Mexico, Réunion, Madagascar, Tahiti, and Indonesia.

Whole dried pods

Good vanilla pods are deep brown or black, long and narrow, somewhat wrinkled, moist, waxy, supple, and immediately fragrant.

Seeds

The tiny, sticky, black seeds may be scraped from the pod with the point of a knife.

Culinary uses

Bourbon vanilla from Madagascar and Réunion has a rich, creamy flavour; Mexican was traditionally considered to be the most delicate and complex; Tahitian smells heady, floral, and fruity; Indonesian vanilla has a smoky, strong flavour. The best pods have a light, white frosting, called givre, of vanillin crystals.

Whole or split pods are most used to flavour creams, custards, and ice cream. The presence of tiny black specks, the sticky seeds, in the dishes indicates authenticity. A whole vanilla pod that has been infused in a syrup or cream can be rinsed, dried, and reused. Vanilla flavours cakes, tarts, and syrups used for poaching fruit. Cut pods can be laid over fruit to be baked in the oven. Vanilla's original use with chocolate is still widely practised, and it also enriches tea and coffee. Vanilla is less commonly thought of as a spice for savoury foods, but it goes well with seafood, particularly lobster, scallops, and mussels, and with poultry. It enhances the sweetness of root vegetables and in Mexico it is used with black beans.

FLAVOUR PAIRINGS

Good with apples, melon, peaches, pears, rhubarb, strawberries, fish and seafood, cream, milk, eggs.

Combines well with cloves, cardamom, chillies, cinnamon, lavender, saffron.

Flavoured sugar
Rather than buy expensive packets of vanilla sugar, caster sugar can be flavoured by putting a fresh or used pod in the jar.

Extract
Made by macerating pods in alcohol, vanilla extract has a sweet aroma and a delicate taste. Avoid synthetic vanilla, derived from pulp waste, which has a cloying smell and a disagreeable, bitter aftertaste.

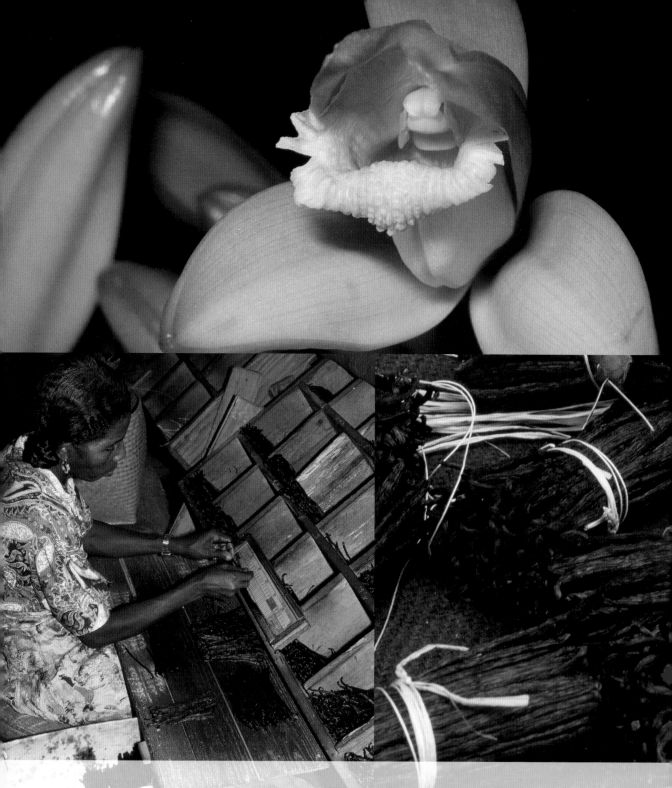

Vanilla *is the second most expensive spice after saffron because, like saffron, its production is very labour-intensive.*

Pollination of the plants has to be done by hand, harvesting the pods is difficult, and there is a lengthy curing process.

TASTING NOTES

The aroma of akudjura suggests baked caramel and chocolate. The taste is of caramel, tamarillo, and tomato, with a bitterish, lingering aftertaste that is quite refreshing.

PARTS USED

Dried fruit.

BUYING / STORING

Bush tomatoes are sold whole – these must be soaked for 20–30 minutes before use – and, more frequently, ground to an orange-brown powder, which is always called akudjura.

HARVESTING

There is, as yet, no cultivation of the bush tomato – what is available has been gathered in the wild. The yellow fruits are left to dry on the plant; they shrink to grape size, turn chocolate brown, and acquire a chewy texture reminiscent of raisins – hence their other name, desert raisins. Drying also reduces the level of alkaloids, especially potentially harmful solanine.

FLAVOUR PAIRINGS

Good with apple, cheese dishes, fish, lean meats, onions, peppers, potatoes.

Combines well with coriander seed, lemon myrtle, mountain pepper, thyme, wattle.

Akudjura

Solanum species

Akudjura, *S. centrale*, is the name of an edible member of a group of wild tomatoes, native to the deserts of western and central Australia – the "bush" that gave the fruit its popular name of bush tomato. Several plants in the group are poisonous. The edible ones have always been gathered by the Aborigines for staple food stores, but recently they have attracted wider attention as a spice. Also collected is *S. aviculare*, which has larger fruit, known as kangaroo apple.

Culinary uses

Akudjura can be used in place of sun-dried tomato or sweet paprika. Those who have become accustomed, even addicted, to its special taste sprinkle it on salads, soups, egg dishes, and steamed vegetables. In Australia it is used whole in casseroles and in an interesting version of damper, the traditional bread-like "bush tucker".

The powder goes into sweet biscuits, chutneys, dressings, relishes, and salsas. A mixture of akudjura, wattle, and mountain pepper is used the same way as Cajun blackening spice, especially for fish; in other mixtures akudjura is used for barbecuing and for marinading meat, especially the very lean kangaroo meat.

Whole fruit
Akudjura suits both sweet and savoury dishes. It gives a distinct flavour to tomato-based sauces and to meat stews, particularly goulash.

Crushed fruit
Akudjura may be orange-red or brownish, depending on rainfall in the growing season.

Pink pepper
Schinus terebinthifolius

Pink pepper is the fruit of the Brazilian pepper tree, native not just to Brazil but Argentina and Paraguay as well. The tree has been introduced in many places as an ornamental or shade tree. It is aggressively invasive and now grows in almost every temperate zone in the world. Mono-terpenes in the volatile oil can cause intestinal irritation, but not in the quantities used in a normal recipe. Réunion is the only place where pink pepper is commercially grown.

Culinary uses

Pink peppercorns flavour a variety of dishes. Use in small amounts, and not, for example, in the quantity needed to prepare a pepper steak. Pickling softens the berries and they can be crushed easily. Dried berries have a brittle, papery outer shell enclosing a hard seed. Pink pepper is mostly recommended for fish or poultry, but goes well with game and other rich foods in the same way as juniper. Pink pepper makes quite delicate sauces to accompany such varied ingredients as lobster, veal escalopes, and pork.

Whole berries
The berries are easily crushed with a pestle and mortar or under the blade of a big knife.

TASTING NOTES

The aroma of crushed berries is pleasantly fruity, with a clear note of pine. The taste is fruity, resinous, and sweetly aromatic, similar to juniper but not as strong. It shares with true black pepper one important constituent, piperine oil, but it has none of pepper's heat.

PARTS USED

Dried fruit.

BUYING / STORING

Dried pink pepper is sold by spice merchants and supermarkets – freeze-dried berries have the best colour and flavour. It is also available pickled in brine or vinegar, bottled or canned. Dried berries are added, for colour effect, to black, white, and green peppercorns, to which they are not related. Keep pink peppercorns whole in an airtight container and crush or grind them as needed.

HARVESTING

In autumn clusters of tiny, white flowers form green and juicy berries that ripen to a bright red. They are harvested when ripe.

FLAVOUR PAIRINGS

Good with fish, game, rich and fatty meats, poultry.
Combines well with chervil, fennel, galangal, makrut lime leaves, lemon grass, mint, parsley, black and green pepper.

TASTING NOTES

The aroma of paprika tends to be restrained and delicate; caramel notes, fruitiness, or smokiness characterize some paprikas, while others have a nose-prickling, light heat. Flavours vary from sweetly smoky to rounded and full-bodied, or gently pungent with bitter notes.

PARTS USED

Dried fruits. There is no single paprika pepper; it is made from a number of different red capsicums.

BUYING / STORING

Hungarian paprika is somewhat hotter than Spanish. Portuguese and Moroccan paprika tend to resemble Spanish; that from the Balkan states is closer to Hungarian. Paprika from the US is mild. All paprika should be kept in an airtight container and away from light: otherwise it will lose its vibrancy. Paprika paste and paprika sauce are also produced in Hungary and the Balkan countries.

HARVESTING

Once dried, the peppers are destalked, seeds and veins are separated, then the wall of the fruit and the seeds are ground separately and blended according to the type of paprika being made. For Spanish pimentón, the peppers are dried over oak fires for a smoky flavour.

Paprika

Capsicum annuum species

Capsicums are native to the Americas and were first planted in Spain after the voyage of Columbus in 1492. It was the Spanish who first dried and ground the peppers to make pimentón, or paprika. Later seeds reached Turkey and were planted there and throughout the Ottoman Empire. Ornamental Turkish pepper was recorded in Hungary in 1604. A century later paprika was mentioned there as a spice used by peasants; it was not until the 19th century that it was considered suitable for "sophisticated stomachs".

Ground paprika

Paprika may be sweet, bittersweet, or hot, depending on whether it is produced from mild or lightly pungent peppers, and also on the amount of ground seeds and veins included in the powder.

Hungarian paprika
Hungarian cooks usually have different grades of paprika in the kitchen and select the one best suited to the dish being prepared.

Culinary uses

Paprika is the predominant spice and colouring in Hungarian cooking. Fried gently with onion in lard (the main cooking fat) it forms the basis of goulash, veal, or chicken paprikás, and duck or goose pörkölt; it gives colour and flavour to potato, rice, and noodle dishes and many vegetables. Serbian cooks use paprika in similar ways. In Hungary, the Balkan countries, and Turkey it is more usual to find paprika or chilli flakes on the table than black pepper.

In Spain, paprika is used in sofrito, the mixture of onions and other ingredients fried in olive oil that forms the basis of many slow-cooked dishes. It appears in rice and potato dishes, is appreciated with fish, in omelettes, and is essential to romesco

sauce. In Morocco it is widely used in spice blends, in tagines, in chermoula (a marinade and sauce for fish); in Turkey it flavours soups, vegetables, and meat dishes, especially offal. In India its principal use is to add a red colour to dishes. Everywhere it is used as an essential flavouring for sausages and other meat products.

Paprika should never be overheated as it becomes bitter.

Essential to romesco sauce.

Good with beef and veal, white cheeses, chicken, duck, most pulses, and vegetables, pork, and rice.

Combines well with allspice, caraway, cardamom, garlic, ginger, oregano, parsley, pepper, rosemary, saffron, thyme, turmeric, soured cream, and yogurt.

Spanish paprika

The D.O. Pimentón de la Vera indicates a high-quality paprika, smoked over wood, to give a distinctive mellow or medium-hot taste, depending on the style chosen.

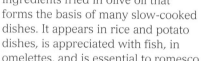

PAPRIKA CLASSIFICATIONS

Paprika is usually sold in sealed tins or bags bearing labels of authenticity.

Hungarian paprika comes from two regions, Szeged and Kalocsa, whose names appear on the packaging.

Különleges (special, delicate) is bright red, finely milled to a silky powder; with only a tiny percentage of seeds, it is sweet with a barely perceptible heat. It has a long shelf life.

Édesnemes (noble sweet) is darker red, sweet, rounded, with restrained heat and no bitterness. Quite finely ground.

Delicatess (delicatessen) is fruity, slightly hot, and bright, light red.

Félédes (semi-sweet) contains more veins, and is therefore less sweet and more pungent.

Rozsa (rose) is pinkish red and has more heat; it is made from the whole fruit.

Eros (strong) is made from lesser-grade whole fruits and has more pungency and a bitter aftertaste. Brownish-red and coarse, it is more like a chilli powder.

Most **Spanish paprika** comes from La Vera and carries a denomination of origin; a small amount of sweet paprika from the ñora pepper is produced in Murcia.

Dulce (sweet, mild) is a brick-red powder with a smoky aroma and a tangy flavour.

Agridulce (bittersweet) is deep red and piquant with a bitter note.

Picante (hot) is rust-red and has a sharp, pleasant heat. Spanish paprika is marketed in different quality grades: extra, select, and ordinary.

TASTING NOTES

Tamarind has little smell, and a sourish but also sweet and fruity taste. The sour element is due to tartaric acid. Different locations give different levels of sourness in the pulp. Thai tamarind has a more rounded, less tart taste than Vietnamese or Indonesian tamarind.

PARTS USED

Pulp of ripe pods; leaves.

BUYING / STORING

From Indian shops and spice merchants tamarind is available as a dried block, with or without seeds, as a thick, fairly dry paste, or as a more liquid, brown-black concentrate. Supermarkets usually have concentrate or paste. In all processed forms tamarind keeps almost indefinitely. Occasionally fresh leaves, slices of dried pulp, and dried powdered tamarind can be found.

HARVESTING

Tamarind trees produce clusters of pale yellow flowers that turn into long, rust-coloured pods. The pods contain a dark brown, sticky, and very fibrous pulp. The pulp is extracted from the brittle outer shell of the pod and pressed into flat cakes; these often include the shiny, black seeds. Further processing results in tamarind paste and concentrate.

Tamarind
Tamarindus indica

Tamarind is obtained from the bean-like pods of the tamarind tree, native to eastern Africa, probably Madagascar, which makes it the only important spice of African origin. The tall, evergreen trees with their handsome crowns were already growing in India in prehistoric times; the name comes from Arabic *thamar-i-hindi*, fruit of India. Tamarind trees remain productive for up to 200 years. The spice has for long been imported – principally from India – for the manufacture of such condiments as Worcestershire sauce.

Whole pods

In Vietnam and Thailand unripe pods are used in tart soups and stews. In the regions where tamarind grows, especially Thailand and the Philippines, young, feathery leaves and flowers are sometimes used in curries and chutneys.

Culinary uses

In India and Southeast Asia tamarind is used as an acidulant (much as the West uses lemon and lime) in curries, sambhars, chutneys, marinades, preserves, pickles, and sherbets. Tamarind gives many hot south Indian dishes, such as Goan vindaloo and Gujarati vegetable stews, their characteristic sourness. With raw sugar and chillies it is simmered to a syrupy dipping sauce for fish. It goes into Thai tom yom soup and Chinese hot-and-sour ones. In Indonesia, where the word *asem* means both tamarind and sour, it is used in sauces, both savoury and sweet, and for marinades. In Java, especially, it is preferred to lemon for the island's sweet-sour dishes. In India ground seeds are used in cakes. In Iran stuffed vegetables are baked in a rich tamarind stock. In the Middle East a lemonade-like drink made from tamarind syrup is popular; Central America and the West Indies also have canned tamarind drinks, which are consumed on their own or in tropical fruit punches, or made into milk shakes with ice cream. Jamaica uses tamarind in stews and with rice; in Costa Rica it makes a sour sauce. In Thailand, Vietnam, the Philippines, Jamaica, and Cuba tamarind pulp is also used as a sweetmeat, dusted with sugar or candied. Try using tamarind with salt as a rub for fish or meat before cooking, or with soy sauce and ginger in a marinade for pork or lamb.

FLAVOUR PAIRINGS

Essential to Worcestershire sauce.

Good with cabbage, chicken, fish and shellfish, lamb, lentils, mushrooms, peanuts, pork, poultry, most vegetables.

Combines well with chilli, asafoetida, coriander leaf, cumin, galangal, garlic, ginger, mustard, shrimp paste (blachan, trassi), soy sauces, sugar (brown or palm), turmeric.

Block
To use tamarind from a block, soak a small piece, about the equivalent of 1 tbsp, for 10–15 minutes in a little hot water. Stir to loosen the pulp, squeeze out, and sieve to remove fibre and, if they are present, seeds.

Concentrate
Tamarind concentrate has a "cooked" smell reminiscent of molasses, and a distinct, sharp, acid taste. To use a concentrate, stir 1–2 tsp into a little water.

Paste
Adding prepared tamarind to dishes moderates the heating effect of fiery chillies and hot spices.

TASTING NOTES

Sumac is only slightly aromatic; the taste is pleasantly tart, fruity, and astringent.

PARTS USED

Dried berries.

BUYING / STORING

Outside the growing regions sumac is normally only available as a coarse or fine powder. In an airtight container this will keep for several months. Whole berries can be kept for a year or more.

HARVESTING

In the autumn sumac leaves turn a beautiful red, and the white flowers eventually develop into dense, conical clusters of fruit – small, round, russet-coloured berries. The berries are picked just before they are fully ripe, dried in the sun, and crushed to a brick-red or red-brown powder.

FLAVOUR PAIRINGS

Essential to fattoush, za'atar.

Good with aubergines, chicken, chickpeas, fish and seafood, lamb, lentils, raw onion, pine nuts, walnuts, yogurt.

Combines well with allspice, chilli, coriander, cumin, garlic, mint, paprika, parsley, sesame, pomegranate, thyme.

Sumac

Rhus coriaria

Sumac is the fruit of a decorative, bushy shrub that grows to a height of about 3m (10ft) and has light grey or reddish stems. The shrub grows wild on sparsely wooded uplands and high plateaux around the Mediterranean in Anatolia (Turkey), elsewhere in the Middle East, and in its native Iran.

Culinary uses

Sumac is an essential ingredient in Arab and, especially, in Lebanese cooking, where it is used as an acidulant. Its taste is tingling and tart and it brings out the flavours of food to which it is added, much as salt does. If the berries are used whole, they are cracked and soaked in water for 20–30 minutes, then squeezed out well to extract all the juice, which is used for marinades and salad dressings, in meat and vegetable dishes, and also to make a refreshing drink. Sumac powder is rubbed onto food before cooking: the Lebanese and Syrians use it on fish, the Iranians and Georgians on kebabs, the Iraqis and Turks on vegetables. Sumac is often sprinkled on flatbreads; it provides the tart element in the Lebanese bread salad, fattoush, and is an essential part of the spice and herb blend za'atar.

Ground berries
Berries vary in colour from brick red to red-brown or maroon, depending on where they come from.

Za'atar
Ground sumac berries are combined with sesame seeds and crushed, dried thyme in this Middle Eastern spice mixture (*recipe, p.283*).

Barberry

Berberis vulgaris

Many species of the *Berberis* genus and of the closely related genus *Mahonia* grow wild in temperate zones of Europe, Asia, northern Africa, and North America. They are dense, spiny, perennial bushes with toothed leaves, and they all have edible berries – the *Berberis* berries some shade of red, the *Mahonia* ones blue. Barberries are used as a spice in central Asia and the Caucasus region. In New England, ripe barberries are used in pies, preserves and syrups; green (unripe) barberries are sometimes pickled.

Culinary uses

Barberries are usually preserved in syrup or vinegar to make a tart flavouring. Being rich in pectin they are easily made into preserves. In central Asia and in Iran, dried berries are used to add a sour flavour and a splash of colour to pilafs; they also go into stuffings, stews, and meat dishes.

Dried berries soon release their flavour if fried gently in butter or oil. They are sprinkled over some rice dishes. In Georgia, I was given a mixture of crushed barberries and salt – this is rubbed on lamb kebabs before grilling, giving the meat a tart piquancy. In India, dried berries are added to desserts, rather like sour currants. Fresh berries strewn over lamb or mutton for the last minutes of roasting will burst and coat the meat with their tart juice.

Whole dried berries

The small, oblong berries have a soft texture and a pleasant, sourish flavour. Berries should be red; dark berries are likely to be old and will have little flavour.

TASTING NOTES

The ripe berries are pleasantly acidulous. Dried berries have a light aroma, reminiscent of currants but with a tart note. The taste is agreeably sweet-tart, with an underlying sharpness that derives from malic acid.

PARTS USED

Berries, fresh and dried.

BUYING / STORING

Dried barberries are difficult to buy outside their region of production, except from Iranian shops. Plants can be had from nurseries and make attractive ornamental shrubs. If you grow one, or have found a bush in the wild, you can easily gather your own berries (provided you wear gloves to do so) and dry them. Dried berries will keep for several months. They retain their colour and flavour best if stored in the freezer.

HARVESTING

The small, oblong berries hang down in tight clusters and can be picked from July until late summer. In Iran, the Caucasian republics, and countries further east, barberries are still gathered from the wild, sun dried, and stored for use in the kitchen.

FLAVOUR PAIRINGS

Good with almonds, lamb, pistachios, poultry, rice, yogurt.
Combines well with bay, cardamom, cinnamon, coriander, cumin, dill, parsley, saffron.

TASTING NOTES
The seeds are fleshy and taste both sweet and acidic. Some fruits have a lovely balance, while others can be decidedly astringent. Indian pomegranates can have a slightly bitter aftertaste. The juice varies in colour from a light pink to a deep red; it is sweet but with a refreshing sharpness.

 PARTS USED

The seeds are used fresh and dried.

 BUYING / STORING

Pomegranates will keep for weeks in a cool place, and storing improves both flavour and juice content. Once extracted, the seeds or the juice can be frozen. Pomegranate molasses is a dark, thick, sticky syrup, stocked in Iranian and Middle Eastern shops and in some supermarkets. Anardana (dried seeds) can be had from Indian stores, either whole, when they should be a deep dark red, or ground. Anardana and molasses keep well.

 HARVESTING

The fruit ripens in October and must be picked before it splits open to release the seeds. In northern India the seeds of the sour and bitterish wild pomegranate are sun dried for 2 weeks to make anardana.

Pomegranate

Punica granatum

The pomegranate is a small, deciduous tree with narrow, leathery leaves, brilliant, orange-red flowers, and large, beige to red-skinned fruits. Native from Iran to the Himalayas, it has been cultivated since ancient times all around the Mediterranean basin. Pomegranates now grow throughout the drier parts of subtropical India and Southeast Asia, Indonesia, and China, as well as in tropical Africa. The trees are very long-lived but their vigour declines after only 15–20 years.

Culinary uses

In the Middle East and central Asia, fresh, whole seeds are sprinkled over salads, pastes like hummus or tahina, or as a garnish on desserts. They are very good with chicken, can be added to stews, and will liven up a fruit or cucumber salad.

The seeds can be pressed, and the juice of the sweeter varieties is a popular beverage in the Middle East; in Georgia tart juice is widely used in sauces for meat and fish.

Pomegranate molasses, a thick, dark syrup, is also made from the juice. Molasses can be brushed on to chicken or meat to act as a marinade, or added to slow-cooked dishes. Its taste and degree of sourness vary

Whole fruit
Choose fruit with the deepest colour you can find. The seeds are really transparent juice sacs holding pulp and one (usually very hard) seed.

greatly from region to region. Arab and Indian molasses tend to be quite tart, even sour. Iran produces a sweeter version, which is an essential ingredient of muhammarah, a Middle Eastern dip made with hot red peppers and walnuts, and of fesenjan, a richly flavoured Iranian duck or chicken dish made with walnuts. There is also a good Iranian winter soup based on pomegranate molasses.

Anardana (dried seeds), which look like red-black raisins, are sticky but have a hard crunch; they have a fruity, tangy flavour, much liked in northern India. They go into curries and chutneys, into stuffings for bread and savoury pastries, and with braised vegetables. In Punjabi cookery they flavour pulses. They give the food a more subtle sweet-sour taste than amchoor (*p.163*) would, and are either soaked in water like tamarind or crushed and sprinkled directly on to food.

(*p.163*)

FLAVOUR PAIRINGS

Good with avocado, beetroot, cucumber, fish, lamb, pine nuts, poultry, pulses, spinach, walnuts.

Combines well with allspice, cardamom, chilli, cinnamon, cloves, coriander seed, cumin, fenugreek, ginger, golpar, rosebuds, turmeric.

Anardana (Dried seeds)
Dried seeds are pleasantly tart to smell and have a sweet-sour taste.

Molasses
Pomegranate molasses may be sweet or sweet-sour, the fruity sweetness tempered by an attractive tartness. The flavour is more concentrated than that of grenadine syrup.

TASTING NOTES

Kokam has a slightly fruity, balsamic smell; a sweet-sour, tannic, astringent taste, often with a salty edge; and a lingering, sweetish aftertaste of dried fruit. Its sourness comes from malic and tartaric acid. The texture is surprisingly soft.

PARTS USED

Whole fruit or rind.

BUYING / STORING

Dried rind can be bought from Indian stores and spice merchants; they may also have kokam paste. In an airtight jar both will keep for up to a year. The deeper the skin colour, the better the kokam. Kokam is often labelled black mangosteen.

HARVESTING

Kokam is a smallish, round, sticky fruit, the size of a plum but with an uneven surface. It is dark purple when ripe. The fruit is dried whole or split – which leaves the pulp full of the half dozen or more fairly big seeds. Alternatively the rind is removed, soaked in the pulp liquid, and then dried in the sun. Its local name is amsul, literally sour rind. The rind is folded into strips that have a leathery appearance.

FLAVOUR PAIRINGS

Good with aubergines, beans, fish and shellfish, lentils, okra, plantain, potatoes, squash.

Combines well with chilli, cardamom, coconut milk, coriander, cumin, fenugreek, garlic, ginger, mustard seed, turmeric.

Kokam
Garcinia indica

Kokam is the fruit of a slender, graceful, evergreen tree that is related to the mangosteen. It is native to India and grows almost exclusively in the tropical rainforests along a thin ribbon of the Malabar (Malwani) coast of India, from Mumbai to Cochin. In its native region, which includes Maharashtra, Karnataka, and Kerala, it is used as an acidulant, much as tamarind is in other parts of India. Fairly recently it has become popular in the US, the Middle East, and Australia, but it still has to make its mark in Britain.

Culinary uses

Kokam is used as a souring agent, milder than tamarind. Dried fruit or rind are usually soaked in water, the pulp softens and is pressed dry, and the liquid is used for cooking pulses or vegetables. Kokam rinds are often rubbed with salt to speed the drying; when using them, check that the dish does not become too salty.

Kokam saar – made by boiling pieces of kokam in water, straining the liquid, and flavouring it with different combinations of grated ginger, chopped onion, and chillies, cumin, or coriander – serves both as an appetizer and a cooling accompaniment to fiery, coconut-based fish curries. In Kerala kokam is known as "fish tamarind".

With coconut milk, and with or without jaggery, kokam makes sol kadhi, a fragrant, carmine-coloured beverage, that may be served with rice or taken as an appetizer.

Amchoor
Mangifera indica

Amchoor is made from mangoes. The evergreen mango, a big, spreading tree with a massive, grey trunk and dark green leaves, is native to India and Southeast Asia and is now widely cultivated for its fruit. The trees crop every other year and continue to do so for well over a century. Every part of the tree is utilized in some way – bark, resin, leaves, flowers, seeds. The fruit are eaten fresh; both green (unripe) and ripe mangoes are made into chutneys and pickles. The spice is made from unripe fruit and is produced in India only.

Culinary uses

Amchoor is used as an acidulant in north Indian cooking in the way tamarind is used in the south. It gives a tang of tropical fruit to vegetable stews and soups, potato pakoras, and samosa fillings. It is good with stir-fried vegetables and in stuffings for breads and pastries. It is an essential ingredient in chat masala, a fresh-tasting and astringent spice blend from the Punjab, used for vegetable and legume dishes and for fruit salads. Amchoor is good in marinades to tenderize poultry, fish and meat, particularly meat to be grilled in a tandoor. It is also much used as a sourish flavouring in dals and chutneys.

Amchoor powder
This lumpy powder is easily crushed and provides acidity without adding moisture.

TASTING NOTES

Amchoor has a pleasant, sweet-sour aroma of dried fruit and a tart, astringent, but also sweetish, fruity flavour. Its acidity comes from citric acid. One teaspoon of amchoor powder has roughly the equivalent acidity of 3 tablespoons of lemon juice.

PARTS USED

Dried fruit, sliced or ground.

BUYING / STORING

Amchoor is available from Indian and some general oriental shops, usually as a powder. It may be labelled in English as "mango powder". Dried slices are normally light brown and look like rough-textured wood. Slices keep for 3–4 months. The finely ground powder has a slightly fibrous texture, and is sandy-beige. It keeps for up to a year in an airtight jar.

HARVESTING

Unripe, green mangoes are taken as windfalls or picked from the many semi-wild trees. They are peeled, sliced thin, and sun dried. Sometimes a little turmeric is dusted over the slices to prevent insect damage. Dried slices are marketed whole, but most of the crop is pulverized to make amchoor powder.

FLAVOUR PAIRINGS

Essential to chat masala.

Good with aubergines, okra, cauliflower, potatoes, pulses.

Combines well with chilli, cloves, coriander, cumin, ginger, mint.

TASTING NOTES

The flavour of lemon grass is refreshingly tart, clean, and citrus-like with peppery notes. Freeze-dried lemon grass keeps its aroma quite well, but air dried lemon grass loses its volatile oils; grated lemon rind gives more flavour than dried lemon grass.

PARTS USED

The lower part of the stem, white and tinged with pale green.

BUYING / STORING

Lemon grass can be found in greengrocers and supermarkets. Buy firm stalks; they should not be wrinkled or dry. Fresh lemon grass will keep for 2–3 weeks in the refrigerator if wrapped in plastic. It also freezes well for up to 6 months. Freeze-dried lemon grass is quite fragrant and has a long shelf life in an airtight container. Dried lemon grass and lemon grass purée are available, but they lack flavour.

HARVESTING

Most gardens in Singapore, Thailand, and Vietnam have a patch of lemon grass from which the cook can pluck a stalk or two. Commercial harvesting is done every 3–4 months. The leaves are removed before lemon grass is sold.

Lemon grass
Cymbopogon citratus

A showy, tropical grass with fibrous, sharp-edged leaves, lemon grass soon forms into large, dense clumps. It flourishes in temperate climates if it is overwintered indoors. The bulbous base imparts an elusive aromatic and lemon fragrance to the cooking of Southeast Asia. Previously hard to find outside that region, fresh lemon grass is now widely available, thanks to the increased appreciation of Thai, Malay, Vietnamese, and Indonesian food. It is cultivated in Australia, Brazil, Mexico, West Africa, and in Florida and California.

Whole fresh stalks
Lemon grass contains citral, the flavour component of lemon rind. It gives the plant a subtle but sustained lemon fragrance.

Culinary uses

Remove the two outer layers and bruise the stalk if the lemon grass is to be used whole to flavour a stew or curry; take it out before serving. If the lemon grass is intended to be eaten as an ingredient of a soup or salad, discard the top part and slice the rest into very fine rings. Start at the bottom and stop slicing when the stalk becomes too hard – big pieces are unpleasantly fibrous to chew. Pounded with other spices and herbs, lemon grass goes into pastes to flavour curries, stews, and stir-fried dishes.

Lemon grass is a key ingredient in the Nyonya cooking of Singapore and the southern part of the Malay peninsula. It is used in Thai larp, curries, and soups, in Vietnamese salads and spring rolls, in Indonesian bumbus (spice blends) for chicken and pork. Sri Lankan cooks use it in combination with coconut. Although it grows in India, it is not much used there except to make tea. If you grow the plant, the upper part of the leaves makes a pleasant, refreshing tea.

Lemon grass has a place in western cooking, too. It suits all fish and seafood, especially crab and scallops. Add it to the stock for poaching fish or chicken. To flavour a vinaigrette, steep a few chopped stalks in it for 24 hours. Lemon grass is also good with fruit; use it alone or with ginger or fennel seeds, to flavour syrups made for poaching peaches or pears.

FLAVOUR PAIRINGS

Good with beef, chicken, fish and seafood, noodles, offal, pork, most vegetables.

Combines well with basil, chillies, cinnamon, cloves, coconut milk, coriander leaf, galangal, garlic, ginger, turmeric.

Finely sliced stalk
Slices cut from fresh lemon grass often show purplish rings.

Bruised stalks
Bruising releases the volatile oils that impart flavour.

TASTING NOTES

Leaves have an explosive fragrance, cleanly floral and citrus – not quite lemon, not quite lime. Their aroma and flavour are assertive and lingering, yet delicate. The rind of the fruit is slightly bitter with a strong citrus note. Dried leaves and dried rind lack the intense aroma of fresh.

PARTS USED

Leaves and rind, preferably fresh.

BUYING / STORING

Fresh leaves are available from oriental shops and online. They keep for weeks in a plastic bag in the refrigerator. The leaves freeze well for up to a year, losing neither texture nor aromatics. Fruits should be firm and feel heavy for their size. Store in the refrigerator or in a cool room, as other citrus fruits. Dried leaves and rind are available; leaves should be green, not yellow or dingy looking. Store both in airtight containers. Leaves will keep for 6–8 months. Some shops also stock rind preserved in brine.

HARVESTING

Makrut limes grow on a shrubby evergreen tree. Leaves and fruit are picked and sold fresh or dried.

Makrut lime

Citrus hystrix

The rind and leaves of the makrut lime have long imparted a clean, citrus flavour to the dishes of Southeast Asia. Cambodia, Indonesia, Malaysia, Myanmar, and Thailand all have fish and chicken dishes, soups, and spice pastes with their instantly recognizable aroma and flavour. Makrut lime is now also grown in Florida, California, and Australia. The original English name kaffir lime may be offensive in some cultures, and the Thai name makrut lime is increasingly used instead.

Whole fresh leaves

The leathery leaves grow in an unusual double form, as two on a single petiole. The upper side is dark green and glossy, the underside lighter and matt.

Shredded fresh leaves

If the leaves are to be eaten, rather than removed before serving, break apart the pairs and remove the thick, central rib. Stack several leaves and shred finely.

Culinary uses

Lime leaves are responsible for the tangy, citrus perfume of many Thai soups, salads, stir-fries, and curries. Grated rind goes into curry pastes, larp, and fish cakes. Both are used in some fish and poultry dishes in Indonesia and Malaysia. Always use fresh leaves when available and never use dried in a salad. Whole leaves may be removed from a dish before serving, but if leaves are to be eaten, for example as a garnish for a clear soup, shred them very finely – as fine as a needle – with a small, sharp knife. The leaves keep their flavour well when cooked.

If you buy rind in brine, wash it well and scrape off the pith before using; shredded, dried rind is best soaked briefly before being added to slow-cooked dishes. The pith makes dried rind bitter, so use sparingly. To give a citrus flavour to a western dish, use leaves in chicken casseroles, with braised or roasted fish, or in sauces to serve with chicken or fish.

Whole fresh fruit
The fruit is pear-shaped, bumpy, and wrinkled, lime green in colour and 7–8cm (2½–3in) long. What little juice it yields is sour and seldom used.

FLAVOUR PAIRINGS

Essential to Thai curry pastes, Indonesian sambals.

Good with fish and seafood, mushrooms, noodles, pork, poultry, rice, green vegetables.

Combines well with oriental basils, chilli, coconut milk, coriander, galangal, ginger, lemon grass, rau ram, sesame, star anise.

Grated fresh rind
The very thin rind is best removed with a small-holed grater rather than a citrus grater, whose fine perforations will reduce the rind to a mushy mass. Proceed with caution to avoid including the bitter pith.

TASTING NOTES

The aroma of greater galangal is mildly gingery and camphorous; the taste has a lemony sourness with a flavour resembling ginger and cardamom mixed. Lesser galangal is more pungent, with a hint of eucalyptus; its taste is piquant, suggesting a mix of pepper and ginger.

PARTS USED

Rhizome.

BUYING / STORING

Fresh galangal can be bought from oriental shops and some supermarkets. It will keep for 2 weeks and can be frozen. Dried slices and powdered galangal are more widely available. Powdered galangal will keep for 2 months; slices keep their flavour for at least a year. Galangal in brine can be substituted for fresh; rinse it thoroughly before use. Greater galangal may be found in oriental shops under its local names: it is called kha in Thailand, lengkuas in Malaysia, and laos in Indonesia. Lesser galangal rhizomes are smaller than greater galangal, reddish-brown outside and pale red inside.

HARVESTING

The rhizomes are lifted, cleaned, and processed much like those of turmeric or ginger.

Galangal
Alpinia species

There are two main types of galangal: greater galangal, *A. galanga*, is native to Java; lesser galangal, *A. officinarum*, is native to the coastal regions of southern China. Greater galangal indeed grows taller than lesser and has larger rhizomes. Both are cultivated extensively throughout Southeast Asia, Indonesia, and India. The popularity of lesser galangal has long declined in favour of greater galangal, which continues to be used in the kitchen, principally in Southeast Asia. The English name stems from Arabic, *khalanjan*.

Greater galangal *A. galanga*

Whole rhizomes of greater galangal are large and knobbly, light orange-brown outside, and marked with darker rings. Young shoots have a pink hue.

Sliced rhizome
The flesh is fibrous and buff-coloured. Unless very young, the rhizomes are tougher and woodier than those of ginger.

Culinary uses

Throughout Southeast Asia greater galangal is used fresh in curries and stews, in sambals, satays, soups, and sauces. In Thailand it is an essential ingredient in some curry pastes, as it is in the laksa spices of Malay Nyonya cooking. In Thai cooking it is often preferred where other Asian cuisines would use ginger, especially to neutralize the smells of fish and seafood. It is good with chicken and in many hot and sour soups, providing the key flavouring in tom kha kai, the popular chicken and coconut milk soup.

Like ginger, fresh galangal is easy to peel and grate or chop. It is always preferred to dried, but dried slices can be added to soups and stews; first soak them in hot water for about 30 minutes. They should be taken out before serving because they remain unpleasantly woody to chew. Powdered galangal is used in spice blends throughout the Middle East and across North Africa to Morocco (in ras el hanout). Grated galangal and lime juice are used to make a popular tonic in Southeast Asia. The use of lesser galangal appears to be largely restricted to tonic and healing soups.

FLAVOUR PAIRINGS

Essential to Thai curry pastes.

Good with chicken, fish and seafood.

Combines well with chilli, coconut milk, fennel, fish sauces, garlic, ginger, lemon grass, lemon juice, makrut lime, shallots, tamarind.

Sliced dried rhizome
Dried slices are satisfactory for flavouring soups and stews and should be soaked in water before use.

Ground rhizome
Tan-coloured lesser galangal powder is ginger-like and sharp; greater galangal is sandy-beige, with a sour aroma and a milder ginger flavour.

Other galangal varieties

Several plants with similar properties to lesser galangal, *Alpinia officinarum*, are also referred to, confusingly, as lesser galangal. While it is often quite hard to make reliable distinctions, at least two of these appear to have individual characteristics and uses.

Aromatic ginger *Kaempferia galanga*

The young leaves of this small, wild plant, also known as the resurrection lily, kencur in Indonesia, cekur in Malaysia, and pro hom in Thailand, are served raw to accompany Thai fish curries and in Malay salads. The reddish-brown rhizome is usually no more than 5cm (2in) long, with yellowish-white flesh. In Indonesia pounded kencur is added to a number of dishes; in China the pounded rhizome is mixed with salt and oil, and served with baked chicken. In Sri Lanka it is roasted and ground for biryanis and curries. Kencur is sold dried, in slices or ground. More like ginger than galangal, the pungent, camphorous rhizome is used in very small quantities. Confusingly, the word kencur is also used for zedoary (*p.198*).

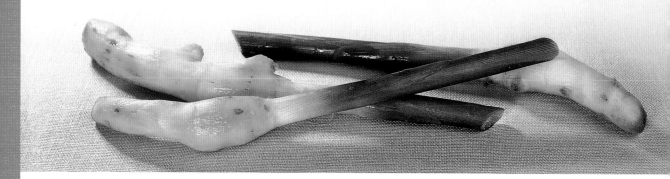

Fingerroot

Boesenbergia pandurata/Kaempferia pandurata

Also called Chinese keys, fingerroot grows throughout Southeast Asia. It is a small plant, up to 50cm (20in) high, with an underground rhizome and slender storage roots. It is used in cooking in Thailand, Vietnam, Cambodia, and Indonesia; elsewhere it tends to be used as a medicinal herb. The rhizome has a crisp texture, a sweet aroma, a refreshing, lemony taste, and lingering warmth. Best used fresh, it is eaten in salads, soups, fish curries, and stir-fries. Also used in Thai curry pastes and Cambodian kroeung spice pastes. If you use dried, soak for 30 minutes. The Thai name is krachai, the Cambodian k'cheay, and the Indonesian temu kunci.

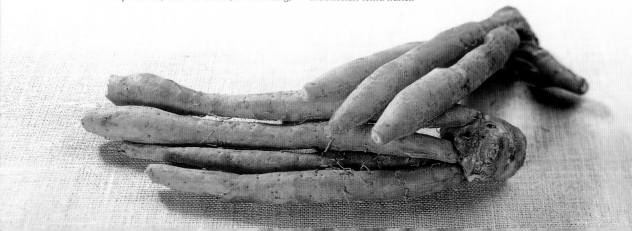

Lemon myrtle

Backhousia citriodora

The tall lemon myrtle tree is native to coastal Australian rainforests, mostly in Queensland. The trees have been introduced to southern Europe, the southern US, and South Africa, and are grown for their essential oil in China and Southeast Asia. So far, lemon myrtle has gained a place in the kitchen only in Australia, and even there quite recently, but it is slowly becoming more widely appreciated.

Culinary uses

Lemon myrtle is versatile and can be used wherever lemon grass or lemon zest is called for. It is best used sparingly. If cooked for too long, the lemony flavour is lost and an unpleasant eucalyptus note can take over. It is therefore better in shortbread, biscuits, and batters for things like pancakes than in longer-baked cakes, and also goes well in stir-fry dishes. It is excellent for fish cakes, and with vinegar, sugar, basil, and olive oil can be used as a dipping sauce or as a salad dressing. It makes good vinegar as well as a lemonade and a herbal tea. It gives a lift to mayonnaise, sauces, and marinades for chicken or seafood. Combined with other spices it makes a good rub for chicken or fish to be barbecued or grilled.

Whole dried leaves
The powerful lemon taste is due to a very high concentration of citral in the volatile oil (30 times that of lemon).

Ground dried leaves
Outside Australia lemon myrtle is usually only available ground.

TASTING NOTES
The aroma is refreshing and intensely lemony, like that of lemon grass and lemon verbena, and is even more pronounced when the leaves are crushed. The taste is stronger still, more like lemon zest. The aftertaste is a lingering note of eucalyptus or camphor.

PARTS USED
Fresh and dried leaves.

BUYING / STORING
Lemon myrtle can be bought as whole, dried leaves or as a coarse, light green powder from herb or spice merchants and some supermarkets. It can also be found via the internet. Both forms should be stored in airtight containers in the dark. Buy powdered leaf only in small quantities.

HARVESTING
Mature, dark leaves are picked all year round. Drying intensifies their flavour, so dried leaves of good quality may taste even better than fresh ones.

FLAVOUR PAIRINGS
Good with chicken, fish and seafood, most fruit, pork, rice.
Combines well with akudjura, aniseed, basil, chillies, fennel, galangal, ginger, mountain pepper, parsley, pepper, thyme, yogurt.

TASTING NOTES

Yuzu juice is aromatic and sharply citrusy; the peel has an attractive, delicate aroma. Crushed and ground dried limes have a sour smell backed by a dried-fruit sweetness; whole limes are less aromatic. Orange peels have a clear, orange scent; the flavours are tart or bitter, depending on the variety.

PARTS USED

Fresh and dried peel; juice.

BUYING / STORING

Fresh yuzu is seldom available outside Japan, but dried peel and bottled yuzu juice are now sold in supermarkets. Oriental shops stock dried tangerine peel; Middle Eastern and Iranian shops have dried bitter orange peel, all forms of dried limes, and Moroccan preserved lemons. In North America commercial mojos and sour orange marinades are sold in Latin American shops, but it is easy to prepare your own. Stored in airtight containers, dried or candied peel and fruits will keep indefinitely.

HARVESTING

Yuzus are only in season for a brief period from November to January; bitter oranges come into the shops in January and February, and there is now an early autumn crop from Chile. Other citrus fruits and dried peels are available all year round.

Citrus

Citrus species

Citrus fruits are universal providers of tartness in the kitchen. The Japanese use the peel of a small citron, called yuzu; the Chinese favour dried orange or tangerine peel; in the Gulf States and Iran dried limes are preferred; in Tunisia bitter orange peel and fruit are used for pickling liquids. In the West cooks use juice and fresh zest for their acidity, and candied peel in desserts and cakes. In the Caribbean islands and Mexico it would be unthinkable to cook without limes.

Preserved lemons

The chopped peel of salted lemons preserved in their juice is used to flavour Moroccan tagines; it combines particularly well with green olives in a renowned chicken dish. The salty juice is good in salad dressings.

Culinary uses

Slivers of fresh yuzu peel, or dried, crumbled peel, add fragrance to Japanese soups, simmered dishes (nabemono), and aromatic yuzu-miso condiments. Yubeshi, a traditional sweet, is made by steaming the shells of yuzus filled with glutinous rice, soy sauce, and sweet syrup. They are dried and sliced to serve. Yuzu juice is now used in salsas and dressings and to flavour chocolate in the West.

Dried tangerine peel is used mostly in the cooking of Sichuan and Hunan. It is soaked in warm water for 15 minutes, then chopped finely for stir-fried dishes or used whole in rich dishes of braised pork or duck. It combines well with Sichuan peppercorns and star anise, with dark soy sauce and rice wine.

In the Gulf States small, dried limes, often called Oman limes, or dried lime powder are used in fish, poultry, and lamb stews and pilafs. Gulf dishes call for a lot of spicing, and dried limes marry well with cardamom, cloves, allspice, pepper, ginger, cinnamon, and coriander. To the north, in Iran they are used in the same way to flavour stews, especially lamb stews, but the Iranians prefer herbs – coriander, dill, parsley, fenugreek – and green vegetables – leeks, spring onions, spinach – in their lime-scented dishes. In some parts of Iran bitter oranges are customary; the juice and rind are added to stews. These flavourings are particularly good with duck, chicken, and rabbit.

The mojos of the Caribbean and South America are made with lime, lemon, grapefruit, or bitter orange juice to which garlic, spices, fruits, and fresh herbs are added. They are used as marinades, dips, and salad dressings, or as refreshing sauces to accompany vegetables, fish, and grilled or roasted meats.

Sliced dried peel

Commercial dried tangerine or orange peel is dark brown and brittle. To dry your own after eating an orange or tangerine, remove all pith from the peel, put the peel on a rack, and leave to dry for 4–5 days. It will remain flexible. The flavour improves with age.

Whole dried limes

Dried limes are pierced and added whole to stews; they soften in cooking and are served as part of the dish, to be squeezed to extract all the juice.

TASTING NOTES

The aroma is fennel- and anise-like – star anise and aniseed both contain essential oil with anethole. Star anise has liquorice notes and an assertive warmth. The flavour is pungent and sweet with a mildly numbing effect, and the aftertaste is fresh and agreeable.

PARTS USED

Whole star anise, or pieces; ground powder.

BUYING / STORING

Star anise is best bought whole or in pieces. It will last for a year if kept out of bright light in an airtight container. Buy ground spice in small quantities; it should last for up to 2–3 months if kept as the whole spice.

HARVESTING

Star anise is the fruit of a Chinese evergreen magnolia tree, which now also grows in India, Japan, and the Philippines. The tree grows to about 8m (26ft) and has small yellow-green flowers. It fruits in its sixth year and continues to bear fruit for up to a century. The fruits are picked before ripening and sun dried, which hardens and darkens the carpels and develops the aromatic compounds.

Star anise

Illicium verum

Certainly the prettiest spice, star anise is native to southern China and Vietnam, where it has a long history of medicinal and culinary use. It was known in Europe in the 17th century, and old recipes indicate that it was used to flavour syrups, cordials, and preserves. Today western cooks use it as a flavouring for fish and seafood, in syrups for poaching figs and pears, and to spice tropical fruits.

Whole pods and seeds

Used whole, star anise makes a decorative addition to a dish. The star anise seed pod is in the shape of an irregular, eight-pointed star. Up to 3cm (1¼in) across, complete pods are tough and red-brown or rust coloured.

Carpels
Each carpel is canoe-shaped and slightly open, revealing a lustrous, brittle, brown seed. The carpels are more aromatic than the seeds.

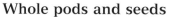

Culinary uses

In Chinese cooking star anise is used in soups and stocks, in marinades for steamed chicken and pork, and in "red-cooked" chicken, duck, and pork – the meat is turned a red-brown colour by braising in a dark broth flavoured with spices and soy sauce. Star anise also colours and flavours marbled tea eggs. It is the main ingredient of Chinese five spice powder. Vietnamese cooks use it in simmered dishes, in stocks, and in pho (beef and noodle soup).

The flavour of star anise can be detected in some of the cooking of Kerala in southern India; in some dishes of north India it may be used as a cheaper substitute for anise.

Star anise is little used in western cookery except as a flavouring in drinks such as pastis and anisette, and in chewing gum and confectionery. In addition to flavouring fish and seafood and some fruit dishes, it enhances the sweetness of leeks, pumpkin, and root vegetables.

FLAVOUR PAIRINGS

Essential to five spice powder.

Good with chicken (in stock for poaching), fish and seafood (in broth for court-bouillon), figs, tropical fruits, leeks, oxtail, pork, pumpkin, root vegetables.

Combines well with cassia, chilli, cinnamon, coriander seed, fennel seed, garlic, ginger, lemon grass, lime peel, Sichuan pepper, soy sauce, dried tangerine peel.

Broken pods
The dried pods are easily broken into pieces when only a little is needed. Star anise is potent, so use it sparingly.

Ground pods
For the best flavour, the pods and seeds should be ground in a mortar or electric grinder and used immediately.

TASTING NOTES

The aroma and taste of the seeds are sweet, liquorice-like, warm, and fruity, but Indian anise can have a hint of bitterness. The leaves have the same fragrant, sweet, liquorice notes, with mild peppery undertones. The seeds are more subtly flavoured than fennel or star anise.

PARTS USED

Seeds, leaves.

BUYING / STORING

Anise can be grown from seed and plants are available from some herb nurseries. As a spice seeds are best bought whole; check that there is no more than a minimum of stalks and husks. In an airtight container anise will retain its flavour for at least 2 years.

HARVESTING

Just before the fruit ripens, plants are pulled up and left to dry. They are threshed and the seeds spread on trays in partial shade to dry further. To dry anise you have grown yourself, put the seed heads in paper bags and hang them in a well-ventilated place.

FLAVOUR PAIRINGS

Good with apples, chestnuts, figs, fish and seafood, nuts, pumpkin, root vegetables.

Combines well with ajowan, allspice, cardamom, cinnamon, cloves, cumin, fennel, garlic, nigella, nutmeg, pepper, star anise.

Anise
Pimpinella anisum

This delicate plant, native to the Middle East and eastern Mediterranean, is related botanically to caraway, cumin, dill, and fennel. It is now widely established throughout Europe, Asia, and North America. Its earliest use was medicinal, but the Romans introduced it as a flavouring in food, especially in cakes served at the end of a meal to aid digestion. The plant, called anise or aniseed, is cultivated for its seeds, but young leaves are also used as a herb.

Culinary uses

In Europe, anise seed is mostly used to flavour cakes, breads, cookies, and sweet fruit dishes. It flavours some rye breads, Scandinavian pork stews, and root vegetable dishes. The Portuguese add a handful of anise seed to the water when boiling chestnuts to impart a delicate fragrance. Figs and anise have a natural affinity; in Catalonia, cakes are made of chopped, dried figs and almonds flavoured with anise, and in Italy, a fig and dried fruit "salami" is flavoured with anise and anisette. Around the Mediterranean, anise often flavours fish stews, and its essential oil is in demand to flavour aperitifs and liqueurs such as ouzo, pastis, and anisette.

In the Middle East and India, anise is mostly used in breads and savoury foods. In India dry-roast seeds enhance the aroma of vegetable and fish curries and, fried in hot oil, they garnish lentils. Anise is also valued for its digestive properties; along with other spices it is offered in the traditional paan at the end of the meal. In Morocco and Tunisia, anise flavours breads; in Lebanon, it goes into fritters and spiced custards.

Whole seeds
Seeds vary in colour from pale brown to grey-green with lighter coloured ridges.

Liquorice

Glycyrrhiza species

Liquorice plants are perennial shrubs with blue or lilac, pea-like flowers. The most important species are *G. glabra*, native to southeastern Europe and southwestern Asia, *G. glandulifera*, which grows further east and is known as Russian or Persian liquorice, and *G. uralensis*, the main form used in Asia, native to the steppes of northern China. Liquorice has been cultivated in Europe for about 1,000 years, in China at least twice as long. It is still used medicinally as a cough repressant, an expectorant, and a gentle laxative.

Culinary uses

In the form of drinks such as sambuca and pastis the flavour enters a variety of dishes, both sweet and savoury. A soft drink is made with it in Islamic countries during Ramadan. In Morocco, the powder flavours snail and octopus dishes and is often an ingredient in ras el hanout. A little liquorice enhances Chinese five-spice powder; it also flavours Chinese soy sauce. Asian spiced stocks or marinades often contain liquorice along with other spices.

The Dutch extrude the extract into black, salty liquorice, called *drop*, in a bewildering variety of shapes and strengths; the English have multi-coloured liquorice allsorts and Pontefract cakes – lozenges named after the Yorkshire monastery where they originated in the 16th century. Liquorice sticks are popular in Asia for chewing. In Turkey, fresh roots are eaten and powder is used in baking. In the West, liquorice is becoming a fashionable flavouring for ice cream.

Powder

Finely powdered liquorice, with its woody, sweet aroma, is most readily available from Chinese shops.

TASTING NOTES

The aroma of liquorice is sweet, warm, and medicinal; the taste is very sweet, earthy, and anise-like with a lingering, bitter, salty aftertaste.

PARTS USED

Rhizomes and roots. Sliced roots are bright yellow.

BUYING / STORING

Dried liquorice roots can be bought from spice merchants. They keep almost indefinitely if they are quite dry; they can be sliced or ground as needed. Powdered liquorice, grey-green and rather strong, needs an airtight container. Sticks and slabs, too, last well if kept dry.

HARVESTING

Liquorice plants are easily grown from seed or root cuttings. They need rich, sandy soil and plentiful sun. The roots can be dug up in autumn; drying them takes several months. Roots are usually crushed to a pulp, which manufacturers boil to a thick consistency and reduce further by evaporation. The resulting soluble substance is called extract of liquorice. Some manufacturers extract glycyrrhizic acid for use as a flavouring.

FLAVOUR PAIRINGS

Combines well with cassia, cloves, coriander seed, fennel, ginger, Sichuan pepper, star anise.

TASTING NOTES

The smell of saffron is unmistakable: rich, pungent, musky, floral, honeyed, and tenacious. The taste is delicate yet penetrating, warm, earthy, musky, bitter, and lingering. The aromatic properties vary slightly depending on the saffron's place of origin.

 PARTS USED

Stigmas.

 BUYING / STORING

Buy dried stamens (known as filaments or threads); ground saffron is easily adulterated. Threads keep their flavour for 2–3 years if stored in an airtight container in a cool, dark place. Buy saffron only from a reliable source; in tourist markets around the world turmeric, marigold petals, and safflower are passed off as saffron. None has saffron's penetrating aroma, so smell before buying. If you use saffron regularly, buy it in larger quantities from a spice merchant.

 HARVESTING

The violet-coloured crocus flowers in autumn. The flowers are picked at dawn and the three red stigmas are plucked from each one. Small quantities are toasted on a drum sieve over a low fire. Dried stamens are deep red to orange-red, wiry, and brittle.

Saffron

Crocus sativus

Saffron consists of the dried stigmas of the saffron crocus, or roses as they are called. Native to the Mediterranean and western Asia, it was used by the ancient civilizations of the region as a dye and to flavour food and wine. Spain is the main producer; at harvest time on the plain of La Mancha, a heady, sensual aroma explodes around you as the stigmas are toasted. It takes about 80,000 roses to yield 2.5kg (5½lb) of stigmas, which produce 500g (1lb 2oz) of saffron after toasting. No wonder it is the most expensive spice in the world.

Whole threads

The best quality saffron is deep red; this is called coupe for Spanish and Kashmiri saffron, sargol for Iranian. A proportion of thicker, yellow threads from the style of the flower is included in the next grade, Mancha if Spanish or Kashmiri, poshal or kayam if Iranian. Good quality saffron is also produced in Greece and Italy. Lesser grades tend to have a brownish colour and stubby, rather scruffy threads.

Iranian poshal
This saffron has deep red, wiry threads with a few yellow styles.

Kashmiri coupe
This saffron has a rich, burgundy colour. The threads are very long, firm, and smooth.

Culinary uses

Saffron has long been renowned as a dye, whether for the robes of Buddhist monks or for paella and risotto. For most dishes saffron is infused in liquid. If an infusion is added in the early stages of cooking it will impart more colour; added at a later stage it contributes more aromatics. Avoid overuse: it can give a bitter, medicinal taste to foods. If a dish does not call for liquid, threads can be ground and stirred in. If they are not quite dry, dry-roast lightly before grinding.

Several cultures flavour specific dishes with saffron, often dishes associated with festivals or celebrations. Saffron provides the characteristic flavour for many Mediterranean fish soups and stews of which Provençal bouillabaisse and Catalan zarzuela are the best known. It adds class to a simple stew of mussels and potatoes or a fish baked in white wine. Saffron rice is excellent whether as a Valencian paella, risotto alla Milanese, an Iranian polo, a Moghul biryani, or a simple vegetable pilaf. In Sweden saffron buns and cakes are made for the festival of light on 13 December, St Lucia's Day. Traditional Cornish saffron cakes and breads have all but disappeared from Britain, but they are not difficult to make and have a fine, rich flavour. Saffron ice cream, whether in the European style, Middle Eastern with mastic, or Indian kulfi is also worth a try.

FLAVOUR PAIRINGS

Good with asparagus, carrots, chicken, eggs, fish and seafood, leeks, mushrooms, pheasant, pumpkin and squash, rabbit, rice, spinach.

Combines well with anise, cardamom, cinnamon, fennel, ginger, mastic, nutmeg, paprika, pepper, rosebuds, rosewater.

Spanish mancha
Spanish Mancha saffron is more orange-red in colour with yellow styles.

Ground threads
Ground saffron is easily adulterated with cheaper and inferior spices.

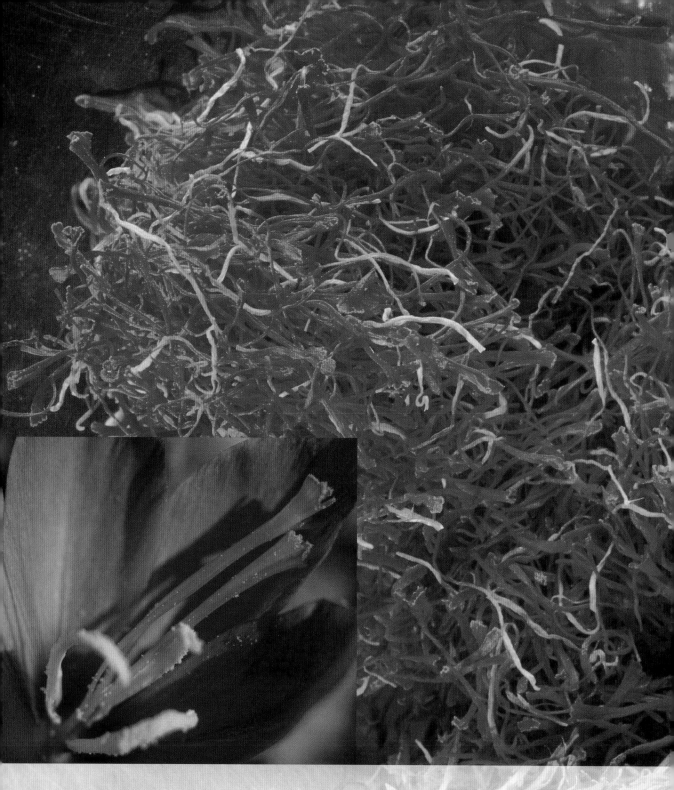

Saffron *is the costliest spice on earth, 10 times as dear as vanilla, because its production still depends on intensive*

manual labour. The fragile stigmas of about 80,000 crocus flowers are needed to produce just 500g (1lb 2oz) of the spice.

TASTING NOTES

The aroma of cardamom is strong but mellow, fruity, and penetrating. The taste is lemony and flowery, with a note of camphor or eucalyptus due to cineole in the essential oil; it is pungent and smoky, with a warm, bittersweet note, yet is also clean and fresh.

PARTS USED

Dried seeds.

BUYING / STORING

Pods will keep for a year or more in an airtight jar but will slowly fade in both colour and aroma. Exposed to air the seeds quickly lose their volatile oils; grinding speeds up the loss. Ground cardamom is easy to adulterate and in any case usually includes the hulls, so it is better to grind your own when needed.

HARVESTING

Fruits ripen from September to December and are harvested at intervals while about three quarters ripe, otherwise they split open. They are dried in the sun for 3–4 days, or more quickly in drying sheds. Dried pods are hard; the best are green to green-amber. Green pods from Kerala traditionally set the standards of quality and price, but Guatemalan cardamom is nearly as good.

Cardamom

Elettaria cardamomum

Cardamom is the fruit of a large, perennial bush that grows wild in the rainforests of the Western Ghats (also known as the Cardamon Hills) in southern India; a closely related variety grows in Sri Lanka. Both are now cultivated in their regions of origin and in Tanzania, Vietnam, and Papua New Guinea; Guatemala has become the main exporter. Cardamom has been used in India for some 2,000 years. It reached Europe along the caravan routes, and the Vikings took it from Constantinople to Scandinavia, where it is still very popular.

Whole pods

Cardamom is best bought as whole pods, which should be plump and green. White pods are bleached green ones; less well flavoured, their production is declining.

Seeds

Inside each oval seed pod, triangular in section, are 15–20 tiny, dark brown or black, sticky seeds. Stickiness is the best indication of freshness.

Culinary uses

Cardamom enhances both sweet and savoury flavours. In India it is one of the essential components in many spice mixes. It goes into sweetmeats, pastries, puddings, and ice creams (kulfi), and is used in a digestive and breath-freshening paan with fennel, anise, and areca nuts. In India it is also much used to flavour tea, while in Arab countries coffee is flavoured with cardamom, often by pouring it over pods put in the spout of the pot – in Bedouin culture the cardamom used is first displayed to guests, bright green and pristine, as a mark of respect. Cardamom is an essential component of spice mixes in Lebanon, Syria, the Gulf States (baharat), and Ethiopia (berbere). Scandinavia is still the biggest importer in Europe; there and in Germany and Russia cardamom is widely used for spiced cakes, pastries, and bread, and occasionally also for hamburgers and meat loaf.

Whole pods, lightly crushed, can be used to flavour rice, poached and braised dishes, and casseroles. They are an important ingredient in many Indian slow-braised meat dishes (kormas), which use a thick marinating liquid to develop a creamy sauce. Hulled seeds can be either lightly bruised and fried, or toasted and ground, before being added to a dish. Cardamom is good in baked apples, poached pears, and fruit salads. It combines well with orange and coffee in desserts, but is equally at home with roast duck or poached chicken, in marinades or spiced wine. It is useful in pickles, especially pickled herring.

FLAVOUR PAIRINGS

Essential to berbere, curry powders, dals, masalas, pilafs, Indian rice pudding (kheer), zhug.

Good with apples, oranges, pears, pulses, sweet potatoes, and other root vegetables.

Combines well with caraway, chilli, cinnamon, cloves, coffee, coriander seed, cumin, ginger, paprika, pepper, saffron, yogurt.

Spices for pilafs

Indian pilafs are flavoured with whole spices, including green cardamom pods, pieces of cinnamon, cloves, cumin seed, and black peppercorns that are simply added whole to the rice before it is cooked (*recipe, p.323*).

TASTING NOTES

The seeds have a tarry smell and a taste of pine with an astringent, smoky, earthy note. They are used to give depth to masalas and tandoori-style spice mixtures.

PARTS USED

Dried seeds.

BUYING / STORING

Buy pods that are whole, not broken, and store in an airtight container. Many of the species are readily available online. Greater Indian is sold in Indian shops; some Chinese shops stock Chinese cardamom.

HARVESTING

Harvesting takes place from August to November, somewhat earlier than that of green cardamom (*p.182*), and drying is always done in sheds. The resulting colour is a very dark brown.

Black cardamom
Amomum and *Aframomum species*

The larger seeds of several species of *Amomum* and *Aframomum* are widely used in the regions where they are grown, and sometimes they are sold, ground, as cheap substitutes for green cardamom. In colour they are various shades of brown and their taste is usually more camphorous than that of green cardamom. The most important is Greater Indian or Nepal cardamom, *Amomum subulatum*, native to the eastern Himalayas. This particular variety, usually referred to as black cardamom, is never used as a substitute for green cardamom and has a distinct and separate role in Indian cooking.

Whole pods
Black cardamom has ribbed, often hairy, fruits that become deep red when ripe.

Ground seeds
Seeds quickly lose their volatile oil when ground, so grind only when needed.

Seeds
Seeds are sticky, but once removed from the pod they soon dry out.

Culinary uses

In contrast to green cardamom, which is considered a "cooling" spice, black cardamom is a "heating" spice. It is therefore an important ingredient in combination with cloves, cinnamon, and black pepper in garam masala blends. Black cardamom also occasionally finds its way into confectionery and pickles. When pods are used whole in vegetable or meat stews they should be removed before serving, but crushed seeds will dissolve into the sauce. The flavour is intense, so use sparingly.

OTHER CARDAMOMS

Bengal cardamom, *A. aromaticum,* is very similar to the Greater Indian and used in the same way.

Chinese cardamom, *A. globosum,* is round, quite large, and dark brown. The flavour is astringent and cooling, leaving a numbing sensation in the mouth. Mostly used medicinally, it also combines well with star anise in stir-fries.

Javanese winged cardamom, *A. kepulaga,* is much used in Southeast Asia.

Cambodian cardamom, *A. krevanh,* from the Krevanh hills of Thailand and Cambodia, is also traded extensively within Southeast Asia.

Ethiopian cardamom, *Afr. korarima,* has a dull, slightly smoky aroma and a rather coarse flavour.

Grains of paradise, *A. melegueta,* are a different spice (*p.219*).

Standard garam masala

This is a basic blend of black cardamom, coriander seeds, black peppercorns, cloves, cinnamon, and tejpat leaves (*recipe, p.275*).

FLAVOUR PAIRINGS

Essential to garam masala.

Good with pilafs and other rice dishes, meat, and vegetable curries.

Combines well with ajowan, green cardamom, cassia leaves, chillies, cinnamon, cloves, coriander seed, cumin, nutmeg, pepper, yogurt.

TASTING NOTES

The smell of cumin is strong and heavy, spicy-sweet, with acrid but warm depth. The flavour is rich, slightly bitter, sharp, earthy, and warm, with a persistent pungency. Use sparingly.

PARTS USED

Dried seeds (fruits).

BUYING / STORING

Cumin seeds are widely available, either whole or ground. Black cumin can be bought online or from Indian shops, as can dhana-jeera, a blend of cumin and coriander seeds. Seeds will keep their pungency in an airtight jar for several months, but ground cumin has a very short shelf life.

HARVESTING

Cumin stalks are cut when the plants begin to wither and the seeds turn brown; they are threshed and the seeds dried in the sun. In many countries the harvest is still done manually.

Cumin
Cuminum cyminum

Cumin is the seed of a small, herbaceous umbellifer, native to just one locality, the Nile valley of Egypt, but long cultivated in most hot regions – the eastern Mediterranean, North Africa, India, China, and the Americas. It was used in medicines in Egypt and Minoan Crete at least 4,000 years ago. The Romans used it the way we use pepper. During the Middle Ages cumin was popular in Europe, but gradually caraway took its place. Spanish explorers took it to Latin America, where it is has become a very popular spice.

Whole seeds
Cumin seeds are oval, brownish-green in colour, about 5mm (¼in) long. They look like caraway but are straighter and show a characteristic pattern of longitudinal ridges.

Ground seeds
For the best flavour, only grind seeds as needed.

Culinary uses

The aroma of cumin is enhanced if the seeds are dry-roasted before they are ground, or fried in oil if they are used whole. Early Spanish dishes combined cumin, saffron, and anise or cinnamon. Now cumin is found in Moroccan couscous and lamb stews, in Tex-Mex chilli con carne, more sparingly in the spice mixes of Mexico itself, and in the merguez sausages of North Africa. It is added to pork sausages in Portugal, cheese in Holland, pickled cabbage in Germany, pretzels in Alsace, the tapas called Moorish kebabs (pinchitos morunos) in Spain, falafel and fish dishes in Lebanon, köfte in Turkey, and a pomegranate and walnut sauce in Syria. In all countries that like spicy food it is used in breads, chutneys, relishes, savoury spice mixes, and meat or vegetable stews. It is present in curry powders and masalas, and in commercial chilli powders. The combination of ground cumin and coriander gives much Indian food its characteristic pungent smell.

Whole black seeds

Darker than plain cumin seeds, black cumin seeds are also smaller. They have an earthy smell and a complex, mellow flavour that lies somewhere between cumin and caraway. Dry-roasted seeds go into pilafs and breads.

FLAVOUR PAIRINGS

Essential to Iranian advieh, baharat, berbere, Cajun spice blend, curry powders, dukka, masalas, panch phoron, sambhar powder, zhug.

Good with aubergines, beans, bread, cabbage, hard or pungent cheeses, chicken, lamb, lentils, onions, potatoes, rice, sauerkraut, squash.

Combines well with ajowan, allspice, aniseed, bay, cardamom, chilli, cinnamon, cloves, coriander, curry leaves, fennel seed, fenugreek seed, garlic, ginger, mace and nutmeg, mustard seed, oregano, paprika, pepper, thyme, turmeric.

OTHER CUMINS

True black cumin (*kala jeera*) and shahi jeera, *Bunium persicum*, seem to be used interchangeably in northern India, Pakistan, Afganistan, and Iran where both are native. Here they are preferred to ordinary cumin and used extensively in Moghul-style dishes like kormas and biryanis. The seeds are usually dry-roasted before being added to spice mixtures or used separately in dishes because dry-roasting gives them an agreeable nutty flavour. Black cumin is sometimes confused with nigella (kalonji, *p.134*).

TASTING NOTES

Caraway has a pungent aroma that, like the flavour, is warm and bittersweet, sharply spicy, with a note of dried orange peel and a slight but lingering hint of anise.

PARTS USED

Dried seeds (fruits).

BUYING / STORING

Caraway seeds can be bought ground, but is often used whole and is best bought that way: the seed will keep for at least 6 months in an airtight jar. The seed is easy to grind or pound when needed, but once ground it will lose strength quite quickly.

HARVESTING

Stems are cut when the fruit is ripening, dried for 7–10 days to complete the ripening, then threshed. In the home garden, caraway plants can be grown from seed in well-drained soil in full sun. The seeds will not ripen until the second year. Cut ripe seed clusters early in the morning when dew is on them, or the seeds may scatter too freely and the plant will self-seed. To dry, hang up the stalks with a paper bag around the seed heads.

Caraway

Carum carvi

Caraway is a hardy umbellifer native to Asia and northern and central Europe. It is cultivated as a biennial, not only in its regions of origin but also in Morocco, the US, and Canada. The Romans used it with vegetables and fish; medieval cooks as a flavouring for soups and bean or cabbage dishes. In 17th-century England it was popular in bread, cakes, and baked fruit; coated with sugar the seeds made comfits. Nowadays, Holland and Germany are the major producers. The essential oil flavours spirits such as aquavit and Kümmel.

Whole seeds

The fruit splits into two curved seeds with tapered ends; the hard, brown shell has five lighter-coloured ridges.

Culinary uses

In central Europe, and especially in the Jewish cooking originating there, caraway is used to flavour brown or rye breads, biscuits, seedcakes, sausages, cabbage, soups, and stews. It gives many south German and Austrian dishes their characteristic flavour, be it pumpernickel bread or roast pork; it is used in coleslaw and in combination with juniper for sauerkraut. It accompanies Munster cheese in Alsace; and is used to flavour Kümmel, schnapps, and Scandinavian akvakvit.

Caraway is used in the cooking of North Africa, mostly in vegetable dishes and in spice blends, such as Tunisian tabil and harissa. Morocco has a traditional caraway soup – as does Hungary, where caraway also figures prominently in goulash. Mention of caraway in Indian recipes usually stems from a mistranslation of the word for cumin; caraway itself is used only in northern India – it grows wild in the Himalayas. Turkish recipes may cite "black caraway", which is not true caraway but nigella (*p.134*).

Young leaves, less pungent than the seeds and resembling dill in taste and appearance, are an interesting addition to salads, soups, or fresh white cheese. They make a good garnish for lightly cooked young vegetables and most other dishes for which parsley could be used.

FLAVOUR PAIRINGS

Essential to tabil, harissa.

Good with apples, breads, cabbage, duck, goose, noodles, onions, pork, potatoes and other root vegetables, sauerkraut, tomatoes.

Combines well with coriander seed, garlic, juniper, parsley, thyme.

Tunisian tabil spices

Used for stews and vegetable and beef dishes, tabil is a blend of caraway seed, coriander seed, garlic, and chilli (*recipe, p.283*).

TASTING NOTES

Nutmeg and mace have a similar rich, fresh, and warm aroma. Nutmeg smells sweet but is more camphorous and pine-like than mace. The taste of both is warm and highly aromatic, but nutmeg has hints of clove and a deeper, bittersweet, woody flavour.

 PARTS USED

Kernel of the seed.

 BUYING / STORING

Nutmeg is best bought whole. In airtight containers it keeps almost indefinitely and is easily ground or grated as required. Once ground, nutmeg loses its flavour rather quickly. Banda and Penang nutmeg and mace are considered superior to the West Indian ones.

 HARVESTING

The yellowish, apricot-like fruits are gathered when ripe and the outer skin, white flesh, and mace are stripped off. The seeds, covered by a hard brown-black shell, are dried on trays for 6–8 weeks, until the kernel, the nutmeg, rattles in its shell. The shells are then cracked open and the smooth, brown nutmegs are removed and graded by size. The yield of nutmeg is about 10 times that of mace, which makes the latter comparatively costly.

Nutmeg
Myristica fragrans

This spreading, evergreen tree, native to the Banda islands of Indonesia, often called the Spice Islands, produces fruit that yields two distinct spices, nutmeg and mace (*p.194*). In the 6th century both spices formed part of the caravan trade to Alexandria; they were probably taken to Europe by the crusaders. Their early use, in China, India, Arabia, and Europe alike, was medicinal. When the Portuguese started trading direct from the islands, nutmeg gained importance as a spice, and by the 18th century a real craze for it developed in England.

Whole seeds
Nutmeg seeds may be bought intact, with the kernel still inside its hard shell, and the lacy aril still clinging to the shell.

Whole nutmegs
The hard, outer shells are stripped from the kernels and discarded.

Culinary uses

In India nutmeg is used more than mace because of the latter's high cost; both are used sparingly, mainly in Moghul dishes. The Arabs have long used both spices in delicately flavoured mutton and lamb dishes. In North Africa they are found in such spice mixtures as Tunisian qâlat daqqa and Moroccan ras el hanout. The Europeans have used nutmeg and mace most extensively, in both sweet and savoury dishes.

Nutmeg is widely used in honey cakes, rich fruit cakes, fruit desserts, and fruit punch. It goes well in stews and in most egg and cheese dishes, as does mace. The Dutch add nutmeg lavishly to white cabbage, cauliflower, vegetable purées, meat stews, and fruit puddings; the Italians add rather more subtle quantities to mixed vegetable dishes, spinach, veal, and fillings or sauces for pasta. In France it is used with pepper and cloves in slow-cooked stews and ragoûts. Half-ripe nutmeg, pricked all over (as is done with green walnuts) and soaked before being boiled twice in syrup, was once a popular sweetmeat from Malaysia. In very large quantities nutmeg's hallucinogenic properties become toxic; drinking alcohol greatly increases their harmful effect.

Grated nutmeg
Nutmeg kernels are best kept whole and only grated when needed. Some graters (below) have a lidded compartment in which the kernels may be stored.

FLAVOUR PAIRINGS

Essential to baking or pudding spices, quatre épices, ras el hanout, Tunisian five spices.

Good with cabbage, carrots, cheese and cheese dishes, chicken, egg, fish and seafood chowders, lamb, milk dishes, onion, potato, pumpkin pie, spinach, sweet potato, veal.

Combines well with cloves, cardamom, cinnamon, coriander, cumin, rose geranium, ginger, mace, pepper, rosebuds, thyme.

Nutmeg and **Mace** *grow together in the same fruit; mace is the bright red aril that shows first when the fruit splits open.*

Both spices are big business in several parts of the world, yet processing them from the pods is still done largely by hand.

TASTING NOTES

Mace has nutmeg's rich, fresh, and warm aroma, but the smell is stronger and shows a lively, floral character with notes of pepper and clove. The taste of mace is warm, aromatic, delicate, and subtle with some lemony sweetness, yet it finishes with a potent bitterness.

 PARTS USED

Aril surrounding the seed.

 BUYING / STORING

Ground mace is more commonly available than whole pieces (the pieces are called blades), but the latter are worth seeking out. They keep almost indefinitely in an airtight container and can be ground in a coffee grinder.

 HARVESTING

The ripe fruit of nutmeg trees is collected and the outer skin and white flesh removed to reveal the seed. The thin, leathery, lacy, bright scarlet aril, the mace, that covers the seed is removed, pressed flat, and dried for a few hours only. Mace from Grenada is stored in the dark for about 4 months, during which time it turns a deep orange-yellow; Indonesian mace remains orange-red.

Mace
Myristica fragrans

Inside the apricot-like fruit of *Myristica fragrans* lies a hard seed, the kernel of which is the spice nutmeg (*p.190*). Around this seed is a lacy covering or aril; this is the second spice, mace. Both nutmeg and mace became important commodities in a trade started by the Portuguese in the 16th century, developed by the Dutch, and taken over by the English when they captured the Spice Islands in 1796. Planting began in Penang, Sri Lanka, Sumatra, and the West Indies, where Grenada now produces almost a third of the world's crop.

Mace and nutmeg
Produced by the same tree, these spices are similar in taste. Mace is preferred when the dish requires a lighter flavouring.

Blades
Mace blades are brittle, yet they exude oil when pressed with the fingernails.

Ground blades
Ground mace keeps its flavour reasonably well, longer than some other ground spices.

Culinary uses

In Southeast Asia and China mace and nutmeg are used more for their medical than for culinary properties. Elsewhere, mace and nutmeg tend to be used interchangeably by cooks, although nutmeg is more widely used because it is cheaper.

Mace gives a lift to béchamel and onion sauce, clear soups, shellfish stock, potted meat, cheese soufflés, chocolate drinks, and cream cheese desserts. Mace should be used in preference to nutmeg to preserve the delicate colour of a dish. Whole blades of mace can be used to flavour soups and stews, but should be removed before serving.

In Indonesia, after the mace and kernel have been removed from the nutmeg fruit, the outer flesh is candied. In Sulawesi, in particular, it is cured in the sun and sprinkled with palm sugar, whereupon it becomes almost translucent.

FLAVOUR PAIRINGS

Essential to pickling spice.

Good with cabbage, carrots, cheese and cheese dishes, chicken, egg dishes, fish and seafood chowders, lamb, milk dishes, onion, pâtés and terrines, potato, pumpkin pie, spinach, sweet potato, veal.

Combines well with cardamom, cinnamon, cloves, coriander, cumin, rose geranium, ginger, nutmeg, paprika, pepper, rosebuds, thyme.

Aromatic garam masala

Cardamom subtly dominates the flavour of this mild masala blend, made from cardamom, cinnamon, mace, black peppercorns, and cloves (*recipe, p.276*).

TASTING NOTES

Fresh turmeric is crunchy, has gingery, citrus aromas, and an agreeably earthy flavour with citrus overtones. Dried turmeric has a complex, rich, woody aroma with floral, citrus, and ginger notes. The taste is slightly bitter and sour, moderately pungent, warm, and musky.

PARTS USED

Fresh and dried rhizomes.

BUYING / STORING

Fresh turmeric is available from oriental shops. Store it in a cool, dry place or in the refrigerator vegetable drawer for up to 2 weeks; it also freezes well. Dried turmeric keeps for 2 years or more in an airtight container. Alleppey and Madras are the best Indian grades of ground turmeric. Alleppey has the higher percentage of essential oil and curcumin (yellow colouring matter), giving it a darker colour and more intense flavour. Stored in an airtight container, it retains its flavour for up to a year.

HARVESTING

Rhizomes are lifted and sold fresh, or boiled to stop further maturation and then sun dried for 10–15 days. When dry and hard, turmeric is polished, graded, and usually ground. It loses three quarters of its weight during processing.

Turmeric

Curcuma longa

A member of the ginger family, turmeric is a robust perennial, native to southern Asia and appreciated there since antiquity as a flavouring, a dye, and a medicine. It is one of the cheapest spices, yet throughout the region it is valued on ritual and ceremonial occasions, whether to colour rice for an Indonesian wedding or to dye the skin of cows (as I once saw during the Sankali festival in Mysore). India is the main producer of turmeric and more than 90 per cent of the crop is used domestically. Other producers include China, Haiti, Indonesia, Jamaica, Malaysia, Pakistan, Peru, Sri Lanka, and Vietnam.

Whole fresh rhizome

Fresh turmeric should be firm and plump. The rhizomes are used sliced, chopped, or grated.

Sliced fresh rhizome

Add pared, sliced turmeric to pickles and relishes; it has a wonderful colour and taste, and is also a preservative.

Culinary uses

Turmeric binds and harmonizes the other spices with which it appears in many combinations. Use it sparingly. Fresh turmeric is used throughout Southeast Asia in spice pastes made with chillies, lemon grass, fresh galangal, garlic, shallots, tamarind, and sometimes dried shrimp paste and candlenuts. Chopped or grated, it goes into laksas, stews, and vegetable dishes. Juice extracted from crushed turmeric flavours and colours rice dishes for festive meals in Indonesia and Malaysia. The fragrant leaves are used to wrap foods in Malaysia, and the shoots are eaten as a vegetable in Thailand.

In India and the West Indies dried, ground turmeric combined with other spices is the basis of masalas, curry powders, and pastes. It imparts a warm flavour and yellow-orange colour to many regional vegetable, bean, and lentil dishes. It occurs in North African tagines and stews, most notably in the Moroccan spice blend ras el hanout, and in harira, the national soup. In Iran turmeric and dried limes flavour gheimeh, a rich stew-sauce that is spooned over rice.

In the West turmeric is used as a colourant for cheese, margarine, and for some mustards. It is widely used in pickles and relishes of both eastern and western manufacture.

FLAVOUR PAIRINGS

Essential to masalas, curry powders and pastes, ras el hanout.

Good with aubergines, beans, eggs, fish, lentils, meat, poultry, rice, root vegetables, spinach.

Combines well with chillies, cloves, coconut milk, coriander leaf and seed, cumin, curry leaf, fennel, galangal, garlic, ginger, makrut lime leaves, lemon grass, mustard seeds, paprika, pepper, rau ram.

Grated dried rhizome
Turmeric stains fingers, utensils, and clothes, so be careful when using it.

Whole dried rhizome
Dried rhizomes look like tough, yellow wood; they are almost impossible to grind at home, but can be grated.

TASTING NOTES

Fresh zedoary has a pleasant, musky taste somewhat similar to young ginger, clean and crisp with a hint of bitterness. The taste is sometimes described as resembling that of green mango, and one of the Indian names reflects this: amb halad means mango turmeric.

PARTS USED

Fresh or dried rhizome; young shoots, flower buds, and leaves.

BUYING / STORING

Fresh zedoary is available from oriental shops, often as "white turmeric". It has a thin, brown skin and lemon-coloured, crisp flesh. It keeps in the refrigerator for 2 weeks. Dried zedoary slices can also be bought in oriental shops. The spice is often available ground; the powder is usually coloured reddish-brown artificially.

HARVESTING

The fleshy, yellow rhizomes take 2 years to reach full development. Then they are lifted and sold fresh, or boiled or steamed, cut into slices, and dried. Dried slices are greyish-brown, hard, and have a rough, somewhat hairy texture.

Zedoary
Curcuma species

Native to subtropical wet forest zones of Southeast Asia and Indonesia, zedoary was brought to Europe in the 6th century, when it was used as a source for medicines and perfume. During the Middle Ages it became popular in the kitchen alongside its close relation, galangal; its culinary use is now largely restricted to Southeast Asia. Increased European interest in the food of that region has led to the availability of fresh zedoary, but the dried spice remains almost unknown. In Indonesia it goes by the misleading name of kencur, which is also used for aromatic ginger, *Kaempferia galanga*.

Fresh rhizome
C. zerumbet is increasingly available in fresh form. Combine with other fresh spices or use as a crisp garnish. The brown skin is removed before use.

Culinary uses

In Indonesia young shoots are eaten, flower buds are used in salads, and the long, aromatic leaves to wrap and flavour fish, as they are in Mumbai, where a fresh zedoary and vegetable soup is popular. In Thailand peeled and shredded or finely sliced fresh zedoary is added to salads or raw vegetables to serve with nam prik. Chopped, fresh zedoary with shallots, lemon grass, and coriander leaf makes a good spice paste for cooking vegetables in coconut milk. In Indonesia and India fresh zedoary goes into pickles. In Southeast Asia dried zedoary is used in the preparation of curries and condiments, and in dishes for which dried turmeric or dried ginger might be used. It goes well with chicken and lamb in southern Indian and Indonesian dishes.

FLAVOUR PAIRINGS

Good with chick peas, curries and stews, fish, lentils, poultry, Asian soups, green vegetables.

Combines well with chillies, coconut milk, coriander leaf, garlic, ginger, makrut lime leaves, lemon grass, turmeric.

OTHER ZEDOARIES

Used interchangeably as a spice by cooks, *C. zedoaria* has round and stubby rhizomes and *C. zerumbet* has long ones. The latter has a milder taste and, because its pale yellow colour contrasts sharply with the darker hue of similar-looking turmeric, it is often called white turmeric, khamin khao in Thai. The roots of two other species, *C. leucorrhiza* and *C. angustifolia*, are used to make the starch called Indian arrowroot or tikor, used as a thickening agent and for baby food.

Crushed dried rhizome
The aroma of dried zedoary is musky and agreeable, with a hint of camphor. The flavour is pungent, resembling that of dried ginger, less acrid but rather bitter and finishing on a citrus note.

When bruised, fresh leaves are intensely aromatic, giving off a musky, spicy odour with a citrus note. The taste is warm and pleasant, lemony and faintly bitter. Dried leaves have virtually no flavour – doubling the amount asked for in a recipe has very little effect on the taste.

PARTS USED

Leaves.

BUYING / STORING

Fresh curry leaves can be bought in Indian and other Asian stores, where they may be labelled meetha neem or kari (or kadhi) patta. They are best stored in an airtight plastic bag in the freezer but even in the refrigerator will keep for a week or more. Dried leaves can be had from the same sources, but don't bother.

HARVESTING

Although the tree is deciduous, leaves are available for picking most of the year in the tropics. From the farms of Tamil Nadu and Andhra Pradesh the stalks are shipped fresh, to be sold in small bundles. Vacuum drying is the best way to retain the fresh colour and preserve at least some of the aroma.

FLAVOUR PAIRINGS

Good with fish, lamb, lentils, rice, seafood, most vegetables.
Combines well with chillies, cardamom, coconut, coriander leaf, cumin, fenugreek seed, garlic, mustard seed, pepper, turmeric.

Curry leaves

Murraya koenigii

Curry leaves come from a small, deciduous tree that grows wild in the foothills of the Himalayas, in many parts of India, northern Thailand, and Sri Lanka. The tree has been cultivated in southern India for centuries, mostly on a small scale in private gardens for use in the kitchen, but more recently, also on a commercial scale. Plantations have recently been established in northern Australia.

Fresh leaves
The slender stalks may have as many as 20 small, bright green leaves.

Culinary uses

Curry leaves are stripped from the stalks just before they are added to the dish. They are used extensively in the cooking of south India. From domestic gardens they go straight into the vegetarian dishes of Gujarat. They are essential to sambhar, and used in long-simmered meat stews and in the fish curries of Kerala and those of Chennai (Madras), the only region of India where curry leaves are a standard ingredient in curry spice mixes. Elsewhere they are usually added to curry dishes only for the last five minutes of cooking.

Sri Lankan curry mixtures also routinely include curry leaves.

These mixtures are darker in appearance and taste than the Indian ones: the ingredients are more highly toasted and include spices native to the island, such as cinnamon and cardamom. Indian emigrants took curry leaves to Fiji, while others made them an important ingredient in South African Tamil cooking.

Quickly shallow-fried in ghee or oil with mustard seeds, asafoetida, or onion, curry leaves may be used as a flavouring at the start of cooking, before other ingredients are added. More often the same spice combination is used as a tempering,

added at the end, for instance as the basic bagaar or tadka that goes over most lentil dishes. Chopped or crushed leaves are used in chutneys (notably coconut chutney), relishes, and marinades for seafood. Whole leaves are added to pickles.

Westerners are just beginning to appreciate the delicate, spicy flavour the leaves impart to curries without the heat often also associated with those dishes. Beginners may want to use whole sprigs and remove them before serving, but cooked leaves are quite soft and the taste soon becomes pleasantly addictive.

Sri Lankan curry powder

This curry powder is made from curry leaves, coriander, cumin, fenugreek, rice, chillies, black peppercorns, cloves, green cardamom, and cinnamon (*recipe, p.278*).

TASTING NOTES

The seeds have a faint flowery or peppermint scent, and a delicate, earthy, slightly peppery taste with a hint of bitterness. They impart an agreeably earthy taste to food if used in quantities much larger than those required for colouring only.

 PARTS USED

Dried seeds.

 BUYING / STORING

Annatto is available as seeds, whole or ground, from West Indian stores and spice merchants. Seeds should be a healthy rust-red; avoid dull, brownish ones. Seeds and powder should be kept in an airtight jar out of the light. Seeds should last at least 3 years. Annatto/achiote paste can be bought online.

 HARVESTING

The large, rose-like flowers develop into prickly, orange-red pods at the end of the branches; each contains about 50 brick-red, angular seeds. When ripe, the pods are harvested, split open, and macerated in water. The pulp embedding the seeds is pressed into cakes for processing into dyes; the seeds are dried as a spice.

Annatto

Bixa orellana

Annatto is the orange-red seed of a small evergreen tree of the same name, native to tropical South America. In pre-Columbian times the seeds were already widely used as a colourant for food, fabrics, and body paint; in the western world annatto (or achiote, its name in the Nahuatl language of Mexico) is still used as such in butter, cheese, smoked fish, and in cosmetics. Brazil and the Philippines are the main producers, but it grows throughout Central America, the Caribbean, and in parts of Asia.

Ground seeds
Dried annatto seeds are very hard and are most easily ground in an electric grinder.

Whole dried seeds
Whole seeds are mostly used as a colourant. Soak ½ tsp in 1 tbsp boiling water for 1 hour, or until the water is a deep orange colour.

Culinary uses

Annatto seeds can be soaked in hot water to obtain a coloured liquid for stocks and stews, or to colour rice. In the Caribbean the seeds are fried in fat, over low heat, then discarded before the now deep-golden or orange fat is used for cooking. The fat, or oil treated the same way, can be stored in a sealed glass jar in the refrigerator for several months.

In Jamaica annatto may be used with onion and chilli in the sauce for saltfish and ackee, often called the national dish. In the Philippines annatto is ground and added to soups and stews, mostly for colour effect; it is an essential ingredient in the famous pork-and-chicken dish, pipián. In Peru it is used in marinades, especially for pork. In Venezuela it is combined with garlic, paprika, and herbs to make a popular condiment called aliño criollo. In Mexico it goes into achiote paste – the Yucatán recado rojo – basis of the region's best-known dish, pollo pibil (marinated chicken wrapped in banana leaves and cooked in a pit oven); the paste is equally good spread on fish or pork before grilling or barbecuing.

In Mexico annatto is also sometimes added to the dough for tamales, corn-based stuffed rolls steamed in a corn-husk wrapping. In Vietnam cooks use oil dyed with annatto as the base of braised dishes to give them colour.

Recado rojo

Red annatto paste is indispensable to the cooking of Mexico's Yucatán peninsula. Annatto seeds are combined with black peppercorns, cloves, cumin, coriander seed, dried oregano, garlic, and bitter orange juice or wine vinegar. Small red chillies may be added (*recipe, p.288*).

FLAVOUR PAIRINGS

Essential to pipián, recado rojo.

Good with beef, egg dishes, fish (especially salt cod), okra, onions, peppers, pork, poultry, pulses, rice, squashes, sweet potatoes, tomatoes, most vegetables.

Combines well with allspice, chillies, citrus juice, cloves, cumin, epazote, garlic, oregano, paprika, peanuts.

TASTING NOTES

The taste of pickled capers (once the vinegar or salt is rinsed off) is piquant, fresh, salty, and somewhat lemony. The pungency in its flavour derives mainly from a mustard oil, glycoside, not unlike those found in horseradish and wasabi.

PARTS USED

Unopened flower buds; unripe fruits.

BUYING / STORING

Capers from southern France are graded from nonpareilles to capottes, according to size – the smaller ones being the best. Other important producers are Italy, notably the tiny island of Pantelleria, Cyprus, Malta, Spain, and California. Pickled capers keep for a long time provided they are kept covered by the pickling liquid, which should not be renewed or added to, least of all with vinegar.

New York chefs are experimenting with pickling ramp seeds in the same way as capers. Ramps are wild leeks, *Allium tricoccum*, similar to ramsons (wild garlic) *see p.76*.

HARVESTING

Caper buds are picked by hand when they are the right size, wilted for a day or two, graded to size, then put in vinegar or dry salted. The intensely flavoured capers from Pantelleria and Sicily are always dry salted. Salting preserves taste and texture better than pickling does.

Capers

Capparis species

The caper bush is a small shrub that grows wild all around the Mediterranean, as far south as the Sahara and as far east as northern Iran, although it may have originated in dry regions of western and central Asia. Capers are successfully cultivated in many countries with a similar climate. In really hot countries the wild variety is likely to be *C. spinosa*, which has, as the name suggests, spines; the cultivated caper is usually *C. inermis*, without spines. In northern India the variety used is *C. decidua*.

Capers

Capers are commonly pickled in vinegar or dry salted. Their quality depends on their place of origin, the preserving method, and on their size.

Culinary uses

Capers are an important ingredient in many sauces, such as ravigote, remoulade, tartare, and tomato-based salsa alla puttanesca. English caper sauce, still mentioned as traditional with mutton, is equally good with firm fish. Most fish can be cooked or garnished with capers in a variety of ways; so can chicken. Salt cod is often accompanied by capers and green olives, a standard combination for fish dishes in Sicily and the Aeolian islands; in Spain, with fried fish, capers are combined with almonds, garlic, and parsley. With black olives, capers are the basis of tapenade and are also good in casseroles of chicken or rabbit. On their own capers enhance many dishes of the fattier meats, and have become one of the standard garnishes on pizza. In Hungary and Austria they flavour Liptauer cheese. Both capers and caper berries may be eaten on their own, like olives, or used as a relish with cold meats, smoked fish, and cheese. Used with discretion they can liven up a salad.

Pickled or salted capers should be rinsed before use. When capers are used in cooking they should be added towards the end; lengthy cooking tends to bring out an undesirable, bitter flavour.

FLAVOUR PAIRINGS

Essential to tapenade, various sauces.

Good with artichokes, aubergines, fish, green beans, gherkins, fatty meats (lamb), olives, potatoes, poultry, seafood, tomatoes.

Combines well with anchovies, basil, celery, garlic, lemon, mustard, olives, oregano, parsley, rocket, tarragon.

Caper berries

Caper berries are the small, semi-mature fruit of *Capparis* species. They are usually preserved in vinegar and their taste is similar, if less intense, to that of capers.

Leaves and shoots

Lightly pickled leaves and shoots are available in jars. The leaves and immature buds have a pleasant caper flavour, but the thicker stalks can be spiny and are best discarded.

TASTING NOTES

Fresh leaves are grassy and mildly pungent with astringent tones. Dried leaves have a fragrant note of hay. The aroma of the raw seeds can be identified as the overriding smell of some curry powders. Their taste is celery- or lovage-like and bitter; the texture is floury.

PARTS USED

Fresh and dried leaves; seeds.

BUYING / STORING

Iranian and Indian shops sell fresh leaves; use within 2–3 days and keep in the refrigerator. Dried leaves should be green with no yellowing; store in an airtight container. Seeds are available from the same sources and from spice merchants; they will keep their flavour for a year if stored in an airtight jar. Roast and grind seeds as needed. Look out for fenugreek sprouts.

HARVESTING

Fenugreek can be grown in rich soil in full sun. Gather both leaves and seeds. The white or yellow flowers develop into narrow beaked seed pods. Harvest when ripe and dry the seeds.

FLAVOUR PAIRINGS

Essential to sambhar powder, panch phoron, berbere, hilbeh.

Good with fish curries, most vegetables, lamb, potatoes, pulses, rice, tomatoes.

Combines well with cloves cardamom, cinnamon, cumin, coriander, fennel seed, garlic, dried limes, nigella, pepper, turmeric.

Fenugreek
Trigonella foenum-graecum

Native to western Asia and southeastern Europe, fenugreek has a long history of use as a flavouring and medicine. The Latin name *Trigonella* refers to the triangular shape of the seeds. Blue fenugreek grows in the Alps and the Caucasus; in Switzerland dried leaves are ground to a green powder, in Georgia seeds are used as a spice.

Culinary uses

A good source of protein, minerals, and vitamins, fenugreek is widely used by vegetarians in India. They make extensive use of fresh fenugreek (methi) leaves as a vegetable, cooked with potatoes, spinach, or rice. The leaves are also chopped and added to the dough for naans and chapattis. Dried leaves are used to flavour sauces and gravies. Fresh or dried leaves are essential to the classic Iranian herb and lamb stew, ghormeh sabzi.

Seeds are used in Indian pickles and chutney, in the southern spice blend sambhar powder, and in panch phoron from Bengal. They are much used in dals and fish curries in the south, and ground with flour to make the local dosai breads. In Egypt and Ethiopia, fenugreek also flavours breads, and it is a constituent of Ethiopian berbere spice mixture. In Turkey and Armenia, ground fenugreek is combined with chilli and garlic and rubbed onto pastirma, the excellent dried beef of the region.

Dress fenugreek sprouts, tomatoes, and olives with vinaigrette for a salad.

Whole seeds
Brief dry-roasting or frying mellows the flavour of the seeds and gives them a nutty, maple-syrup taste. Prolonged heat intensifies bitterness. Use immediately after roasting. Seeds should be soaked for several hours if they are to be used in a paste.

Ajowan

Trachyspermum ammi

Ajowan, native to southern India, is a small, annual umbellifer closely related to caraway and cumin. The seeds are a popular spice throughout India, and the plant is also grown and used in Pakistan, Afghanistan, Iran, and Egypt. Ajowan's essential oil was the world's main source of thymol (an antiseptic phenol) until the introduction of synthetic thymol.

Culinary uses

Ajowan should be used judiciously: too much will make a dish taste bitter. Cooking mellows the flavour to resemble that of thyme or oregano, but stronger and with a peppery note.

Ajowan has a natural affinity with starchy foods, and in southwestern Asia is used in breads (paratha) and fried snacks (especially those made with chickpea flour). Cooked with dried beans it helps relieve flatulence. It is also used to flavour pickles and root vegetables and in some curry mixes. It is very popular in the vegetarian cuisine of Gujarat, where it is used in batters for bhajias and pakoras, and with chilli peppers and coriander to flavour the crêpes called pudlas. In northern India, ajowan is fried in ghee with other spices before being added to a dish. Probably its best-known use in the West is in the flavouring of a crunchy snack called Bombay mix.

Ground seeds
Seeds are often used whole or crushed. Do not grind until needed.

Whole seeds
The seeds are small, ridged ovals, greyish-green to reddish-brown, and resemble celery seeds.

TASTING NOTES

When crushed, ajowan seeds have a strong, rather crude smell of thyme. The taste, largely determined by thymol in the essential oil, is hot and bitter. If chewed on their own, ajowan seeds numb the tongue.

PARTS USED

Dried seeds.

BUYING / STORING

Ajowan can be bought from Indian shops, where it may also be called ajwain or carom. The seeds will keep indefinitely in an airtight jar. Bruise them before use to release their flavour; they are easily ground in a mortar.

HARVESTING

Ajowan stalks are cut in May or June, when the seeds are ripe; they are dried, then threshed.

FLAVOUR PAIRINGS

Essential to berbere, chat masala.

Good with fish, green beans, pulses, root vegetables.

Combines well with cloves, cardamom, cinnamon, cumin, fennel seed, garlic, ginger, pepper, turmeric.

TASTING NOTES

Mastic has a light, pine aroma; the taste is pleasantly mineral-like, lightly bitter, and very mouth-cleansing.

PARTS USED

Tears of dried resin. Mastic is powdered before use so that it blends evenly into a dish.

BUYING / STORING

Mastic is expensive and is sold in small quantities, but you need only a small amount at a time. It is available from Greek and Middle Eastern shops and spice merchants. Store in a cool place.

HARVESTING

The slow-growing evergreen trees start to produce mastic when 5–6 years old, and continue producing for another 50–60 years. Mastic is harvested from July to October; the gnarled trunks are cut diagonally and the sticky resin oozes out; some collects on the trunk, some falls to the ground. In contact with the air the resin hardens into tears, which are collected, washed, then cleaned by hand and laid out to dry.

FLAVOUR PAIRINGS

Good with almonds, apricots, fresh cheese, dates, milk desserts, pistachio nuts, rosewater and orange flowerwater, walnuts.

Combines well with allspice, cardamom, cinnamon, cloves, mahlab, nigella, poppy seed, sesame.

Mastic
Prunus mahaleb

Mastic is a resin produced by cutting the bark of one variety of lentisk tree native to the Greek island of Chios. The tree has many veins, rich in mastic, just beneath the bark of the trunk. The pieces of resin, some oval, some oblong, are called tears. They are semi-transparent, with a light, golden colour. Mastic has a brittle texture, but when chewed it takes on the consistency of chewing gum.

Culinary uses

Mastic's main use is in baking, desserts, and sweetmeats. Greeks use mastic to flavour festive breads, especially the Easter bread tsoureki, and Cypriots in their Easter cheese pastries, flaounes. Most of the crop is exported to Turkey and the Arab states. With sugar and rose or orange flower water, mastic is used to flavour milk puddings, dried fruit, and nut fillings for pastries, Turkish delight, and preserves. It gives a pleasant, chewy texture to ice creams. Mastic soup, mastic stew, and a mastic sweetmeat are made in Izmir, the Turkish port city in sight of Chios.

Mastic tears
Used as a breath-freshener and digestive aid, mastic was the original chewing gum.

Safflower
Carthamus tinctorius

The thistle-like safflower is an ancient crop, traditionally grown on small plots for local consumption, whether as medicine, dye, food colourant, or spice. Today it is grown in many parts of the world, mainly as an oilseed crop. Unscrupulous merchants sometimes pass it off to tourists as the much more expensive saffron, and indeed it is known as bastard or false saffron in some countries.

Culinary uses

Safflower will colour rice, stews, and soups a light gold but it does not give the depth of colour or complex flavours of saffron. It is often used in this way in India and in the Arab world. Petals may be added straight to the dish or infused in warm water to obtain a colouring liquid. Portuguese cooks use safflower in seasoning pastes for fish stews and in the vinegar sauces that accompany fried fish. In Turkey it is used in cooking or as a garnish; in Georgia it is essential to khmeli suneli spice mix.

Safflower oil is high in the mono-unsaturated fatty acids that are beneficial in the prevention of heart disease.

Dried petals
Safflowers are the globe-shaped flowers of a tall, upright plant with prickly edged, oval leaves. When growing the flowers are deep red with yellow tips; when dried they are yellow to bright orange to brick-red in colour.

TASTING NOTES
Safflower has little aroma, but smells herbaceous and somewhat leathery; the flavour is bitter and lightly pungent. Although safflower contains the colouring agents carthamin and saflor yellow, it lacks essential oils to provide aroma.

PARTS USED
Dried flowers.

BUYING / STORING
Safflower is available online, from some spice merchants, and in countries where it is used it can be bought in markets. It may be sold as loose, dried petals or as compressed flower heads. In Turkey, where it is in common use, it may be sold as Turkish saffron. Store in an airtight container. The flavour fades after 6–8 months.

GROW YOUR OWN
Flowers are gathered in summer and sun dried, then crushed.

FLAVOUR PAIRINGS
Good with fish, rice, root vegetables.
Combines well with chilli, coriander leaf, cumin, garlic, paprika, parsley.

TASTING NOTES

Black pepper has a fine, fruity, pungent fragrance with warm, woody, and lemony notes. The taste is hot and biting with a clean, penetrating aftertaste. White pepper is less aromatic, and can smell musty, but it has a sharp pungency with a sweetish afternote.

PARTS USED

Immature and ripe fruits.

BUYING / STORING

Sun drying is preferable for peppercorns; if dried at high temperatures in artificial heat some of the volatile oils are lost. Black and white pepper rapidly lose their aroma and flavour when ground, so it is best to buy whole berries and grind in a pepper mill or crush in a mortar, as needed. In airtight containers peppercorns will keep for a year.

HARVESTING

To produce black pepper, immature green berries are picked, briefly fermented, and then dried. During drying the pepper shrivels, becomes wrinkled, and turns black or dark brown. For white peppercorns, berries are picked when yellowish-red and almost ripe, then soaked to soften and loosen the outer skin. Once this is removed they are rinsed and sun dried.

Pepper
Piper nigrum

The history of the spice trade is essentially about the quest for pepper. Peppercorns and long pepper from India's Malabar coast reached Europe at least 3,000 years ago; trade routes were fiercely protected, empires were built and destroyed because of it. In 408CE the Goths demanded pepper as part of their tribute when they laid siege to Rome; later, pepper was traded ounce for ounce for gold and used as currency to pay rents, dowries, and taxes. In volume and value pepper remains the most important spice. India, Indonesia, Brazil, Malaysia, and Vietnam are the main producers.

Whole peppercorns
Large, uniform, dark brown to black, peppercorns command the highest price. Aroma and flavour are more important than pungency. The best white pepper is considered to be Muntok from Indonesia.

Ground pepper
Ground white pepper is more attractive in creamy sauces than black.

Crushed pepper
Crushed peppercorns can be pressed into steaks to be grilled, and release their flavours in marinades.

Pepper has different characteristics in different places of origin and is therefore classified according to where it is grown. Broadly speaking, the flavour of pepper is determined by its essential oil content, while its content of the alkaloid piperine accounts for its bite. Black pepper has both aroma and pungency. White pepper contains less essential oil than black because the oil is present in the hull and is removed in cleaning; that also explains why white pepper, although pungent, has little aroma. Over time the strength of the flavour compounds in the essential oil diminishes.

The essential oil and piperine content varies according to the origins of the pepper. The best-quality pepper is from the Wyanad district on India's Malabar coast; it has a fruity aroma and a clean bite. Tellicherry is the grade with the largest berries. Indonesian lampong pepper has more piperine and less essential oil, so it is more pungent than aromatic; the berries are smaller and grey-black in colour. Sarawak pepper from Malaysia has a milder aroma than Indonesian berries, but is hot and biting. Brazilian pepper has a low piperine content and is rather bland. Vietnamese is light in colour and mild.

Red peppercorns

Red or pink peppercorns are fully ripe fruits, usually available preserved in brine or vinegar. They have a soft outer shell with a delicate, almost sweet, fruity taste. The inner core provides a moderate, lingering heat.

Green peppercorns

Green pepper has a light aroma, and an agreeable, fresh pungency; it is not overpoweringly hot. Green peppercorns are preserved by freeze-drying or dehydration, or packed in brine or vinegar. Keep fresh green and red pepper berries in the refrigerator.

Pepper *growing peacefully on its vine gives no hint of the fierce warfare and empire-building that have marked its past.*

As the condiment that invariably accompanies salt in the West, pepper remains the most important spice in volume and value.

FLAVOUR PAIRINGS

Essential to baharat, berbere, garam masala, ras el hanout, quatre épices.

Good with most foods.

Combines well with basil, cardamom, cinnamon, cloves, coconut milk, coriander, cumin, garlic, ginger, lemon, lime, nutmeg, parsley, rosemary, thyme, turmeric.

OTHER PEPPER

The long pepper species *P. longum* and *P. retrofactum* originated in India and Indonesia respectively. Long pepper is mostly used in Asia, East Africa, and North Africa in slow-cooked dishes and pickles. The spikes of minute fruits are harvested green and sun dried, when they resemble grey-black catkins. Long pepper is usually used whole. It smells sweetly fragrant, and initially resembles black pepper in taste, but it has a biting, numbing aftertaste. Indonesian long pepper is slightly longer and more pungent than the Indian.

Culinary uses

Pepper is neither sweet nor savoury, it is aromatically pungent. Although mostly used in savoury foods, it can be used with fruits and in some sweet breads and cakes. It brings out the flavour of other spices and retains its own flavour well during cooking.

The aroma of black pepper can be detected in foods all round the world. Even the chilli lovers of Latin America and southern Asia reach for the peppercorns to flavour cooking liquids, stocks, salad dressings, and sauces, or crush them to add to spice mixtures and marinades. Ground pepper is rubbed on fish and meat to be grilled or baked, it flavours rich stews and curries, and is used to season simple buttered vegetables and smoked fish.

White pepper is used in pale sauces and cream soups to preserve their attractive appearance. Use it judiciously because the bite is sharp.

In France, mignonette pepper, a mixture consisting of black and white peppercorns, black for aroma and white for strength, is often used.

Rinse brined peppercorns before using. Green pepper combines beautifully with sweeter spices, such as cinnamon, ginger, bay, fennel seed, and lemon grass, to flavour pork, chicken (rub butter mixed with crushed peppercorns and ginger under the skin before baking), lobster, crab, and fish, especially salmon. It makes an excellent steak au poivre and combines well with Dijon mustard. Red peppercorns can be used in similar ways.

Mignonette pepper

Black and white *P. nigrum* peppercorns are combined in this French seasoning.

Cubeb

Piper cubeba

Cubebs are the fruit of a tropical vine of the pepper family native to Java and other Indonesian islands. They were cultivated in Java from the 16th century, and for 200 years cubebs were a popular substitute for black pepper in Europe. By the 19th century they had become almost unobtainable. Cubebs are now scarcely known in the West, but there is a revival of interest in them among spice aficionados.

Culinary uses

Cubebs, also known as Java pepper and tailed pepper, are used locally in Indonesian cuisine and to a lesser extent in Sri Lanka, where they are also grown. They were traded from the 7th century onwards by Arab merchants and formerly had a role in Arab cooking, one that persists mainly in their presence in the Moroccan spice mixture ras el hanout. Cubebs are used to flavour North African lamb or mutton tagines, and as a substitute for allspice in long-cooked stews. Cubebs are best suited to meat and vegetable dishes.

Cubebs are sometimes confused with the Ashanti pepper, *P. guineense*, an African species, and the Benin pepper, *P. clusii* – these also have stalks and are often called false cubebs.

Whole fruits

Cubebs are furrowed and wrinkled, slightly larger than peppercorns, and have a short, straight tail. Some berries contain a single seed, others are hollow.

TASTING NOTES

Cubebs have a warm, pleasant aroma, lightly peppery but also allspice-like, with a whiff of eucalypt and turpentine. When raw, the flavour is strongly pine-like, pungent, and glowing with a lingering, bitter note, but cooking brings out the allspice flavour.

PARTS USED

Immature fruits.

BUYING / STORING

Cubebs can be bought from online spice merchants. Buy sparingly; although they keep their aromatic properties well, they are only used in small amounts. Stored whole in an airtight container they will keep for 2 years or more. Grind as needed.

HARVESTING

Cubebs are harvested green and sun dried to a deep brown-black.

FLAVOUR PAIRINGS

Combines well with bay, cardamom, cinnamon, curry leaf, rosemary, sage, thyme, turmeric.

TASTING NOTES

For aromas and flavours, see individual captions.

PARTS USED

Fresh and dried leaves.

BUYING / STORING

Most dried aromatic leaves are available by mail order and via the internet. Dried leaves hold their flavour quite well, but if you can get fresh leaves it is worth freezing them between sheets of plastic film. Fresh and dried hoja santa leaves are available in Latin shops in the US; fresh lá lót leaves in Southeast Asian shops. Dried salam leaves are available in Holland from Indonesian shops; dried avocado leaves in Latin shops in the US.

HARVESTING

Avocado trees are sold in some US nurseries; salam trees can be bought in Holland. Aromatic leaves can be picked at any time from the tree and used fresh. Leaves are also laid out in the shade to dry before being packed for sale.

Aromatic leaves
Various species

The aromatic leaves of a variety of trees are used as flavourings in many parts of the world. They are often described, somewhat misleadingly, as being rather like bay leaves. The way they are used may be similar, but their aromatic properties are very different. Included here are a few that are little known, but which are slowly becoming available outside their region of origin.

Hoja santa *Piper auritum*

This relative of *P. nigrum* grows in Central America and Texas. Fresh leaves have a lightly pungent, musky aroma and flavour, with a hint of mint and anise; dried leaves have a warm, anise-fennel aroma with a citrus note.

Lá lót *Piper sarmentosum*

The lightly spicy leaves of this pepper are used in Thailand (where it is called chaa phluu) and Vietnam (where it is lá lót). These large, glossy, round to heart-shaped leaves are sometimes mistaken for betel pepper leaves (*P. betle*), which are chewed in India as a digestive aid.

Culinary uses

Large, soft, heart-shaped hoja santa leaves feature in Mexican cooking, particularly in the states of Veracruz and Oaxaca. They are used to wrap fish or chicken to be steamed or baked; to line or layer casseroles of fish or chicken; and as a flavouring for tamales. They are also used with other herbs in green mole sauces. The leaves combine well with chillies, garlic, Mexican mint marigold, and paprika. Avocado leaves make a differently flavoured substitute as a wrapping, or use chopped fennel leaves in tamales to achieve a flavour

similar to that of hoja santa. The Thais wrap morsels of food – roasted coconut, peanuts, young ginger, shallots, chillies, and cubes of lime or other fruits – in lá lót leaves and serve them as a snack. In Vietnam the leaves are used to wrap spring rolls and small pieces of beef to be grilled, and are added to soups.

Salam leaves are used fresh in soup-like mixed vegetable dishes, in stir-fried vegetables, or with beef, braised chicken, or duck, and in Bali with roast or barbecued pork. Dried leaves are less fragrant than fresh.

The aroma and flavour develops with cooking. Salam leaf combines well with other Southeast Asian aromatics: chillies, garlic, galangal, ginger, lemon grass, tamarind, and coconut milk, as well as pepper, cinnamon, cloves, and nutmeg.

Avocado leaves are used, fresh and dried, in some regions of Mexico to flavour tamales, stews, or barbecued meats, or as wrappers. The leaves are usually toasted lightly and used whole or ground.

Salam *Eugenia polyantha*

The salam tree, a relative of the clove tree, is native to Malaysia and Indonesia. The leaf is used in Indonesian cooking. There is no real replacement for the lemony, aromatic leaves, but you could try curry leaves.

Avocado *Persea americana*

The glossy leaves of the avocado have a light hazelnut-anise or liquorice flavour. If you live in a climate where the avocado will grow, it is worth cultivating for its wonderful fruit alone; the scented leaves come as a bonus.

TASTING NOTES

All parts of the tree are aromatic. The leaves have a warm, woody aroma with a citrus note; the taste is similar. Fresh berries initially taste of sweet fruit; a camphor turpentine note soon follows, with an intensely pungent bite that leaves a numb sensation in the mouth.

PARTS USED

Fresh and dried leaves; fresh and dried berries.

BUYING / STORING

In Australia fresh and dried whole leaves and berries are available; fresh berries will keep for several weeks in a sealed plastic bag in the refrigerator. Berries are more potent than leaves, and both are stronger than true pepper, so use with caution. Elsewhere dried, ground leaf is most commonly found. Buy both leaf and berries in small quantities since they are used sparingly and the flavour diminishes once they are ground, even when stored in an airtight container.

HARVESTING

Leaves may be used fresh, or dried flat in the same way as bay leaves. Ripe berries are dried or preserved in brine.

FLAVOUR PAIRINGS

Good with game meats, beef, lamb, pulses, pumpkin and squash, root vegetables.
Combines well with bay, garlic, juniper, lemon myrtle, oregano, mustard, parsley, red wine, rosemary, thyme, wattle.

Mountain pepper
Tasmannia lanceolata

Mountain pepper comes from a genus of small trees, native to the uplands of Tasmania, Victoria, and New South Wales; it is unrelated to the pepper vine, *Piper nigrum*. Early colonists soon discovered that ground berries could be used as a condiment; in 1811 the colonial historian Daniel Mann noted that this "spice tree possesses a more pungent quality than pepper".

Culinary uses

When substituting mountain pepper for true pepper, use half the amount of ground leaf as you would true pepper, and even less if you are using the berries. It combines well with other Australian spices, such as wattle (*p.137*) and lemon myrtle (*p.171*). A rub of pepper leaf, lemon myrtle, and thyme is good for lamb and for local meats such as kangaroo. Use a few berries crushed or whole in a long-cooked meat stew or bean dish; prolonged cooking dissipates their sharpness and pungency. The berries may also go into a classic French sauce poivrade, which is good with beef and rich, well-flavoured game, in particular hare or venison. The leaves and berries of a related tree, *T. stipitata*, are sold as Dorrigo pepper, named for the Dorrigo mountains where it grows.

Fresh leaves
Mountain pepper leaves have a lingering heat and a kick that recalls Sichuan pepper (*p.220*) rather than black pepper. Dried leaves are stronger than fresh.

Dried berries
Dried mountain pepper berries can be ground in a peppermill and are often sold crushed, looking rather like oily, cracked black pepper.

Grains of paradise

Amomum melegueta

Grains of paradise are the seeds of a perennial, reed-like plant with showy, trumpet-shaped flowers, indigenous to the humid tropical coast of West Africa, from Liberia along the Gulf of Guinea to Nigeria. Among their other names are Guinea pepper, Melegueta pepper, and, less often, alligator pepper. The spice, originally brought to Europe in the 13th century via Saharan caravan routes, was appreciated as a replacement for true pepper. Present-day production is still in the same region, with Ghana the main exporter.

Culinary uses

Grains of paradise are little used in Western cooking now, but did remain popular long after true pepper became more readily and cheaply available. They were used to spice wine and beer, and in hot sack (Spanish white wine) they were a popular 17th-century tonic. But by the mid-19th century, interest in the spice had all but disappeared. In Scandinavia, they are still used in akvavit. Only in West Africa, and to a lesser degree in the West Indies, are they still a much-used seasoning; in the Mahgreb they are one of the components of Moroccan ras el hanout and Tunisian qâlat daqqa. Grains of paradise are excellent in mulled wine, in braised lamb dishes, and with vegetables, including eggplant, potatoes, and pumpkin. Grind them before use and add at the last stage of cooking. Pepper mixed with a little cardamom and ginger may be used as a substitute.

Crushed seeds
Crushing breaks down the red-brown coats of the seeds to reveal the white flesh inside.

Ground seeds
Grains of paradise grind down into a fine, aromatic powder.

Whole seeds
The seed head encloses a white pulp in which there are embedded 60–100 small, red-brown seeds, the grains of paradise.

TASTING NOTES
Grains of paradise are related to cardamom, but their taste does not have that spice's camphor element. Grains of paradise taste pungently hot and peppery, with a fruity note. The aroma is similar but fainter.

PARTS USED
Seeds.

BUYING / STORING
Grains of paradise are not easy to obtain: try online, or a specialist spice merchant. They are sometimes available in West Indian or African stores, or from health food shops. Stored whole in an airtight container they keep their flavour for several years. Grind them as needed.

HARVESTING
The fruit is a capsule, yellow streaked with red, fig-shaped and fig-sized. The capsule dries and becomes brown, hard, and nut-like; the seeds are chestnut brown and look like tiny, blunt pyramids.

FLAVOUR PAIRINGS
Essential to qâlat daqqa, ras el hanout.
Good with aubergines, lamb, potatoes, poultry, rice, squash, tomatoes, root vegetables.
Combines well with allspice, cinnamon, cloves, cumin, ginger, nutmeg.

TASTING NOTES

Sichuan pepper is very fragrant, woody, somewhat pungent, with notes of citrus peel. Sansho is tangy and quite sharp. Both have a numbing or tingling effect in the mouth. Sansho leaves, called kinome and used as a garnish in Japan, have a minty-basil aroma.

PARTS USED

Dried berries; fresh leaves.

BUYING / STORING

Sichuan pepper is sold whole or ground by oriental shops and spice merchants. Sansho is usually available as a coarse powder from the same sources. Split berries will keep their fragrance longer than the powder; store in an airtight container. The season for kinome is short and the leaves are not easily found outside Japan. If you do find the leaves, they keep for a few days in a plastic bag in the refrigerator.

HARVESTING

The reddish-brown berries are sun dried, then split open and the rather bitter, black seeds are usually discarded. Kinome leaves are gathered and used fresh in spring.

Sichuan pepper and sansho

Zanthoxylum simulans and *Z. piperitum*

These two spices, one traditional to the cooking of Sichuan province in China, the other to Japan, are the dried fruits of prickly ash trees. Also called flower pepper, Japanese pepper, and formerly fagara (the prickly ashes are no longer classified in the genus *Fagara*), the spice should not be confused with black and white peppercorns harvested from the *Piper nigrum* vine.

Whole and split berries

Remove the bitter seeds from whole berries. Split berries are sold with the seeds removed, but check the packet and discard any seeds you find.

Ground berries

Berries are dry-roasted alone or with salt, then ground and used as a condiment.

Culinary uses

Sichuan pepper is an important constituent of Chinese five spice powder. For many dishes, the berries are dry-roasted for 3–4 minutes to release their aromatic oils. Control the heat carefully for if they blacken they are not good and should be discarded. Leave to cool, then grind; an electric grinder does the job well. Sieve and discard the husks and store in an airtight container to use as a condiment. It is best to make only a little at a time because the flavour soon dissipates. The roasted pepper is also used to make spiced salt (*see p.272*). Sichuan pepper is used with poultry and meat to be roasted, grilled, or fried, and also with stir-fried vegetables. Try it with green beans, mushrooms, and aubergines.

Sansho is used as a table condiment in Japan, and is also an ingredient of seven spice blend, shichimi togarashi. The spice is most commonly used with fatty fish, meat, and poultry to mask the smell.

Kinome has a refreshing, mild flavour and a tender texture, which make it a popular flavouring herb or garnish for soups, simmered dishes, grills, and cooked salads.

FLAVOUR PAIRINGS

Essential to five spice powder, Chinese spiced salt (Sichuan pepper); seven spice blend (shichimi togarashi).

Combines well with black beans, chillies, citrus, garlic, ginger, sesame oil and seeds, soy sauce, star anise.

Seven spice powder

This is the Japanese spice blend shichimi togarashi, or seven flavours chilli, which is used to flavour udon (wheat noodles), soups, nabemono (one-pot dishes), and yakitori. In addition to chilli flakes and sansho it includes black and white sesame seeds, dried tangerine peel, flakes of nori (laver), and poppy seeds (*recipe, p.271*).

TASTING NOTES

Fresh ginger has a rich and warm aroma with a refreshing, woody note and sweet, citrus undertones. The flavour is hot, tangy, and has a bite. Rhizomes harvested young are milder and less fibrous than those harvested later in the season.

PARTS USED

Fresh rhizomes.

BUYING / STORING

Fresh ginger rhizomes should be hard, unwrinkled, plump, and heavy. They keep well in the vegetable drawer of the refrigerator for a week to 10 days. Ginger is also available chopped and preserved in an acid medium, and frozen as a paste. Ginger in syrup and crystallized ginger will keep for up to 2 years in a cool, dry place. Pickled ginger keeps for 6 months.

HARVESTING

Ginger rhizomes are dug up 2–5 months after planting, while still tender. When they are to be used fresh, they are washed, dried for a few days, and then stored. Ginger to be preserved or crystallized is peeled, cut into pieces, soaked in brine for some days, then in water. It is boiled in water, then in syrup, and either left in syrup or dried and dusted with sugar.

Fresh ginger
Zingiber officinale

Ginger is a rhizome, an underground stem of a lush plant that is somewhat like a small bamboo. It has been an important spice for more than 3,000 years. Cultivated in the southern provinces of China and in India, it was a staple in the diet of Confucius, and Sanskrit literature records its pungent spiciness in Indian cookery. In Asia ginger is most commonly used fresh, except in masalas and other dry spice mixtures. Most recently ginger has begun to be cultivated in Queensland in northern Australia.

Whole fresh rhizome
Fresh ginger has a pale tan skin stretched tautly around the yellow flesh, which should be crisp and not fibrous.

Sliced fresh rhizome
Sliced rhizome can be left unpeeled for use in marinades or dishes from which it will be removed before serving.

Culinary uses

Fresh ginger is used in savoury dishes throughout Asia. In China it is grated, chopped, sliced, or shredded for cooking fish and seafood, meat, and poultry because it neutralizes fishy and meaty smells. Large, crushed pieces are left unpeeled for extra flavour and discarded when the dish is ready. Among vegetables it is particularly used with cabbages and greens. It goes into soups, sauces, and marinades. In Japan fresh ginger has many uses; one of the principal ones, as in China, is to mask fish odours. Freshly grated ginger and its juice are used in tempura dipping sauce, in dressings, and with grilled and fried foods. Koreans add a little chopped ginger to many dishes, and the popular pickle, kimchi, relies on ginger and garlic for its flavour.

Galangal is generally preferred to ginger in Southeast Asia, although the two are used together in some dishes. Ginger and garlic are natural partners; many north Indian dishes are based on a ginger-garlic-onion paste, used to flavour cooking oil before meat or vegetables are added. In the south the combination is more likely to be ginger, garlic, chillies, and turmeric. It goes into chutneys and relishes, marinades for meat and fish, and into salads. Ginger and lime juice with chat masala makes a good salad dressing for pulses; with chillies, sugar, fish sauce, and water a Vietnamese dipping sauce for fish.

To obtain ginger juice, grate fresh ginger (a fine Japanese grater does the job well) or grate pieces in a food processor, then squeeze the juice from the shredded or chopped ginger through muslin or a tea towel. You could also add a little water to ginger in the processor and then strain. Ginger juice is used in sauces and marinades where a subtle flavour of ginger is needed, and is also sprinkled on meat. Fresh ginger has been readily adopted in Europe and America and is now often found in dishes of western origin.

FLAVOUR PAIRINGS

Good with green beans, beef, beetroot, broccoli, cabbage, chicken, citrus fruits, crab, fish, melon, parsnips, pineapple, pumpkin, and squash.

Combines well with basil, chillies, coconut, coriander, fish sauce, galangal, garlic, makrut lime, lemon grass, lime juice, mint, soy sauce, spring onions, tamarind, turmeric.

Fresh juice
Fresh ginger rhizomes are easily grated to produce an aromatic juice for use in sauces and dressings.

Young ginger

Very pale, young ginger with a moist, translucent skin is sometimes found in oriental shops in early summer. The flesh is creamy-white, the tips of the shoots pink, and the flesh crisp. It has a pure, clean fragrance; the taste is definitely of ginger, but without bite. The tender rhizomes can be used without peeling. Slices can be stir-fried and eaten as a vegetable or lightly cooked with fish and seafood, especially crab. In China it is often pickled. Add finely sliced young ginger and "wet" garlic to salads of green beans, tomatoes, or young beetroot. It is surprisingly good with cold roast beef.

Pickled ginger

In Japan knobs of ginger are pickled in sweet vinegar and served in wafer-thin slices with sushi as a digestive condiment, called gari. The taste is quite mild and pickling turns the ginger pink. I have found that well drained gari can be shredded and used to good effect in fish, seafood, and vegetable salads.

Beni-shoga is shredded ginger, dyed to a striking red by pickling and by being preserved with perilla leaves. More pungent than gari, it is good with crab and other seafood.

Hajikami shoga are pickled ginger shoots that are served with grilled fish. Gari, beni-shoga, and hajikami shoga are all available in packs or jars from oriental shops.

Pickled shoots
Sometimes garishly coloured, sometimes a delicate pink, hajikami shoga is made with the tender, young shoots of the ginger plant.

Shredded rhizome
Pungent beni-shoga is preserved first in salt, then vinegar. This vivid red pickle offers a sharp contrast in colour and taste when served with seafood.

Sliced rhizome
Familiar to sushi lovers, gari is finely sliced ginger rhizome that is pickled in sweet vinegar.

Preserved ginger
Ginger in syrup and crystallized ginger may be eaten as sweetmeats on their own or used as flavourings for sweet sauces, ice cream, cakes, and tarts. China and Australia are the main producers and both kinds are widely available.

Mioga ginger
The Japanese and Koreans share an enthusiasm for the mildly flavoured young shoots and buds of mioga ginger, *Z. mioga*. They are sliced and used to flavour soups, tofu, salads, vinegared dishes, and pickles to accompany grilled foods. This cold-tolerant ginger is now being grown in New Zealand for export. It is available pickled, and fresh when in season, from oriental shops.

Ginger flower
Also called torch ginger, the showy flowers of a wild ginger, *Nicolaia elatior*, are used in Thailand and Malaysia. Buds and young shoots are eaten raw with nam prik, sliced into salads, shredded over laksa soups, or used to add a mild pungency to fish curries. The buds are difficult to find outside Asia.

Aromatic ginger, see p.170.

Ginger in syrup
Knobs of young ginger are poached several times in a dense syrup so that the syrup penetrates the flesh. It is sometimes called stem ginger because both stems and rhizomes are used.

Fresh mioga buds
Mioga buds are gathered in spring. They are fragrantly herbal rather than hot, and have a delicate, crunchy texture.

Crystallized ginger
To make this lightly pungent sweetmeat, knobs of young ginger are cooked in a thick syrup, air dried, and rolled in sugar.

TASTING NOTES

Whole, dried ginger is less aromatic than fresh (*p.222*), but once bruised or powdered it is warm and peppery with light, lemony notes. The taste is fiery, pungent, and penetrating.

PARTS USED

Dried rhizomes.

BUYING / STORING

Dried ginger can be bought as pieces of rhizome, slices, and powder. Quality is important in buying dried ginger; the best is pungent and lemony; poor-quality ginger is sharp and biting with a fibrous texture. Rhizomes are hard to grind; they can be rasped on a fine grater, but it is easier to buy a small amount ready ground. Stored in an airtight container, good-quality rhizomes will keep their flavour for 2 years or more.

HARVESTING

Ginger to be dried is harvested 9–10 months after planting, when it is fully mature, more pungent, and more fibrous. The rhizomes are dried in the sun. For the best quality, the skin is scraped off first; other grades may be left unpeeled or boiled before peeling and drying. Ginger may also be bleached.

Dried ginger
Zingiber officinale

Middle Eastern and European dishes developed using dried ginger rather than fresh because it was in the dried form that ginger arrived via the caravan routes. The Assyrians and Babylonians used it in cooking, as did the Egyptians, Greeks, and Romans. Ginger was in use as a table condiment throughout Europe by the 9th century; such was the demand by the 16th century that the Spanish and Portuguese were planting it in their new tropical territories.

Ground dried rhizome
Ground ginger is essential to many breads, cakes, and pastries. Dried ginger has a different taste to fresh, and the one should not be substituted for the other.

Dried rhizome pieces
Dried, pale beige rhizomes release a warm aroma when bruised. Whole pieces are most used in pickling spices.

Culinary uses

In Asia dried ginger is used in many pungent spice mixtures. In the West it was one of the cornerstones of early spice blends and today is used in quatre épices and pickling spice. It is an excellent flavouring for squash, pumpkin, carrots, and sweet potato.

In the Arab countries it is used with other spices in tagines, couscous, and slow-cooked meat dishes with fruit. It is a popular baking spice for ginger bread, cake, and biscuits, and in commerce is much used for ginger beer and wine, and soft drinks. Fruits marry well with ginger, especially bananas, pears, pineapples, and oranges, and it is good for spicing jams.

Types of dried ginger

The quality and flavour of ginger vary greatly according to its origin. In commerce, different grades indicate how the ginger has been prepared before drying. Peeled Jamaican ginger has long been considered the best for its delicate aroma, pale colour, and fine-textured powder. It is expensive and in short supply. India is the main exporter of dried ginger; the best quality is Cochin, which is light brown, partly peeled, and has a pungent, lemony odour and taste. Chinese dried ginger is more lemony and less pungent than Cochin. The African varieties, principally from Sierra Leone and Nigeria, are often unpeeled and tend to be harsh and peppery with a note of camphor. Ginger from Australia has distinct lemon notes.

FLAVOUR PAIRINGS

Essential to berbere, curry and masala blends, five spice powder, pickling spice, quatre épices, ras el hanout.

Good with apples, bananas, beef, citrus fruits, lamb, pears, root vegetables, pumpkin, and squash.

Combines well with cloves, cardamom, cinnamon, dried fruits, honey, nutmeg, nuts, preserved lemons, paprika, pepper, rose water, saffron.

Quatre épices

This classic French blend is used in the preparation of pork and other meats. The four spices are black peppercorns, cloves, dried ginger, and nutmeg (*recipe, p.285*).

TASTING NOTES

Allspice has a pleasantly warm, fragrant aroma. The name reflects the pungent taste, which resembles a peppery compound of cloves, cinnamon, and nutmeg or mace. Most of the flavour is in the shell rather than in the seeds it contains.

PARTS USED

Dried berries.

BUYING / STORING

Allspice can be bought whole or ground. Whole berries, which look like large, brown peppercorns, are infinitely preferable; they crush easily if you need just a little allspice, and they keep in an airtight jar almost indefinitely.

HARVESTING

In Jamaica berries are mostly harvested from trees cultivated in plantations. They are hand-picked when full size but still green. After a few days' sweating they are dried on black concrete platforms for up to a week. As they dry the berries turn red-brown. When dry – determined by the seeds rattling inside the shell – they are winnowed and graded by size. Larger, inferior, wild berries are still gathered in the rainforests of Mexico and Guatemala.

Allspice
Pimenta dioica

Allspice is native to the West Indies and tropical Central America. Columbus found it growing in the Caribbean islands and thought he had found the pepper he was looking for, hence allspice's Spanish name pimenta (pepper), which was anglicized as pimento. That name was later altered to Jamaica pepper because most of the crop, and certainly the best quality, came and still comes from that island. Allspice is the only important spice that still comes almost exclusively from its region of origin – which also makes it the only one grown almost exclusively in the New World.

Whole dried berries
Jamaican allspice has the highest level of the essential oil that determines the taste. One of the main components of the oil is eugenol, which is also the principal flavouring element of cloves.

Ground berries
Ground allspice can lose its strength rather quickly.

Culinary uses

Long before the discovery of the Americas, the people of the islands used allspice to preserve meat and fish. The Spaniards learned from them and used allspice in escabeches and other preserving liquids. In Jamaica it is still an important ingredient in jerk seasoning pastes that are rubbed onto chicken, meat, or fish for barbecuing. It is also used extensively, crushed rather than ground, in breakfast breads, soups, stews, and curries. In the Middle East allspice is used to season roasted meats. It is used in pilafs and goes into some Indian curries. In Europe allspice is either used whole, as a pickling or mulling spice, or ground, to give a gentle, warm flavour to cakes, puddings, jams, and fruit pies. Allspice enhances the flavour of pineapple, plums, blackcurrants, and apples. Most of the world's crop goes to the food industry for use in commercial ketchups and other sauces, as well as sausages, meat pies, Scandinavian pickled herrings, and sauerkraut.

FLAVOUR PAIRINGS

Essential to jerk spice mixtures.

Good with aubergines, most fruit, pumpkins and other squash, sweet potatoes, and other root vegetables.

Combines well with chilli, cloves, coriander seed, garlic, ginger, mace, mustard, pepper, rosemary, thyme.

Baking or pudding spice

Ground together, allspice berries, coriander seed, cloves, mace, nutmeg, and cinnamon make up the baking or pudding spice that is sometimes called mixed spice (*recipe, p.286*).

TASTING NOTES

The aroma of cloves is assertive and warm, with notes of pepper and camphor. The taste is fruity but also sharp, hot, and bitter; it leaves a numbing sensation in the mouth. As in allspice, eugenol in the essential oil is mainly responsible for the characteristic taste.

PARTS USED

Dried flower buds.

BUYING / STORING

Whole cloves vary greatly in size and appearance, but should be clean and intact. Good cloves exude a small amount of oil if pressed with a fingernail. They will keep for a year in an airtight jar. They are hard and must be ground in an electric grinder. Ground cloves should be dark brown; lighter, gritty powders are likely to be mostly made from flower stems, which contain less of the volatile oil. The powder loses its strength quite quickly.

HARVESTING

Clove buds appear in small clusters, twice a year, from July to September and November to January. They are picked before flowering, when they are mature but only just turning pink at the base. Drying in the sun on woven mats they lose most of their weight and turn reddish to dark brown.

Cloves

Syzyium aromaticum

The clove tree is a small, tropical evergreen with fragrant leaves. Its crimson flowers seldom develop, as unopened flower buds constitute the spice. Native to the Moluccas, volcanic islands now part of Indonesia, cloves reached Europe overland through Alexandria in Roman times. The Spice Islands were conquered by the Portuguese and then the Dutch, who harshly defended their monopoly until, in 1772, a French official smuggled seedlings to Ile-de-France (Mauritius). These days Zanzibar, Madagascar, and Pemba in Tanzania are the main exporters; Indonesia uses nearly all its vast production itself.

Whole cloves
Good-quality cloves have reddish-brown stems and a lighter crown. They are rough to the touch and should snap cleanly.

Ground cloves
Ground cloves contribute their assertive warmth to most masalas and curry powders, to five spice powder, berbere, and baharat.

Culinary uses

Cloves are used in many of the world's cuisines. They are good with savoury and sweet foods. They go into baked goods, desserts, syrups, and preserves almost everywhere. In Europe cloves are used as a pickling or mulling spice. The French press a single clove into an onion to flavour a stew, stock, or sauce, the English sometimes use one or two in apple pie, the Dutch use them in a cheese called Nagelkaas (nail cheese) because of the shape of the cloves. In Germany they are found in spiced breads, in America in ham glazed with brown sugar. The candied walnuts of Turin have a clove stuck into one end. In the Middle East and North Africa cloves go into spice blends used to flavour meat dishes or rice, often in combination with cinnamon and cardamom. In much of Asia they appear in curry powders. In India they are essential to garam masala, in China to five spice powder, in France to quatre épices (with black pepper, nutmeg, and dried ginger). In Indonesia cloves are mixed with tobacco for the very popular kretek cigarettes, which crackle as they burn and have a unique aroma.

FLAVOUR PAIRINGS

Essential to quatre épices, five spice powder, garam masala.

Good with apples, beets, red cabbage, carrots, chocolate, ham, onions, oranges, pork, pumpkin and winter squash, sweet potatoes.

Combines well with allspice, bay, cardamom, cinnamon, chilli, coriander seed, curry leaves, fennel, ginger, mace, nutmeg, tamarind.

Five spice powder

This Chinese blend of cloves, star anise, cassia, fennel seed, and Sichuan pepper goes well with chicken, duck, and pork (*recipe, p.272*).

Cloves *grow in plantations of tall, dense trees that would produce remarkably delicate flowers if the buds were not*

picked before opening. The buds are still dried and sorted in the traditional way, without recourse to modern equipment.

TASTING NOTES

Powdered asafoetida has a strong, unpleasant smell, reminiscent of pickled garlic and as pervasive as that of truffles. The taste is bitter, musky, and acrid – nasty when sampled alone but becoming pleasantly onion-like when the spice is briefly fried in hot oil.

PARTS USED

Dried resin from the stems and rhizomes or taproots.

BUYING / STORING

In India asafoetida is sold in a wide range of qualities; the lighter, water-soluble hing is preferred to dark, oil-soluble hingra. In the West buy it in solid or powdered form. In an airtight tin (which also contains the smell), solid asafoetida keeps for several years while the powdered form lasts for about a year.

HARVESTING

Just before the flowering, the stalks of plants, which are at least 4 years old, are cut and earth scraped away to expose the large taproots, which are also cut. A milky latex exudes; this hardens and darkens to a reddish-brown on exposure to the air. Care is taken to shield this process from sunlight, which would spoil the juice. The gum is collected and more cuts are made until the root dries up, usually after about 3 months.

Asafoetida

Ferula species

Asafoetida is a dried, resinous gum obtained from three species of *Ferula*, giant fennel, a tall, fetid-smelling, perennial umbellifer native to the dry regions of Iran and Afghanistan, where it is also cultivated. Imported from Persia and Armenia it was much appreciated in Roman cooking when silphium from Cyrenaica was no longer obtainable. It came to India via the Moghul empire and has remained a popular spice there, although it is only cultivated in the north, in Kashmir.

Whole tears and lumps
Asafoetida is available either as "tears", small individual pieces, or "lumps" consisting of tears processed into a uniform mass. Solid asafoetida has little smell, but crushing releases the sulphur compounds in the volatile oil responsible for the odour.

Culinary uses

Asafoetida is essentially an Indian spice. In western and southern India it flavours pulses and vegetable dishes, soups, pickles, relishes, and sauces. Its flavour is particularly appreciated in the cooking of the Brahmin and Jain sects, whose diet forbids the use of garlic or onions. It is very good in many fish dishes. In its native Iran it is not used at all, and in Afghanistan it is only used, with salt, to cure meat that is dried in the sun for winter use.

Asafoetida should always be used sparingly. It can be used in any cooked dish where garlic would be appropriate; even a tiny amount enhances the flavour of a dish or spice mix, such as sambhar powder. A piece may be rubbed on a grill or griddle before cooking.

FLAVOUR PAIRINGS

Essential to chat masala, some curry powders, sambhar powder.
Good with fresh or salted fish, grains, grilled or roasted meat, pulses, most vegetables.

Crushed tears
Solid asafoetida is prepared for use by grinding it in a mortar with an absorbent powder such as rice flour. Only a small piece is needed for an individual dish.

Ground tears
Asafoetida is most widely available as a powder, mixed with a starch or gum arabic to keep it from lumping. Brown powder is coarse and strong; yellow powder (which owes its colour mostly to added turmeric) is more mellow.

TASTING NOTES

Whole mustard seed has virtually no aroma. When ground it smells pungent, and cooking releases an acrid, earthy aroma. When chewed, black seeds have a forceful flavour; brown ones are slightly bitter, then hot and aromatic; the larger white seeds have an initial sickly sweetness.

 PARTS USED

Dried seeds.

 BUYING / STORING

White and brown mustard seed is widely available. Black is hard to find; brown can be used instead but is less potent. Ground white mustard is relatively coarse as it contains the husk. Mustard powder is the finely sieved flour of seed kernels; its bright colour is due to added turmeric. All forms keep well provided they are kept scrupulously dry.

 HARVESTING

Mustard is harvested by cutting the stalks when the seeds are fully developed but not quite ripe, to avoid the pods bursting open and spilling their contents. Black mustard is particularly prone to this, which is why it has largely been replaced by brown in commercial production. The stalks are dried, then threshed.

Mustard

Brassica species

Black mustard, *B. nigra*, and white or yellow, *B. alba/ Sinapsis alba*, are native to southern Europe and western Asia; brown, *B. juncea*, to India. White mustard, of mustard and cress, has long been naturalized in Europe and North America. The Romans, who made prepared mustard, introduced the plant to England. In medieval Europe mustard was the one spice ordinary people could afford. The French started to add other ingredients in the 18th century, while the English refined the powder by removing the husks before grinding the kernels.

Whole seeds

Mustard's pungent taste is determined by an enzyme, myrosinase, which is activated by water.

White seeds

Sandy-yellow European seeds are larger than the oriental variety used in Japan.

Black seeds

Black seeds are larger than brown and are oblong rather than round. Their heat affects the nose and eyes as well as the mouth.

Culinary uses

In western cooking, whole white mustard seeds are used primarily as a pickling and preserving spice, and in marinades.

Brown seeds (known as rai) have increasingly taken the place of black in much Indian cooking. They figure prominently in the cooking of southern India, where whole seeds are usually first dry-roasted or heated in hot oil or ghee to bring out an attractive nutty flavour for a tadka or baghar. The dishes are not pungent because the hot oil does not activate myrosinase. In Bengal ground raw seed is used in pastes for curries, especially fish in mustard sauce. Mustard oil – viscous, deep golden, and quite pungent – is made from brown mustard seed and several lesser varieties. It is widely used as a cooking oil, most of all in Bengal, where it is heated to smoking point to reduce the smell, then cooled before use. Its piquant flavour contributes to the distinctive taste of many Indian dishes.

Powdered mustard flavours barbecue sauces and meat dishes and works well with most root vegetables. Add it towards the end of cooking because heat dissipates its strength fairly quickly.

The seeds are not the only part of the mustard plant to be used. Fresh shoots are often used in salads, as in mustard and cress. In Japan, and now in Europe, the beautiful, feathery mizuna is grown as a salad herb; it makes its appearance alongside Chinese red mustard and other varieties in supermarket mixtures. Shredded leaves make a pleasant garnish for root vegetables and potato and tomato salads. In Vietnam leaves are used to wrap stuffings of pork, shrimp, and herbs.

FLAVOUR PAIRINGS

Essential to panch phoron, sambhar powder.

Good with roast and grilled beef, cabbage, strong cheeses, chicken, curries, dals, fish and seafood, cold meats, rabbit, sausages.

Combines well with chillies, coriander, cumin, dill, fennel, fenugreek, garlic, honey, nigella, parsley, pepper, tarragon, turmeric.

OTHER MUSTARDS

B. juncea has a yellow variety, used in Japan in cooking (stuffed into lotus roots fried in tempura batter) and as a condiment, made English-style and very hot, to go with oden, a choice of cold raw or cooked food.

Field mustard *B. campestris*, and rapeseed, *B. napus*, are both used to produce mustard oil.

Mustard oil
Mustard oil is easier to digest after brief exposure to a very high temperature.

Brown seeds
Brown seeds have a long-lasting pungency, almost as intense as that of black seeds.

PREPARED MUSTARDS

To prepare blended mustards, the seeds are soaked in water to activate the enzyme myrosinase; once the required heat has been achieved the enzyme's activity is stopped. The resulting flavour is determined largely by the acidic liquid used – vinegar gives a mild tang, wine or verjuice a more spicy pungency, beer a real heat. Water gives the sharpest, hottest taste but will not stop the enzyme's activity and therefore does not make a stable mustard. Prepared mustards are best kept at room temperature even when opened; they will keep for 2–3 months, but they may dry out a little and will steadily lose their flavour.

French mustards, milder than the English, are made in three forms. Bordeaux is brown, although made from white seed, and contains sugar and herbs, usually tarragon. Dijon, from brown (but husked) mustard seed, is paler and stronger, made with white wine or verjuice and fewer additives. Meaux is quite hot, made from crushed and ground grains, a step towards the many wholegrain mustards, some of them made even more fiery by the addition of green peppercorns or chillies.

In Germany, Bavarian mustard is of the Bordeaux type, but Düsseldorf mustard is a pungent version of Dijon.

Meaux mustard

The town of Meaux has produced mustard since the 17th century. Usually sold in stoneware jars, this grainy mustard has a bite followed by a mouth-filling roundness. An excellent table mustard.

Bordeaux mustard

In Bordeaux mustard some of the hulls are left in the mixture, giving a darker appearance. It is mildly spicy with a hint of sweetness, and is good with sausages and in cheese dishes.

Dijon mustard

Dijon mustard has an appellation contrôlée; the name refers to a style of mustard that is pale, smooth, and clean tasting. The classic mustard for sauces and salad dressings, it is highly prized throughout the world.

Zwolle, in Holland, makes a mustard flavoured with dill that would be great with gravad lax. Mild and runny American mustard is made from white mustard, with rather too much turmeric. The aromatic, mild Savora mustard was developed in England around 1900 and is popular throughout South America. English mustard powder is made up with cold water, then left for about 10 minutes to develop its clean and pungent taste. Once made up it will not keep.

   Prepared mustards are mainly used as a condiment with oxtail or other meat casseroles, or a tracklement with roast beef, ham, and other cold meats. The various kinds are equally good in many cold sauces, from vinaigrette to mayonnaise, as dressings for green or other salads, vegetable dishes, and plain cooked or smoked fish. Added towards the end of the cooking process they will spice up a wide variety of casseroles, such as rabbit with mustard sauce. They also go well with many cheese dishes. Sweet mustards, made with honey or brown sugar, make good glazes for chicken, ham, or pork, and can be a piquant addition to some fruit salads.

English mustard
English mustard powder is a mixture of finely ground brown and white seeds, rice or wheat flour, and spices. Fiery and slightly acidic, it is good with roast beef and oxtail stew.

American mustard
Mild, sweet American mustard has devoted followers among hot dog fanciers, but the turmeric that colours it bright yellow can also make the taste dusty.

Moutarde au cassis
This wholegrain mustard from Dijon contains crème de cassis liqueur, which gives it a rich, fruity flavour and its red colour.

Tarragon mustard
Tarragon mustard is made by adding tarragon and sometimes green food colouring to a pale mustard. It is good in sauces for fish and chicken dishes.

TASTING NOTES

Chillies range in taste from mild and tingling to explosively hot. The fruits of *C. frutescens* are generally hotter than those of *C. annuum*, and those of *C. chinense* are hottest of all. Large, fleshy varieties tend to be milder than small, thin-skinned ones.

PARTS USED

Fresh and dried fruits. Immature chillies are green; they ripen to yellow, orange, red, brown, or purple, and may be used fresh or dried.

BUYING / STORING

All fresh chillies should be shiny, smooth-skinned, and firm to the touch. They keep in the refrigerator vegetable drawer for a week or more. They can be blanched and frozen, but if frozen raw, most lose their flavour and piquancy. Dried chillies vary in appearance according to the variety. A specialist merchant will tell you the country of origin, the type, flavour characteristics, and heat level. Dried chillies keep almost indefinitely in an airtight container.

HARVESTING

Most chillies are grown as annuals. Green chillies are picked 3 months after planting; varieties normally used ripe are left longer on the plant. Chillies may be dried, in the sun or artificially.

Chillies
Capsicum species

Native to Central and South America and the Caribbean islands, chillies have been cultivated there for thousands of years. Columbus took plants back to Spain; the Spaniards named them *pimiento* (pepper) because of their pungency, and capsicum fruits are still called sweet peppers, cayenne peppers, and so on, even though they are not related to the pepper vine. Today chillies are the biggest spice crop; hundreds of different varieties are grown in all tropical regions and eaten daily by about a quarter of the world population.

Whole fresh chillies

Chillies come in many colours, shapes, and sizes; they can be as tiny as a young pea or as long as 30cm (12in). Many of them stimulate the appetite not only with pungency but with fruity, floral, smoky, nutty, tobacco, or liquorice flavours.

Culinary uses

Chillies are an excellent source of vitamins A and C, and provide that added benefit to the millions of people who eat them as a cheap means of pepping up a bland and unvarying diet. Chillies are used extensively in their native region, throughout Asia, in Africa, and in the American southwest. India is the largest producer and consumer of chillies, fresh green or dried red (which are usually ground), and each region uses its local varieties. Mexican cooking makes the most sophisticated use of chillies, both fresh and dried.

The pungent bite of chillies is due to the presence of capsaicin in their seeds, white, fleshy parts, and skin. The capsaicin content depends on the variety of chilli and its degree of ripeness; removing seeds and veins will reduce the heat of the chilli. Capsaicin stimulates the digestive process and the circulation, which induces perspiration and has a cooling effect on the body. Chilli flakes are important in Middle Eastern cooking. Dark, almost black, Urfa from Turkey is smoky and rich flavoured. Aleppo chilli flakes from Syria are mid-red and have more heat.

FLAVOUR PAIRINGS

Essential to berbere, chilli powder (which is actually a combination of spices), curry powders and pastes, harissa, jerk seasoning, kimchi, moles, nam prik, pipián, romesco sauce, sambals.

Combines well with most spices, bay, coriander, rau ram, coconut milk, lemon, and lime juice.

The heat of chillies is rated on a scale of 1–10, from 1 for mild peppers to 10 for extremely hot scotch bonnets.

Ground chilli
Ground chilli is made from hot, dried, red chillies. Heat rather than flavour is often the characteristic of these products, 5–9/10 on the heat scale, depending on the variety.

Whole dried chillies
Drying changes the flavours of chillies. Similarly, the taste of green, immature chillies alters as they ripen and redden.

Chilli flakes
Produced from mild to moderately hot chillies, 2–5/10, these are often used as a table condiment in Hungary, Turkey, and the Middle East. Hotter chilli flakes are used as a condiment in Korea and Japan.

Chilli threads
Red chillies are an essential Korean ingredient. Very fine chilli threads are used as a garnish.

Chilli products

Ground chilli, chilli pastes, sauces, and oils are produced worldwide. Good-quality ground chilli smells fruity, earthy, and pungent and contains traces of natural oils that will stain the fingers slightly. A light orange colour indicates the inclusion of a high proportion of seeds, which makes for a sharper taste. Thin, pungent sauces are labeled salsa picante or hot pepper sauce; thick sauces, based on tomatoes, onions, garlic and herbs, may be mild or hot and may be sweetened. Indonesian sambals and Thai chilli jam are among the hottest. Chilli pastes are widely used in South America. The Chinese use soy sauce, black beans, ginger, and garlic to create medium to hot sauces. Korean gochu-jang is a sticky condiment made with chillies, soy bean paste, and rice flour.

Chilli oil
Seasoning oil made with dried red chillies is available commercially, but it is easy to make your own; fill one third of a bottle with dried chillies, top up with sunflower oil, close tightly, and leave for 1 month. In Sichuan crushed chillies are added to very hot oil, left to cool for several hours, then strained to produce a bright red oil, used in many cold sauces and on its own as a dip.

Chilli powder
This blend of ground chilli, cumin, dried oregano, paprika, and garlic powder is used to flavour chili con carne and other southwest US dishes. 1–3/10

Yellow chilli powder
The colour of ground chillies ranges from yellow to red and mahogany. Yellow chilli powder is used in South America; it can be mild or hot.

Cayenne powder
The most common powdered chilli, cayenne, is intensely pungent and made from small, ripe chillies, grown worldwide. The flavour is tart, slightly smoky, and pungent. 8/10

Thin sauces

Thin sauces are made from crushed chillies blended with spices and vinegar to produce fiery liquids. Tabasco sauce is the best-known example.

Chilli sauces

Chilli sauces are made in most regions where chillies are grown. The simplest types are made from whole chillies preserved in brine or vinegar. Thick sauces, which may be cooked or made from raw ingredients, are used as dips and condiments.

Chilli jam and sambal

Chilli pastes and thick sauces enliven stir-fries and slow-cooked dishes. At the end of this book are recipes for chilli jam (*p.293*) and sambals (*p.295*).

Mexico

In Mexico fresh and dried versions of a chilli often have different names. Specific chillies are required for specific dishes; using the wrong one can significantly alter the balance of flavours. Large, fleshy poblanos are used as a vegetable, often stuffed; jalapeños and serranos in salsas, stuffings, and pickles; dried anchos and pasillas are often ground to thicken a sauce. When used fresh, green chillies tend to be preferred and they are often charred and peeled before being used.

Serrano *C. annuum*

Mid green, cylindrical, crisp-textured, with a concentrated, fresh, grassy flavour and very pungent seeds and veins. It ripens to bright red. Commonly used in sauces. **6–7/10**

Jalapeño *C. annuum*

Bright green, some with dark patches, torpedo-shaped, quite fat with crisp, thick flesh. Sometimes roasted and peeled. Jalapeños have a light flavour and are medium-hot. Red and fully ripe they are sweeter and less hot. Also sold canned en escabeche (pickled) and widely used as a table condiment. **5–6/10**

Habanero *C. chinense*

Lantern-shaped, mid green ripening to yellow, orange, and deep red, thin-fleshed, and fruity. Mostly used in Yucatán, raw or roasted, to flavour beans and sauces. For a hot sauce, blend roasted habaneros with salt and lime juice. **10/10**

Chilaca *C. annuum*

Thin, deep red and shiny, with vertical ridges. The deep flavour has a hint of liquorice. Roasted and peeled, they are used in vegetable dishes, with cheese, and in sauces. Sometimes available pickled. **6–7/10**

OTHER CHILLIES

Mulato (*C. annuum*) is similar to ancho, but chocolate brown; the taste is full-bodied, sweeter than ancho, with notes of dried cherries, and mild to medium-hot. Mostly toasted and ground for sauces. 3–5/10

De arból (*C. annuum*) is seldom found fresh; it remains bright red when dried. Slender, curved, pointed, with thin flesh and a smooth skin, this chilli is searingly hot and has a somewhat tannic flavour. Soaked and puréed, de arból chillies are used in stews and as a table sauce. 8/10

Poblano (*C. annuum*) is dark green and shiny, with a ridge around the base of the stem. The chilli is triangular and tapering, with thick flesh. Roasted and peeled, poblanos are stuffed or fried. They pair well with corn and tomatoes, and have a rich flavour. 3–4/10

Pasilla (*C. annuum*) is the dried chilaca, slender, wrinkled, and almost black. It has an astringent yet rich flavour with herby notes that are complex and long-lasting. Toasted and ground it is used in table sauces or in cooked sauces for fish. 6–7/10

Güero (*C. annuum*) is pale yellow, smooth, long, and pointed, with thin flesh. The taste is lightly floral, mild to medium-hot. Güeros are used fresh in salsas and moles. 4–5/10

Cascabel *C. annuum*

This chilli is round, brown-red, with a smooth, translucent skin; the seeds rattle when you shake it. It has a lightly acidic, smoky flavour and is agreeably nutty after toasting. Moderately hot, it is toasted and blended with tomatoes or tomatillos to make a salsa, and crumbled in stews. 4–5/10

Chipotle *C. annuum*

The smoke-dried jalapeño. Tan to coffee-coloured, wrinkled, leathery, it has a smoky, sweet, chocolate smell and taste. Often used whole to flavour soups and stews. Soaked and puréed, it goes into sauces. Available canned in a light pickle for use as a condiment. 5–6/10

Ancho *C. annuum*

This is the dried poblano chilli. Deep red-brown, wrinkled, fruity, and sweet with rich flavours of tobacco, prune, and raisin, and slightly hot. Anchos are toasted and ground for sauces, or can be stuffed. Also available as powder and blocks of paste. The most popular dried chilli. 3–4/10

Guajillo *C. annuum*

This chilli is long and slender, with a blunt point; maroon with brown tones and a smooth, tough skin, it has high acidity, giving a tangy, pleasantly sharp taste. It is soaked and blended for enchilada sauces or crumbled in stews. It colours foods well. 4/10

Southwest US and Caribbean

West Indians tend to prefer hot chillies for marinades, relishes, and stews. Early hot sauces mixed chillies and cassava juice; now garlic, onion, and other spices give depth to Caribbean chilli sauces. In the American southwest Mexican chillies are used in Mexican-inspired dishes, but the local New Mexican chilli, used green, red, and dried, is mild. These chillies are hung out to dry in colourful ristras, and once dried they are often ground and sold as Chimayo chilli powder or chile colorado.

Jamaican hot *C. chinense*

Bright red and squat with thin flesh, this chilli tastes sweet and very hot. Use in salsas, pickles, and curries. 9/10

New Mexico *C. annuum*

Bright green or a deep, intense red, these have a sweet, earthy flavour. They are roasted and peeled, and keep well frozen after roasting. Green are good in guacamole, tacos, and tamales; red go into sauces, soups, and chutneys. Dried, they have rich, dried-fruit flavours. They are used for red chilli sauce and other relishes. 2–3/10

Scotch bonnet *C. chinense*

Yellow-green to orange-red, similar in appearance to the closely related habanero but with a wrinkled top and flattened base. Very hot and with a deep, fruity, smoky flavour. Used in many Caribbean hot sauces and in jerk seasoning. 10/10

Tabasco *C. frutescens*

Thin-fleshed and yellow, turning orange or red when ripe, this chilli has a sharp, biting taste with a hint of celery. It is mostly used for Tabasco sauce. 8/10

Latin America

Called ají, chillies are much used in the Andean countries as a flavouring and as a condiment; a bowl of uchu llajawa – a salsa of chillies and quillquiña (*Porophyllum ruderale*) – is always on the table. Many varieties have only local names; some are mild, others hot or bitter, and some dried chillies have rich flavours of raisin and prune. Chillies are also important in the cooking of Bahia in Brazil; elsewhere chilli pastes and bottled sauces are more common.

Rocoto *C. pubescens*

Native to the Andes; plump and rounded, yellow to orange-red, rocotos are always used fresh in sauces and condiments, or as a vegetable, often stuffed with meat and cheese. 8–9/10

Mirasol *C. annuum*

A popular Peruvian chilli, also found in Mexico, where the dried form is known as guajillo. Used green, yellow, or at its ripe, red-brown stage. Fruity and lively, it colours dishes well. Good with meats, beans, and vegetables. 5/10

Ají amarillo *C. baccatum*

Common in Peru, both fresh and dried, when it is called cusqueño. Pointed and hot with raisiny aromas, it is used with root vegetables, guinea pig, ceviche, and other seafood dishes. Also used in paste form, available online. 7/10

OTHER CHILLIES

Ají dulce (*C. annuum*) is sweet, mild, musky, and herbal-like. It is used extensively in Central America, Colombia, and Venezuela, especially with beans. 1/10

Rocotillo (*C. chinense*) is a mild Andean chilli, bright red and squashed-looking, that is eaten as a condiment with corn, beans, root vegetables, and roast meats. 3–4/10

Malagueta (*C. frutescens*) is pale or mid green, thin-fleshed, tapered, and tiny. It is native to Bahia in Brazil and widely used in Afro Brazilian cooking and as a table condiment. Malagueta is also the name given in Portugal to small chillies pickled in vinegar. 8/10

Asia

Asian chillies are even harder to pinpoint by name than Latin American ones. They are usually distinguished by types: large red and green ones, which are roasted and used in dips and sauces in Southeast Asia; medium-sized, shiny-skinned chillies, moderately hot, used in Indonesian and Malay cooking; and more pungent varieties for Thai and Indian curries. Japanese santakas and hontakas resemble cayennes.

Thai *C. annuum*

Used fresh and dried, these chillies are slender, dark green or bright red, with meaty flesh and lingering heat. Add whole to curries and stir-fries or chop for pastes and dips. **8/10**

Korean *C. annuum*

The bright green, curved, Korean chilli is related to the Thai. Fresh chillies are cooked in fish, meat, and vegetable stews, in stir-fries, or stuffed and fried. **6–7/10**

Bird *C. frutescens*

The tiny green, orange, and red chillies are all used, often whole, to give a "finishing" flavour to a dish. They are fiercely hot. **9/10**

Kashmir *C. annuum*

Grown not only in Kashmir but in other parts of India, this chilli is deep red and has sweet notes yet a distinct bite. In India it is called lal mirch. **7/10**

Europe

A few chillies are specific to Europe, and many more are imported or are now grown here as enthusiasm for chillies has spread. Hungary, Spain, and Portugal are the countries where local chillies are most used, and they are usually only mildly hot.

OTHER CHILLIES

Cherry (*C. annuum*) is orange to deep red when fresh, mahogany when dried. This chilli has thick flesh and lots of seeds. It has a fruity flavour and ranges from mild to medium-hot. Often sold pickled. **1–5/10**

Peri peri (*C. chinense*) is the Portuguese name for small chillies. It crops up in those parts of the world colonized by the Portuguese. In Africa it is used for the jindungo chilli, similar to the bird chilli. **9/10**

Piment d'Espelette (*C. annuum*) from the Basque country has an appellation contrôlée. Bright red, wide-shouldered, and tapering, it is sweetly fruity and mildly piquant. Available dried, whole, or as a powder, and also as a purée or coulis. **3/10**

Guindilla *C. annuum*

Brick-red and smooth, this long, tapering Spanish chilli is used dried. Large pieces are soaked and added to a dish for extra piquancy; remove before serving. **5/10**

Ñora *C. annuum*

This chilli is mild and pleasantly earthy. It is soaked and used to flavour rice dishes and stews. Ñoras are essential to romesco sauce and for sweet paprika. The larger, bell-shaped choricero is similar and, as its name suggests, is used to flavour chorizo and other meat products. **1–2/10**

Banana *C. annuum*

Yellow-green ripening to red, curved, with a waxy skin, this mild chilli is related to the hotter Hungarian wax. Use fresh in salads, stews, roasted whole, with pulses or potatoes, pickled, and as a garnish. **1/10**

Peperoncino *C. annuum*

These chillies are slender, wrinkled, and often curved, with thin flesh. Used fresh, green or red, in pickles and tomato-based dishes, the flavour is sweetish. **1–4/10**

Preparing
spices

Bruising, grating, slicing, and shredding spices

Many spices need some preparation before being added to a dish or used in a spice blend or paste. Bruising, cutting, and grinding serve to release the volatile oils and perfume of a spice. Large, bruised pieces of a spice are intended only for flavouring and should be removed before a dish is served. Mild spices are sometimes cut into bite-sized pieces and eaten as part of the dish; otherwise, spices should be grated, finely sliced, or shredded.

Bruising spices

Soft-textured fresh spices such as lemon grass, ginger, galangal, aromatic ginger, and zedoary (white turmeric) are often bruised before cooking to release their flavours, then added whole for later removal.

1 Remove the upper stalk of lemon grass (or peel a knob of the other spices).

2 Crush the lower part of the lemon grass stem (or the peeled knob) using the back of a heavy knife or a wooden kitchen mallet.

Extracting juice from ginger

Many Asian dishes call for the pure flavour of ginger juice, which can be quickly extracted from a fresh root.

1 Grate the ginger or chop finely in a food processor.

2 Wrap the shavings in a piece of muslin or a tea towel and squeeze the juice into a bowl.

Slicing and shredding spices

Some dishes require discs of fresh spices, while others call for spices to be shredded or chopped.
The procedure for spices such as ginger, galangal, or zedoary (white turmeric) is given below.
Lemon grass is cut into fine rings from the base, stopping when the texture becomes fibrous.
Makrut lime leaves should be shredded as fine as a needle if they are to be eaten.

1 Peel as much fresh rhizome or root as you need, cutting off any woody or dry bits.

2 Using a sharp knife, slice the root thinly across the grain into a series of fine discs.

3 Stack the discs, press down firmly, and shred them into fine slivers.

4 Line up the slivers and cut them across to chop. To chop more finely, mound up the pieces and chop as herbs (p.119).

Grating fresh spices

Fresh roots and rhizomes, such as wasabi and ginger are best grated. A Japanese oroshigane, designed specifically for grating wasabi and ginger (p.113), grates more finely than any western grater.

Grating galangal
A very sharp western grater will produce a pulp that is suitable for some purposes, such as extracting the juice.

Grating dry spices

Although most spices are ground, some of the larger ones are more easily grated. For nutmeg use a nutmeg grater or the finest holes of a normal grater.

Grating dried ginger
Dried ginger, turmeric, and zedoary are very hard and therefore best grated on a fine citrus grater or rasp.

Dry roasting and frying spices

Roasting whole spices in a dry frying pan is especially common in Indian cooking. The process concentrates the flavours and makes the spices easier to grind. Other dishes call for spices to be fried before other ingredients are added. Frying brings out the flavour, which is imparted to the oil. The aroma of fried spices permeates a dish more fully than that of raw spices, but once a liquid is added the amount of fragrance they release is reduced.

Dry roasting spices

Some seed spices, notably mustard seeds, tend to jump about as they roast, so have a lid available to cover the pan. A tablespoon of spices will be ready in 2–3 minutes, whereas a large quantity can take up to 8–10 minutes to brown evenly. With large quantities, roast each spice separately.

1 Heat a heavy-based pan until it feels hot when you hold your hand above the base.

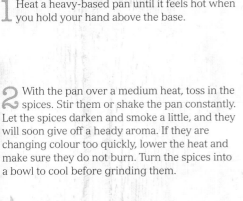

2 With the pan over a medium heat, toss in the spices. Stir them or shake the pan constantly. Let the spices darken and smoke a little, and they will soon give off a heady aroma. If they are changing colour too quickly, lower the heat and make sure they do not burn. Turn the spices into a bowl to cool before grinding them.

Dry roasting in an oven or microwave

◀ **Dry roasting in an oven**
Dry roasting a large quantity of spices may be easier in an oven preheated to 250ºC (500ºF/Gas 9). Spread the spices on a tray and leave in the oven until they darken and are aromatic, shaking and stirring from time to time. Cool before grinding.

Dry roasting in a microwave
Spread the spices in one layer on a plate or dish and cook uncovered at full power. Roasting 2–4 tbsp will take 4–5 minutes. Stir the spices once during cooking. Cool before grinding.

Frying spices

Prepare all the ingredients of a dish before frying its spices. Some spices are fried for only a few seconds, others for up to a minute. All will darken, and some, such as cardamom pods, will puff up. Remove the pan from the heat to add more ingredients, and stir quickly to prevent them burning in the oil.

1 Pour a thin film of sunflower oil into a heavy-based frying pan and heat until you can see a faint haze rising over the pan.

2 Fry whole spices before ground ones, adding them in the order they appear in the recipe. Spices should sizzle when they hit the hot oil and brown almost instantly. Watch them closely to prevent burning.

Grinding, crushing, and making spice pastes

Freshly ground or crushed spices are always more aromatic than spices bought ready-ground. You will soon appreciate the difference if you take the trouble to grind, say, a teaspoon of coriander seeds and put them to one side for an hour or two. Then grind another spoonful. Smell the older batch and then the freshly ground seeds – you will find that some of the aroma of the first batch has already dissipated.

Grinding spices

Some whole spices – allspice, cinnamon, and cloves, for example – are aromatic, but most need to be crushed or ground to release their aroma. A blender can be used for a large quantity, but most spices are too hard to grind evenly in a food processor.

◄ **Using a pestle and mortar**
Choose a mortar that is deep, sturdy, and roughly textured, for many spices are very hard and it needs considerable force to grind them by hand.

Using an electric coffee grinder
Most spices can be ground in an electric coffee grinder kept specially for the purpose, although a few, such as anardana (*see p.161*), are too sticky.

Crushing spices

Some spices need only to be crushed, rather than pulverized to a powder. A pestle and mortar works well because you can easily see and control how much the spice is broken up – and you can enjoy its fragrance at the same time.

◄ **Using a rolling pin**
Put the spice in a plastic bag, spread out the seeds on a hard surface, then crush firmly with a rolling pin.

Making spice pastes

Spice pastes are made by crushing fresh spices (such as garlic, ginger, galangal, or zedoary) together with dry spices or herbs and sometimes a little liquid. The technique is widely used in India and Southeast Asia, and in Mexico. Use a pestle and mortar or the small bowl of a food processor.

◄ **Making a dry spice mixture**
If dry spices are to be added, grind them first, either in the mortar or in a coffee grinder.

◄ **Making a wet spice mixture**
Crush the garlic or ginger, then work in the ground spices, and finally the liquid if needed.

Preparing fresh chillies

Chillies come in many shapes, colours, and sizes, and the flavour changes from the young, green state to the mature, red or red-brown state. When chillies are dried, their flavour changes again. Often fresh chillies are used whole or sliced in a recipe, but sometimes they benefit from seeding or roasting, especially if they have tough skins.

Roasting fresh chillies

Most chillies can be used without peeling, but some are peeled because the skin is tough or because peeling will improve the texture and give an attractive charred flavour. Small chillies can be roasted on a preheated dry griddle or heavy frying pan. Turn them until they darken and soften.

1 Hold large chillies directly over a gas flame, turning from time to time so that they are charred evenly and the flesh doesn't burn. If you have an electric hob, lay the chillies on a roasting rack over the element. Alternatively hold them close to the preheated element of the grill and turn them as they blister and blacken.

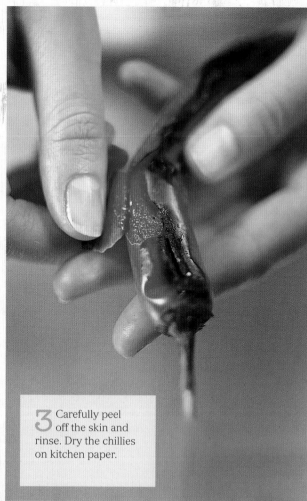

3 Carefully peel off the skin and rinse. Dry the chillies on kitchen paper.

2 Once they are evenly charred, put the chillies into a polythene bag or a bowl covered in clingfilm and leave to sweat for 10–15 minutes.

Freezing chillies

Fresh chillies can be frozen after roasting. There is no need to peel them because the skin will come off when the chillies have thawed.

◄ Freezing unroasted chillies
Blanch unroasted chillies with stalk intact for 3 minutes, then drain in a colander. Cool completely, place in a polythene bag, and freeze.

Removing seeds and veins from fresh chillies

Capsaicin, the pungent principle that gives chillies their heat, is present to varying degrees in the seeds, white veins, and skin. Capsaicin can sting the skin and eyes (*see below*). Removing seeds and veins before cooking reduces the heat of a dish.

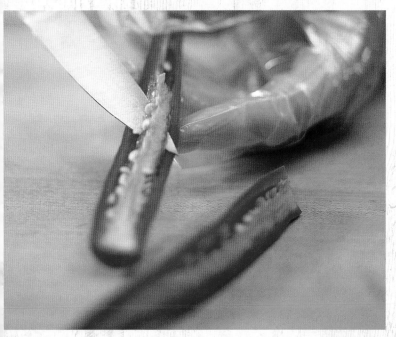

1 Cut off and remove the stalks and slice each of the chillies in half.

2 Cut out the veins and scrape out all the seeds, then rinse.

CAUTION

• If you are not used to handling chillies or have any cuts or a sensitive skin, wear thin rubber or plastic gloves to protect against the capsaicin.

• Remember that the seeds and veins are the hottest part of chillies. Avoid rubbing your eyes – if you do, wash them at once with cold water.

• When you have finished handling chillies, use soapy water and thoroughly wash your hands, as well as the work surface and any utensils.

• If your hands do suffer chilli burn, put them in a bowl of cold water or light vegetable oil.

• If you burn your mouth from eating too much chilli, a drink of water will make it worse. Instead, chew a piece of bread or try yogurt or milk.

Preparing dried chillies

Large dried chillies, widely used in the cooking of Mexico and the American southwest, are usually toasted, then soaked and puréed before use in a sauce. Toasting enhances their flavour; for a milder dish, the chillies are just soaked. In Mexico, smaller varieties of dried chillies are frequently ground or puréed straight into a sauce; Asian cooks are more likely to toast small dried chillies before grinding them.

Removing seeds and veins from dried chillies

As with fresh chillies, removing the seeds and veins from dried chillies before use reduces the heat of the dish. Seeds and veins are best removed before toasting, so that the skins are ready for soaking or grinding immediately after the chillies have been toasted.

◀ **Shaking out seeds**
Wipe the chillies clean, then either tear them apart or break off the stalks and shake out the seeds.

Toasting dried chillies

Toasted dried chillies darken in colour, blister, and crackle as they release their aroma. Don't let them scorch or they will taste acrid and bitter. Once toasted they are ready for soaking or grinding.

◀ **Using a griddle**
Place cleaned dried chillies onto a preheated griddle or heavy frying pan for 1–2 minutes, turning so that they don't burn. Alternatively, toast them for 2–3 minutes in an oven preheated to 250°C (500°F/Gas 9).

Soaking dried chillies

If you need small, soaked dried chillies for an Asian spice paste, tear them into pieces and add to water. They should be ready for use in 15 minutes.

1 Place toasted or cleaned, dried chillies into a bowl and cover with almost-boiling water. Keep the chillies submerged by leaving a saucer or plate on top of them and soak for 30 minutes or until soft – large, thick ones may need longer.

2 Sieve the soft chillies to remove tough skins, then form a sauce by blending them with other ingredients and some of the soaking liquid.

Grinding dried chillies

Wipe the chillies clean, remove the stalks, and tear the skins into pieces. Retain the seeds and veins if you need additional heat in the dish: otherwise remove them before grinding.

◀ **Using an electric grinder**
Dried chillies can be ground to a fine consistency in an electric coffee grinder. Better results are obtained when the dried chillies have first been toasted.

Salt

Sodium chloride

Salt is a mineral, primarily composed of sodium chloride (NaCl), and is found in most parts of the world. It is the main mineral constituent (78%) of the world's oceans, and is also found in crystalline form known as rock salt. It is essential to animal life, yet we call it common salt and tend to take it for granted without much thought to its production or its history.

EARLY HISTORY

Some of the earliest salt works recorded date back 6000 years ago to the Chinese province of Shanxi, where wars were fought over control of the saltwater Lake Yuncheng. The water evaporated in summer, leaving deposits of salt crystals to be harvested. Conflicts between producing states and consumers were common throughout history; it was a high-value commodity, salt routes were established across the classical world, cities on these routes became rich by taxing traders. It led to private fortunes being amassed, and also to government riches, for salt was usually a state monopoly and salt taxes were levied (not unlike oil in the 20th century). At times the Roman army was paid in salt, which is the origin of the word "salary".

Salt has been viewed as a gift from the gods, myths and superstitions abound; it was among the offerings found in Egyptian tombs; in Vietnam, salt, water, and rice are also

Maldon sea salt
Salt has been harvested from the Essex marshes for 2000 years. Seawater was heated in pots over open fires until the water vaporated, then the pots were broken open to take out the salt. Today Maldon salt, a family business started in 1882, produces one of the finest sea salts with a distinctive flaky texture.

Cheshire rock salt
The Romans settled in this part of North West England partly due to the presence of brine springs, and salt has been produced here for about 2000 years. Today only one vast underground mine is active, producing salt for the table and for gritting roads in winter.

offerings for life in the next world, and in the countryside are symbols of survival when faced with typhoons, floods, and poor harvests. In the Christian and Jewish religions salt signifies longevity and permanence. Bread and salt were the offerings given to a new household, bread the symbol of food and salt its preservation.

SOURCES OF SALT

The sea is one source of salt; salt lakes like Yuncheng in China, Uyuni in Bolivia, and the lakes of the Rocky Mountains in the USA are others, but the main deposits are underground rock salt. Germany, for example, is estimated to have some 100,000km³ of salt underground.

Sea and lake salts are produced by controlled evaporation to ensure the product is virtually pure: symmetrical, small crystals indicate pure salt. Rock salt is mined all over the world; the largest mines are at Goderich in Canada and Khewra in Pakistan. Sold as Himalayan salt, in recent years, this has become very popular. Rock salt has even been used to impressive

effect as a wall in the ageing room of a Sydney butcher, to help with the ageing process. Wieliczka in Poland was one of the oldest and biggest mines in Europe, and is now a museum. Towns in mining regions are often named for their salt connections: Halle in Germany, Hallstatt and Salzburg in Austria, Salt Lake City in the USA and Middlewich, Northwich and other -wich towns in Cheshire.

USES OF SALT

From earliest times salt has preserved both bodies and food. The Egyptians used salt in preserving mummies, in central Asia and in South America bodies have been preserved in salty desert soils.

Thousands of years ago when people moved from a diet based on hunting and fishing and started rearing animals and cultivating crops, they needed salt for themselves and their animals because there is more salt in animal tissue than in plant tissues. Early Mediterranean civilizations used salt in their diet, some

Trapani sea salt
Trapani on the coast of Sicily is a landscape of pyramids of white salt, large, shallow pans, and windmills. The salt is harvested manually after the seawater has evaporated from the pans and piled up in pyramids. It is crushed to various grades as required.

Fleur de sel
Fleur de sel (flower of salt) is sea salt collected by scraping only the top layer of salt before it sinks to the bottom of the salt-pans. The crystals are purer and finer than coarse sea salt. In France it is produced at Guérande in Brittany, the Ile de Ré and in the Camargue. Spain, Portugal, and Vancouver Island also produce high quality fleur de sel.

like the Romans ate very salty food. They also used salt to preserve fish, olives, and other vegetables. They salted fresh vegetables to remove bitterness and gave us the word "salad". Meats and cheeses were salted to preserve food for winter.

The Romans also made garum and liquamen, sauces made by layering fish scraps and salt weighted down in earthenware jars. In earlier times, in China and Japan, fish and vegetables were fermented, using salt and allowing fermentation to take place to produce lactic acid which acts as a preservative. Pickles still have an important place in the East Asian diet, and salt is seldom found as a condiment on the table. Salted and dried fish are found throughout the region, as are fermented sauces and pastes based on fish or seafood, and spices or soybeans soaked in brine: nam pla and kapi in Thailand, teuk trey and prahok in Cambodia, nuoc mam and tuong ot in Vietnam, blachan and trassi in Indonesia and Malaysia.

Salt as a condiment and a preserving agent has been part of life since the Neolithic era, adding taste and flavour to foods and ensuring our survival. Almost every

Himalayan rock salt
The salt can be reddish or pink or almost transparent when used in small crystals. It is popular with health food advocates because it has fairly abundant trace minerals. Blocks of the salt can be used as serving dishes or for food preparation.

Seaweed salt
Seaweed salt is produced in a growing number of places where sea salt is harvested. The most common seaweeds used are wrack, dulse, nori (laver) and sea lettuce. They are dried, ground, and mixed with salt crystals. Most seaweeds add a tangy note to the salt, but nori has a mellow, sweet-salty taste. Seaweed salt is good with potatoes and eggs.

Spiced salt
Many different spices are used to make spiced salt: allspice, cayenne or chilli powder, clove, coriander, cumin, mace, peppercorns are the most common. Grind the spices finely and mix into coarse salt. Use as a rub for meat before grilling or roasting. It is good with vegetables and pulses too.

Falk salt
This Swedish company has been producing salt since 1830. The salt is harvested in the traditional way in Cyprus. Vegetable carbon is added to the salt to give black salt its colour. The large crystals can be crumbled in your fingers and look striking when sprinkled over rice with some finely chopped parsley.

Celery salt
Commercial celery salt is made with ground celery seed or the essential oil. It can soon develop a stale taste, so buy in small amounts. If you grow celery (p.80) chop some leaves (or leaves from garden celery) and combine with salt crystals for a mild-flavoured celery salt. It is traditionally used in a Bloody Mary.

part of the human body contains salt, which, with water, is necessary to the nourishment of cells. Sodium allows the body to move oxygen around, transmit nerve pulses, and move muscles; chloride is needed for digestion and respiration. The body loses salt constantly through bodily functions and it has to be replaced. That said however, only a small amount is needed; excess can lead to high blood pressure and kidney failure. Today we are in danger of abusing salt. Five to six grams a day is sufficient to remain healthy; but many people consume far more, often in processed foods.

Table salt, which has anti-caking agents added to make it free-flowing, is best avoided. Kosher salt has a larger grain size than other salts due to the way it is processed. It derives its name from its use in the koshering process for meat; the salt itself is not kosher.

Herbs and spices have a useful role in adding flavour to food without using salt. Fresh herbs are good in pasta dishes, with vegetables, fish, meat and rice. Marinating meat and fish adds flavour (*see pp.302–03*), chilli, garlic, and ginger pep up stir-fries, and sauces and dips (*see pp.289–301*) add zest to just about any food.

Green tea salt

This Japanese salt is a combination of matcha tea powder and salt crystals. Matcha is the finest green tea; its delicate green colour is attractive when the salt is sprinkled over food or used as a dip for fried foods. Japanese shops sell green tea salt, but it is easy to make at home: stir together 2 tsp salt crystals and ½ tsp matcha.

Goma shio

Goma shio is a Japanese mixture of roasted sesame seeds and coarse salt. Black sesame gives a more striking appearance, and the aroma and flavour of sesame are pleasantly dominant. Use as a dip, or condiment for rice, vegetables, and salads. Goma shio is sold in health food shops, but it is very easy to make your own. See the recipe on *p.271*.

Cornish smoked salt

Smoked salts are produced by the cold smoking process. The woods most commonly used are alder, apple, hickory, and mesquite. The subtlety or strength of the smokiness depends on the wood used. Smoked salt can give food, if not a barbecue flavour, at least a smoky taste.

Murray river salt

This salt is harvested from aquifers in the Murray-Darling basin in Australia. The salt has a soft texture, mild taste, and a white or pale pink colour, thanks to the natural minerals in the aquifer.

Recipes

Herb mixtures

Dried or fresh herbs can be used in many combinations. The composition of even the classic mixtures is usually determined by the kind of dish they are to go with – a guiding principle, whether in European bouquets garnis, Iranian blends, or Latin American blends in which spices are often included with the herbs. If the balance of a mixture is not quite to your taste, change the proportions so that you have a mix you like.

Bouquets garnis

A bouquet garni is a little bundle of herbs used in French cooking to flavour slowly-cooked dishes. Tied with string, or wrapped in muslin, the bouquet garni is removed before serving. A basic bouquet garni consists of a bay leaf, 2–3 fresh parsley stalks, and 2–3 sprigs of thyme, but flavourings can be varied according to the dish to be cooked. Here are a few suggestions:

FOR LAMB

Rosemary, garlic, oregano or marjoram, and thyme
Lavender, savory, and myrtle
Lemon thyme, mint, and parsley

FOR POULTRY

Parsley, bay, tarragon, and bruised lemon grass
Marjoram, rosemary, and savory
Lemon thyme, lovage, parsley, and an outer piece of leek

FOR GAME

Parsley, juniper berries, thyme, and bay
Lemon balm, marjoram, mint, and celery
Rosemary, myrtle, and a strip of orange peel

FOR FISH

Parsley, tarragon, thyme, and a strip of lemon peel
Fennel, bay, and lemon thyme
Dill, parsley, green onion, and lemon balm

FOR BEEF

Bay, parsley, thyme, and a piece of leek
Oregano, bay, garlic, and a strip of orange peel
Thyme, savory, marjoram, and a small piece of hyssop

FOR PORK

Sage, celery, parsley, and thyme
Lovage, rosemary, and savory
Orange thyme, tarragon, and bay

Blackcurrant sage

Fines herbes

Another classic mixture from French cookery, fines herbes is a blend of delicately flavoured summer herbs: chervil, chives, parsley, and tarragon, with equal proportions of the first three and half the amount of tarragon. The chopped herbs make an excellent seasoning for omelettes and other egg dishes, for cream sauces, and for salads of soft leaves.

Tarragon

Persillade

Chop together finely 1 garlic clove and a small handful of flat-leaf parsley sprigs. Stir the mixture into a dish for a few minutes before serving or scatter, raw, over the dish before it goes to the table. Persillade makes a fresh-tasting topping for poultry, fish, and vegetables. Mixed with breadcrumbs it can also be pressed over a rack of lamb towards the end of cooking.

Gremolata

Prepare a persillade (above) but include the grated rind of half an unwaxed lemon. The classic garnish for Milanese osso buco, gremolata is also good with grilled or baked fish, lentil and bean soups, and salads. It is also sprinkled over or stirred into meat and poultry stews.

Herbes de Provence

This is traditionally a variable blend of dried herbs, but there is no reason not to use fresh when available. One version is described below, but fennel seed, sage, basil, bay, and hyssop are also used. Use for braised meat and game dishes, especially those cooked in a red wine sauce, and with tomato dishes and root vegetables.

3 tbsp dried thyme

2 tbsp dried marjoram

1 tsp dried rosemary

1 tbsp dried savory

1 tsp dried lavender flowers

Crumble or grind the herbs and store in an airtight jar for 2–3 months.

Farcellets

Farcellet is the Catalan word for a little bundle, and these little bundles, tightly bound in bay leaves, contain sprigs of dried savory, oregano, and thyme. Use to flavour long-cooked dishes of meat, poultry, or vegetables. Remove before serving.

Chilean aliño

Aliño means seasoning or dressing and is used throughout South America for herb and spice mixtures, either to rub onto meat, poultry, or fish, or to flavour soups and casseroles. In every market you can buy bundles or little packets of aliño. This version comes from *Three Generations of Chilean Cuisine* by Mirtha Umaña-Murray.

1 tbsp dried thyme

1 tbsp dried rosemary

1 tbsp dried oregano

1 tbsp dried sage

1 tbsp dried mint

1 tbsp dried lemon balm

1 tbsp dried marjoram

1 tbsp dried tarragon

Mix and crush the herbs and store in an airtight container or in a plastic bag in the freezer.

Cuban adobo

In the Spanish-speaking Caribbean islands many dishes start with a sofrito, a mixture of herbs, spices, and vegetables cooked together to give the basic flavouring to a dish. The other flavouring blends are adobos; used dry as rubs or liquids as a marinade. To use this recipe as rub, omit the orange juice. Adobos are also used in much Central and South American cooking; the flavours change according to the region.

1 tbsp thyme leaves

1 tbsp oregano leaves

2 handfuls of coriander leaves and sprigs

3 garlic cloves, crushed

1 tsp ground cumin

2 tsp ground black pepper

100ml (3½fl oz) bitter orange juice or lime juice

Blend everything in a food processor and keep in a non-reactive jar in the refrigerator for 4–5 days. Use as seasoning (*p.269*).

Winter herbs

This is a simple blend Richard Olney used regularly, as I found when helping him prepare his winter supplies. Coarsely crumble or grind roughly equal amounts of dried thyme, oregano, and winter savory, and store. Marjoram can replace oregano.

Herbed pepper

Only use dried herbs and vary them if you wish. The blend is good with root vegetables, as a stuffing for chicken, and in winter soups.

1 tbsp dried rosemary

1 tbsp dried winter savory

1 tbsp dried thyme

1 tbsp dried marjoram

1 tbsp ground black pepper

1 tbsp ground mace

Rosemary

Crush or grind all the herbs finely. Sieve and combine with the pepper and mace. Store in an airtight jar for 2–3 months. A clove of crushed garlic and a little grated lemon peel can be used with the herbed pepper to good effect.

Mediterranean herb and spice blend

1 tbsp dried mint

1 tbsp dried savory or hyssop

1 tbsp dried oregano

1 tbsp fennel seeds

1 tbsp ground cumin

1 tbsp ground coriander

Crumble or grind the herbs and combine with the fennel seed, cumin, and coriander. Store in an airtight container or in a plastic bag in the freezer. Use as a rub for meats to be grilled or roasted, or add to long-cooked dishes of meat, poultry, or vegetables.

Green masala

This Indian masala is excellent with fish or chicken.

60g (2oz) fresh ginger

2 garlic cloves

4–6 fresh green chillies

large handful of coriander leaves and young stems

½ tsp salt

Peel and chop the ginger and garlic; remove the seeds from the chillies and slice the flesh. Put all the ingredients into a food processor and blend to a paste with a little water. The mixture will keep for up to 2 weeks in a tightly closed container in the refrigerator, or it can be frozen for up to 3 months. A simpler masala can be made without the coriander, if you prefer.

Adjika

This chilli and herb-based paste is popular in Georgia and the neighbouring countries.

2 fresh red chillies, deseeded

5 garlic cloves, crushed

handful of chopped parsley

handful of chopped dill

3 tbsp chopped walnuts

salt

3–4 tbsp olive oil

Put all the ingredients except the oil into a blender and pulse until you have a rough paste. Add the olive oil, little by little, until it is smooth. Add to meat and poultry dishes or slow-cooked beans.

Khmeli-suneli

This mixture is from the Republic of Georgia. Many varieties of mixed herbs and spices are sold under the name khmeli-suneli in markets in Tbilisi. Every region and every family has its own version of khmeli-suneli. Here is one:

1 tbsp ground coriander

1 tsp dried fenugreek leaves

1 tsp ground marigold petals

1 tsp dried mint

1 tsp dried dill

1 tsp dried summer savory

½ tsp fennel seeds

½ tsp ground cinnamon

large pinch of ground cloves

Pound or grind all the ingredients to a powder. Store in an airtight container or in a plastic bag in the freezer for 2–3 months. Use the mixture in a marinade for or rubbed onto meats to be grilled, and in vegetable dishes, soups, and stews.

Savory

Svanuri marili

This piquant flavouring, sometimes called Svaneti salt comes from the Svaneti mountain region of Georgia. Blue fenugreek, somewhat milder than the fenugreek that is widely available, grows up in the Caucasus and is used in this salt and garlic based blend. If you can't find it use ordinary fenugreek.

1 tsp ground coriander

1 tsp ground fenugreek

½ tsp ground chilli

3 garlic cloves, crushed

2 tbsp sea salt

Mix the spices into the garlic and stir in the salt. Use to season vegetables and salads or combine with olive oil to serve as a dip.

Seasoning

Seasoning is a paste used for flavouring meat, poultry, and fish in the English-speaking Caribbean islands. Ingredients and recipes vary from island to island and cook to cook, but they commonly include fresh herbs: parsley, mint, thyme, celery, oregano, coriander, culantro, chives, green onions, and garlic. Spices used include ginger, cloves, cinnamon, allspice, curry powder, paprika, pepper, and chillies, along with other flavourings such as Worcestershire sauce, bitter orange juice, lime juice, vinegar, and oil.

Seasoning is most often used as a marinade, but it can also be used in sauces or stirred into a stew. To use as a marinade, rub the seasoning onto food and leave for 1–2 hours for small fish and seafood, up to 3–4 hours for large, whole fish, pieces of chicken, or meat, and up to 12 hours for large pieces of meat or a whole chicken.

Bajan seasoning

As its name indicates, this version of seasoning comes from Barbados.

6–8 spring onions, coarsely chopped

4 garlic cloves, crushed

handful of parsley leaves and small stems

1 tbsp thyme leaves

small bunch of chives

1 scotch bonnet chilli, deseeded and coarsely chopped

4 tbsp lime juice

Combine all the ingredients in a food processor and blend to a paste. Taste, add more lime juice if necessary, and salt if you wish. Refrigerate in a non-reactive jar for 4–5 days.

Trinidad seasoning

6–8 spring onions, coarsely chopped

1 small onion, coarsely chopped

3 garlic cloves, crushed

1 bunch culantro or coriander leaves, coarsely chopped

small handful of mint leaves

small piece of fresh ginger, coarsely chopped

1 green chilli

good grinding of black pepper

4 tbsp lime juice

Blend all the ingredients to a paste in a food processor. Taste and add more lime juice as necessary. Salt may also be added. Store as Bajan seasoning (above).

Jamaican jerk seasoning

This seasoning is spice- rather than herb-based. It is used primarily as a rub for pork and chicken.

3–6 scotch bonnet chillies, deseeded and coarsely chopped

4–6 spring onions, coarsely chopped

3 shallots, quartered

3 garlic cloves, crushed

small piece of fresh ginger, coarsely chopped

3 tbsp fresh thyme leaves

1 tbsp ground allspice

2 tsp ground black pepper

1 tsp ground cinnamon

½ tsp grated nutmeg

½ tsp ground cloves

3–4 tbsp sunflower oil

Combine all the ingredients in a food processor and blend. If necessary, add a little water or more oil. Store, refrigerated, for up to 6 weeks.

Nutmeg

Mixed herb platters

A bowl of herbs accompanies almost every Iranian meal. The freshest possible herbs – mint, chives, spring onions, parsley, dill, tarragon – are put on the table as an appetizer or to eat with other dishes.

In Lebanon a platter of fresh vegetables and herbs is always part of a mezze table: cucumbers, radishes, tomatoes, cos lettuce, parsley, mint, purslane, watercress, and spring onions are those most often encountered.

The Vietnamese share this passion for fresh herbs. No meal is complete without a bowl of fresh herbs: basil, coriander, rau ram, red and green perilla, mint, cucumber, and lettuce leaves.

Iranian herb mixtures

The Iranian passion for herbs carries over to their cooked dishes. Large quantities of fresh herbs are used in summer; in winter dried herbs are used. Herbs dry well in Iran's hot climate, retaining their flavour and colour; they are available from Iranian shops:

Rice mixture (sabzi polo) has equal quantities of parsley, coriander, chives, and sometimes dill.

Stew mixture (sabzi ghormeh) includes parsley, chives, and coriander with a little fenugreek; dried lime powder is invariably included, and sometimes dill and mint.

Soup mixture (sabzi âshe) has parsley, chives, and coriander as staples, and sometimes mint and fenugreek.

Chubritsa

Chubritsa is the Bulgarian name for summer savory, and is widely appreciated there. A simple table condiment of dried savory, paprika, and salt, called Sharena Sol (mixed or colourful salt) is regularly on the table. Savory is also combined with smaller quantities of dried fenugreek leaves, dried spearmint, paprika, a dash of chilli, and salt to make a more robust mixture that is used to flavour meat stews and bean dishes. Almonds or seeds such as pumpkin seeds can also be added.

Grind the dried leaves and pass through a sieve to make a powder. If you use the nuts or seeds, dry roast them, cool, and grind. Combine them with the herb powder and then add the remaining ingredients.

Moroccan mint

Fenugreek

Spice mixtures

The art of blending spices has been practised for centuries in many parts of the world. In much of China, Japan, the Indian subcontinent, the Middle East, Africa (especially East and North Africa), the Caribbean islands, and Latin America these mixtures are an important element in distinguishing regional cuisines. If the balance of a mixture is not quite to your taste change the proportions so that you have a mix you like.

Japan

In Japanese cooking emphasis is placed on bringing out the pure flavours of the food itself. A number of aromatic ingredients – soy products, seaweeds, dashi, dried bonito – are used, but few spices. Wasabi, sansho, chilli, mustard, ginger, and sesame are used in moderation.

Seven spice powder

Shichimi togarashi, often just called shichimi, translates as seven flavours chilli. Plain chilli powder is ichimi togarashi; shichimi is chilli with six additions. There are variations to the formula depending on the region; perilla, mustard seed, toasted and dried chilli may all be used. Even if there are more than seven ingredients, the name doesn't change. Hemp seeds are usual in Japan, and available online, but you can use poppy seeds as an alternative.

The aroma is primarily of tangerine peel with iodine notes from the nori (laver); chilli is the dominant but not overwhelming flavour and the texture is gritty. The mixture can be bought mild or hot, so adjust the amount of chilli to your taste when making your own. Yuzu peel may be added to seven spice powder to give it a tart note. Use as a condiment for spicing udon (wheat noodles), soups, nabemono (one-pot dishes), and yakitori.

2 tsp white sesame seeds

1 tsp crushed dried tangerine peel

2 tsp nori flakes (aonori)

2 tsp chilli flakes

1 tbsp sansho

1 tsp black sesame seeds

1 tsp hemp or poppy seeds

Grind the white sesame seeds and tangerine peel coarsely. Add the nori and chilli flakes and grind again. Stir in the remaining ingredients and store in an airtight container or in a plastic bag in the freezer.

Goma shio

Goma means sesame and this simple mixture is used as a condiment for rice, vegetables, and salads.

4 tsp black or white sesame seeds

2 tsp coarse sea salt

Dry roast the sesame seeds lightly for a minute or two, stirring and shaking the pan. Cool, then grind briefly with the salt to keep a coarse texture. Store in an airtight jar. Sesame is a popular flavouring in Korea, and a similar Korean blend would use up to 60g (2oz) toasted sesame seeds to 2 tsp salt.

Sesame

China

Chinese cooks use single spices and five spice powder for a more complex flavour, and a rich blend of mixed spices with soy sauce and sugar to flavour the broth for slow-cooking pork or beef.

Chinese spiced salt

Spiced salt is widely used with barbecued or grilled meat and poultry. It is usually served in small dishes and sprinkled onto the food as it is about to be eaten.

3 tbsp coarse sea salt

1 tbsp five spice powder

Combine the salt and five spice powder in a heavy-based frying pan and dry roast, shaking and stirring to ensure they are well mixed and don't stick to the pan. In about 5 minutes the mixture should be fragrant and look lightly toasted. Transfer to a plate and leave to cool, then store in an airtight container.

In Sichuan, spiced salt is made by dry roasting 1 tbsp Sichuan pepper until fragrant, grinding it when cool, and stirring it into the salt.

Five spice powder

In Chinese culture the balance of the five flavours (salty, sour, bitter, pungent, and sweet) ensures medicinal and culinary potency. Five spice powder is sometimes extended to seven with the addition of dried ginger, cardamom, or liquorice. Use sparingly to flavour slow-cooked dishes, in marinades, and to season meat or poultry to be roasted or grilled.

6 star anise

1 tbsp Sichuan pepper

1 tbsp fennel seeds

2 tsp cloves

2 tsp ground cassia or cinnamon

Grind all the spices together to a powder. Sieve and store in an airtight container or in a plastic bag in the freezer.

Thailand

The success of Thai cooking depends on the complex combination of flavours in a curry paste, sauce, soup, or dip. The skilful blending of herbs, spices, and other flavourings, such as fish sauce, dried shrimps, and shrimp paste, gives zest to vegetables, fish, meat, and poultry. Curry pastes differ from region to region and from house to house; they are usually prepared when needed and not stored, but these pastes will keep for about 2 weeks in a closed jar in the refrigerator, or can be frozen in small pots if you prefer to make larger amounts.

Red curry paste

10 dried red chillies

1 tsp shrimp paste (kapi)

1 tbsp coriander seeds

2 tsp cumin seeds

5 garlic cloves, chopped

6 shallots, chopped

2 stalks lemon grass, lower third only, sliced

6 slices galangal

1 tsp grated makrut lime peel

2 tbsp chopped coriander roots

1 tsp ground black pepper

Cut the chillies and soak them in a little warm water for 10–15 minutes. Wrap the shrimp paste tightly in foil and dry roast for 1–2 minutes on each side. Dry roast the coriander and cumin seeds, cool, and grind.

Put the chillies and their water and all the other ingredients into a food processor and blend to a smooth paste, or pound in a mortar. Red curry paste goes well with beef, game, duck, and pork.

Sichuan pepper

Green curry paste

Green curry paste is the hottest type you can make, but you can reduce the number of chillies or leave out the seeds. Green curry paste is good with fish, seafood, chicken, and vegetables.

2 tsp coriander seeds

1 tsp cumin seeds

1 tsp shrimp paste (kapi)

2 tsp chopped galangal, or 1 tsp dried

2 tsp chopped fingerroot (krachai), or 1 tsp dried

2 stalks lemon grass, lower third only, chopped

1 tsp grated makrut lime peel

4 shallots, chopped

3 garlic cloves, chopped

1 tsp ground black pepper

½ tsp ground nutmeg

small bunch of coriander – leaves, young stems, and roots – chopped

4 tbsp chopped Thai basil leaves

15 small green chillies, chopped

Dry roast the coriander and cumin until they darken. Cool, then grind. Dry roast the shrimp paste, wrapped tightly in foil, for 1–2 minutes on each side. Allow to cool.

Combine all the ingredients and blend in a food processor or in a mortar and pestle until you have a smooth paste.

Chillies

Massaman curry paste

This paste derives its name from the Muslim traders who brought spices to Thailand. Some of its spices are more commonly used in India and it has a rich, warm flavour.

2 tbsp coriander seeds

2 tsp cumin seeds

6 green cardamom pods

½ cinnamon stick

6 cloves

10 dried red chillies

½ tsp grated nutmeg

½ tsp ground mace

1 tsp shrimp paste (kapi)

2 tbsp sunflower oil

5 shallots, chopped

4 garlic cloves, chopped

1 tbsp chopped galangal

1 tbsp chopped coriander root

2 stalks lemon grass, lower third only, sliced

Dry roast all the whole spices and chillies, leave to cool, then remove the pods from the cardamoms and grind all to a powder. Combine with the nutmeg and mace. Wrap the shrimp paste in foil and dry roast until its aroma rises.

Heat the oil and lightly fry the shallots and garlic until they start to colour, then add the galangal, coriander root, and lemon grass. Fry for a minute or two longer then transfer to a food processor or a mortar and pestle.

Add all the other ingredients and blend to a smooth paste or pound in the mortar and pestle. Use with meat and poultry.

Cumin seeds

Cambodia

Cambodian food is as intensely spiced as that of its neighbours; market stalls are piled high with chillies, garlic, ginger, galangal, coconuts, herbs, fish pastes (prahok), and sauces. Cambodian fish sauce also includes ground peanuts, an ingredient not used elsewhere. Many dishes are based on herb pastes called kroeung. These are made with seven or eight basic ingredients, which may be added to depending on the dish to be made. Pastes may be predominantly red (from chillies), yellow (from turmeric), or green (from lemon grass).

Kroeung

Pastes are made fresh and used immediately, but in a sealed container the paste will keep for 2–3 days in the refrigerator. Traditionally ground with a mortar and pestle, the paste is now easily made in a food processor, adding a little water if necessary.

50g (1¾oz) lemon grass, lower part, sliced

1 tbsp fresh galangal, chopped

1 large garlic clove, chopped

2 shallots, chopped

5 makrut lime leaves

80g (3oz) peanuts, dry roasted

2 tbsp palm sugar or brown sugar

1 tsp ground turmeric

1 tsp salt

2 tsp fish sauce

125ml (4fl oz) thick coconut milk

Blend all the ingredients in a food processor until smooth. Sometimes more coconut milk or a little stock or water is needed to achieve a smooth paste. The paste can be used as any curry paste, adding vegetables, fish or seafood, meat or poultry, and some liquid.

Green kroeung

100g (3½oz) lemon grass, chopped

50g (1¾oz) fresh galangal, chopped

1 tbsp ground turmeric

½ tbsp lesser galangal, chopped

4 garlic cloves, chopped

4 shallots, chopped

3 dried red chillies

Blend all the ingredients in a food processor until smooth. Use as described opposite.

Lemon grass

Turmeric

India and beyond

The first requirement of an Indian cook is to become a good masalchi, or spice blender. A masala is a blend of spices; it may contain two or three, or a dozen or more. It may be added to the dish, whole or ground, at different stages of cooking. For rice and some meat dishes, whole spices are traditional; the most common ground mixtures are the garam masalas (hot spices) used in northern Indian cooking. A garam masala is usually added towards the end of the cooking time to draw out the flavours of the other ingredients and preserve the aromas. Indians have taken their masalas to other parts of the world where they have settled: Malaysia, South Africa, the Caribbean islands. Curry powder originated in Chennai (Madras), where local cooks working for British households in the 18th century introduced Indian dishes to the newcomers.

Standard garam masala

This masala and its variations are best for meat and poultry dishes, especially those cooked in tomato or onion gravy. It also makes a good flavouring for spiced bean or lentil soups.

2 tbsp black cardamom pods

1½ sticks cinnamon

3 tbsp cumin seeds

2 tbsp black peppercorns

1 tbsp cloves

4 tbsp coriander seeds

2 tejpat leaves, crumbled

Extract the seeds from the cardamom pods and discard the pods. Break the cinnamon. Dry roast all the spices over a medium heat – this will probably take 4–6 minutes.

Let the spices cool, grind them to a powder, then sieve. The masala will keep in an airtight jar or in a plastic bag in the freezer for 2–3 months.

VARIATIONS
Gujarati masala
Add 1 tbsp sesame seeds, 2 tsp fennel seeds, 1 tsp ajowan seeds, and 3–4 dried chillies.

Kashmiri masala
Use black cumin seeds, green cardamoms instead of black, and add 2 blades of mace and ¼ nutmeg, grated.

Punjabi masala
Reduce coriander to 2 tbsp and black cardamoms to 1 tbsp. Add 1 tbsp green cardamoms, 2 tsp fennel seeds, 2 blades of mace, 1 tbsp black cumin seeds, 2 tsp ground ginger, and 1 tbsp dried rose petals.

Dhana jeera powder

This simple mixture of 4 parts coriander seeds to 1 part cumin is a common seasoning in Gujarat and Maharashtra, and is often used ground as the basis for masalas.

Bombay masala

This masala has richness and texture from the use of coconut, sesame, and poppy seeds. It is particularly good with lentils and vegetables. If it is added to the dish at the beginning, it will give a subtle flavour; for a more pronounced taste, add it when the cooking is almost completed.

8 green cardamoms

small piece cinnamon

2 tejpat leaves or 1 sprig curry leaves

1 tsp black peppercorns

2 tsp coriander seeds

1 tsp cumin seeds

6 cloves

2 tbsp unsweetened dessicated coconut

2 tsp sesame seeds

1 tbsp poppy seeds

Extract the seeds from the cardamoms and discard the pods. Break the cinnamon, crumble dried tejpat leaves, or strip curry leaves from the stalk. Dry roast cardamom seeds, cinnamon, leaves, peppercorns, coriander, cumin, and cloves until lightly coloured. Set aside to cool.

Dry roast the coconut and sesame and poppy seeds over gentle heat until they colour; the coconut should be dark brown. Leave to cool, then grind with the spices. Store in an airtight container or in a plastic bag in the freezer for 2–3 months.

Tandoori masala

Tandoori chicken is one of the dishes most westerners think of when Indian food is mentioned. The smoky flavour of tandoori meat or fish comes from the clay oven in which it is cooked; the slightly sour flavour from the spicing and the yogurt marinade. You can use the masala for food cooked in the oven or on a barbecue. To get the deep red colour of restaurant tandoori food, you will need some red colouring from an Indian shop.

Black salt is a rock salt, sold as a pink powder or in reddish lumps in Indian shops. It has a pronounced sulphurous smell that dissipates in cooking. If you can't find it, use a little extra sea salt.

½ stick cinnamon

1 tbsp coriander seeds

2 tsp cumin seeds

6 cloves

3 blades mace

2 tsp turmeric

2 tsp ground ginger

1 tsp ground chilli

1 tsp amchoor

1 tsp black salt

1 tsp sea salt

Amchoor

Crush the cinnamon lightly and dry roast the whole spices until they darken and start to smoke. Cool and then grind them. Combine all the spices with the salts.

To use, beat 200ml (7fl oz) yogurt and combine with 2–3 teaspoons of the masala.

Bengali panch phoron

This mixture of whole spices is used to flavour pulses and vegetarian dishes.

1 tbsp cumin seeds

1 tbsp fennel seeds

1 tbsp mustard seeds

1 tbsp nigella seeds

1 tbsp fenugreek seeds

Combine all the spices and store in an airtight container Use to flavour hot oil before other ingredients are added, or to spice ghee (clarified butter) that is poured over dal before serving.

Aromatic garam masala

This masala blend is mild, with a subtle emphasis on cardamom. It is used for kebabs and classic moghul dishes made with butter and cream or yogurt.

2 tbsp green cardamom pods

½ cinnamon stick

2 blades mace

2 tsp black peppercorns

1 tsp cloves

Remove the seeds from the cardamom pods and discard the pods. Break the cinnamon into pieces. Combine all the spices in an electric grinder and grind to a powder, then sieve. Store in an airtight container or in a plastic bag in the freezer for 2–3 months.

Chat masala

This masala is used in small quantities with fruit and vegetable salads. It has a fresh, sourish taste.

1 tsp cumin seeds

1 tsp black peppercorns

½ tsp ajowan seeds

1 tsp anardana

1 tsp black salt (see *left*)

1 tsp coarse sea salt

3 tsp amchoor

¼ tsp asafoetida

½ tsp crushed dried mint leaves

½ tsp ground chilli

Grind all the whole spices and salts to a powder, then stir in the remaining ingredients. Store in an airtight container or in a plastic bag in the freezer for 2 months.

Masala for fish

1 tbsp cumin seeds

2 tbsp coriander seeds

½ tsp ajowan seeds

1 tbsp ginger juice (*p.223*)

Grind the spices and combine with the ginger juice. Add a little water if the mixture is too dry. Rub into the fish and leave to marinate for up to 1 hour before cooking.

Sambhar powder

This powder is much used in south Indian cooking, which is mostly vegetarian, to flavour pulses, vegetable dishes, sauces, and soups. The dal in the blend serves as a thickening agent and provides a nutty taste.

4 tbsp coriander seeds

2 tbsp cumin seeds

1 tbsp black peppercorns

1 tsp mustard seeds

2 tsp fenugreek seeds

10 dried chillies

¼ tsp asafoetida

1 tbsp turmeric

1 tbsp channa dal (yellow split peas)

1 tbsp urad dal (split black lentils)

1 tbsp sunflower oil

Dry roast the whole spices for 4–5 minutes. When the spices have darkened and give off their aroma, add the asafoetida and turmeric and stir for 1 minute. Transfer to a bowl.
  Fry the dal in the oil until they darken. Keep stirring to prevent burning. Add them to the spices, mix well, cool, then grind. Store in an airtight container and use within 2 weeks.

Mustard seeds

Madras curry powder

2 dried chillies

4 tbsp coriander seeds

2 tbsp cumin seeds

1 tsp mustard seeds

1½ tbsp black peppercorns

6 curry leaves

½ tsp ground ginger

1 tsp turmeric

Roast the whole spices in a dry frying pan and leave to cool. Dry the curry leaves in the pan briefly then add to the whole spices. Grind to a powder, sieve, and stir in the ginger and turmeric. Keep in an airtight container or in a plastic bag in the freezer for 2 months.

Tamil curry powder

This southern Indian blend is used to flavour rice or is stirred into a vegetable curry just before serving.

10 sprigs curry leaves

1 tbsp sunflower oil

1 tbsp coriander seeds

3 dried chillies

pinch of asafoetida

1 tsp toor dal (yellow lentils)

1 tsp urad dal (split black lentils)

Strip the leaves from the stalks and fry in the oil until lightly coloured. Remove from the pan and fry the other items until they change colour, shaking and stirring the pan. Leave to cool.
  Grind the curry leaves; add the other ingredients and grind to a powder. Store in an airtight container for up to 2 weeks.

Massalé

Massalé is the spice blend of the French islands of the Indian Ocean – Mauritius and Réunion. The proportions of ingredients vary. It is used, with turmeric, to flavour dishes variously called caris, curries, or massalés.

2 tbsp coriander seeds

2 tsp cumin seeds

2 tsp black peppercorns

1 tsp green cardamom pods

1 tsp cloves

small piece of cinnamon

1 tsp ground chilli

1 tsp grated nutmeg

Dry roast the whole spices until lightly coloured and set aside to cool. Grind finely and stir in the chilli and nutmeg. Store for 2–3 months in an airtight jar.

Grated nutmeg

Sri Lankan curry powder

1 tbsp raw rice

2 tbsp coriander seeds

½ cinnamon stick

3 green cardamoms

3 cloves

1 tsp black peppercorns

1 tbsp cumin seeds

2 sprigs curry leaves

Dry roast the rice. Add the spices and curry leaves, stripped from the stalks. Stir over low heat to prevent burning, until all the spices turn dark brown. Leave to cool, then grind finely and sieve. Stir a teaspoon or two into a curry just before serving. Fenugreek and chilli may be added to the blend.

Malay curry paste

2 stalks lemon grass, lower third only

thumb-sized piece of galangal, chopped

6 garlic cloves, chopped

2 shallots, chopped

6 fresh chillies, deseeded and chopped

1 tsp ground mace

1 tsp black peppercorns

1 tbsp sunflower oil

½ tsp salt

1 tbsp turmeric

Blend all the ingredients in a food processor, adding a little more oil or water if necessary to make a smooth paste. Store in a closed jar in the refrigerator for a week.

Galangal

Malay curry powder

Malay curry spices show the influence of the large Indian population. The curries are usually cooked in coconut milk; lemon grass and garlic are sometimes added.

½ stick cinnamon

5 dried chillies

1 tsp green cardamom seeds

6 cloves

1 tsp cumin seeds

1 tbsp coriander seeds

2 tsp ground turmeric

1 tsp ground galangal

Grind the whole spices to a powder and stir in the turmeric and galangal. Store for 2–3 months in an airtight container or in a plastic bag in the freezer.

Indonesia

These spice pastes are used throughout Indonesia; they vary from island to island and vary according to traditional regional cooking styles. There are generic bumbus used throughout the country based on colour - white, yellow, red, and orange.

Bumbu Bali

2 garlic cloves, chopped

20 shallots, chopped

6 red chillies, deseeded and chopped

finger-length piece of fresh galangal, chopped

finger-length piece of fresh turmeric, chopped

small piece of aromatic ginger or fingerroot, chopped

5 candlenuts (substitute macadamias)

2 tsp shrimp paste (trassi)

1 tsp black peppercorns

1 tbsp coriander seeds

3 cloves

1 tbsp palm sugar or brown sugar

3 tbsp coconut or vegetable oil

2 stalks lemon grass, lower part only, finely sliced

2 makrut lime leaves, shredded

Put all the ingredients except the oil, lemon grass, and lime leaves into a blender and pulse to a smooth paste. Add a little water if needed.

Heat the oil in a wok or heavy pan and add the paste together with the lemon grass and lime leaves. Cook over high heat, stirring constantly, until the paste smells aromatic and has darkened slightly.

Pour into a sterilized jar and cool before use. To keep, top with oil and keep in the refrigerator, or freeze.

Middle East and North Africa

Iranian spicing tends to be mild, using sesame, saffron, cinnamon, rose petals, coriander, and small amounts of cardamom, caraway, and cumin. Souring spices such as sumac, dried limes, barberries, or pomegranate also play an important part. Spice mixtures, advieh, vary greatly from the Gulf to the central plateau, and are prepared for specific dishes.

The people of the Gulf have a taste for highly spiced food. Each country has its spice blends, called baharat (meaning spice). Enthusiasm for spicing spreads throughout the Arab countries to Israel and Turkey, where spices and herbs are often combined in milder blends; the widely used red pepper flakes may be fiery or subtle. The spicing of the eastern Mediterranean continues in North Africa, where sophisticated blends are used, particularly in Tunisia and Morocco.

Advieh for stews

2 sticks cinnamon

2 tbsp coriander seeds

1½ tbsp green cardamoms

1 tbsp black peppercorns

1 tbsp cumin seeds

2 tsp grated nutmeg

2 tsp ground dried lime powder

Break the cinnamon into pieces, grind all the whole spices, sieve, and combine with the nutmeg and lime powder. Keep in an airtight container or in a plastic bag in the freezer for 1 month.

Advieh for rice

2 tbsp ground cinnamon

2 tbsp ground dried rose petals

1 tbsp ground cumin or green cardamom seeds

Combine the spices and use to flavour steamed rice or rice cooked with herbs in the Iranian way (p.324). Store in an airtight jar or in a plastic bag in the freezer for 1 month.

Iranian advieh

Lebanese seven spice mixture

This is Anissa Helou's recipe.

1 tbsp ground black pepper

1 tbsp ground allspice

1 tbsp ground cinnamon

1 tsp grated nutmeg

1 tsp ground coriander

1 tsp ground cloves

1 tsp ground ginger

Mix all the spices together and store in an airtight container or in a plastic bag in the freezer.

Bizar a'shuwa

This blend comes from Oman, thanks to Philip Iddison, and is based on a recipe from *Al Azaf, the Omani Cookbook* by Lamees Abdullah Al Taie.

1 tbsp cumin seeds

1 tbsp coriander seeds

1 tbsp cardamom seeds

2 tsp ground chilli

½ tsp turmeric

2–3 tbsp vinegar

2 garlic cloves, crushed

Grind the whole spices and mix with the chilli and turmeric. Combine with enough vinegar and the garlic to make a stiff paste. Add to slow-cooked dishes or use as a rub for meat or chicken.

Basic baharat

In these baharats the balance between the spices varies from one country or region to another. If you dry roast the whole spices briefly, the flavours will be enhanced. Use a small heavy pan, toss and shake so that the spices don't burn and when they are fragrant, after 3–4 minutes, tip onto a plate to cool. When cool, grind and combine with the other ingredients.

2 tbsp black peppercorns

1 tbsp coriander seeds

small piece cassia or cinnamon

2 tsp cumin seeds

2 tsp cloves

seeds of 6 green cardamoms

½ nutmeg, grated

2 tbsp paprika

Grind all the whole spices and mix with the nutmeg and paprika. Sieve and store in an airtight container or in a plastic bag in the freezer for 2 months. Fennel seed and turmeric are sometimes added to baharat.

The mixture is used in kibbeh, in meat stuffings for pastries, in tomato and other sauces, and in stews and soups.

Iranian baharat

1 tbsp freshly ground black pepper

1½ tbsp cumin seeds

2 tsp allspice

1 tbsp coriander seeds

1 tbsp green cardamom seeds

1 tsp cloves

1 tbsp ground cinnamon

2 tsp turmeric

1 tsp ground ginger

1 tsp grated nutmeg

1 tbsp paprika

1 tbsp ground dried lime

Dry roast the whole spices and leave to cool. Grind them and mix with the ground spices. If grinding the dried lime yourself, make sure you discard the seeds before grinding. Store in an airtight container or in a plastic bag in the freezer.

Syrian baharat

1 tbsp black peppercorns

2 tbsp allspice

15 cloves

1 tsp green cardamom seeds

2 tsp grated nutmeg

1 tbsp ground cinnamon

Dry roast the whole spices if you wish, leave to cool then grind them and mix thoroughly with the cinnamon. Store in an airtight container. Some recipes include ground galangal.

Nutmeg

Saudi baharat

This is sometimes called Gulf Baharat or Kabsa spices, the former because a mixture akin to this is found around the Gulf and the latter because the spice blend is used in kabsa, a popular Saudi rice dish with chicken.

1 tbsp green cardamom seeds

1 tbsp cumin seeds

1 tbsp black peppercorns

1 tbsp coriander seeds

1 tbsp fennel seeds

1 tsp saffron threads, crushed

2 tsp ground cinnamon

1 tsp grated nutmeg

2 tsp ground dried lime

Dry roast the whole spices if you wish, grind them when cool, and mix with the other ingredients. Store in an airtight container.

Saffron

Turkish baharat

2 tbsp black peppercorns

2 tbsp cumin seeds

1 tbsp coriander seeds

10 cloves

1 tsp green cardamom seeds

1 small piece cassia or cinnamon

1 tsp grated nutmeg

1 tbsp dried mint

Dry roast the whole ingredients, leave to cool, then grind. Rub the mint between your fingers so that it crumbles. Combine all the ingredients and store in an airtight container.

Turkish red chilli paste

Tomato and red chilli pastes are widely used in southeastern Turkey. The town of Gaziantep, surrounded by orchards of almond and pistachio trees, is renowned for its excellent food. These pastes are made at home after the peppers and chillies have spent time drying in the sun. Jars of the pastes can be bought in Middle Eastern shops and you can make your own as long as your peppers and chillies have dried out in the hot sun.

3 red peppers

6 long red chillies

juice of 1 lemon

1 tsp freshly ground black pepper

2 tsp sea salt

Grill the peppers and chillies, or roast in the oven at 200°C (400°F/Gas 6) for 15–20 minutes, turning them as needed. When the skins have charred, put them into a plastic bag or a bowl with a lid and leave to cool. This makes it easier to get the skin off.

Peel the peppers, if the chillies won't peel easily scrape the flesh from the skins with a sharp knife. Discard the membranes and seeds. Cut the flesh into pieces and blend to a purée.

Add lemon juice, pepper, and salt. Taste for seasoning. Store in a sterilized jar and keep in the refrigerator. Use in meat dishes, in marinades, with wheat and bean dishes, or as a condiment.

Yemeni hawaij

This blend is recommended for soups, grilled meat, and vegetable dishes.

1 tbsp black peppercorns

1 tbsp caraway seeds

1 tsp green cardamom seeds

1 tsp saffron threads

2 tsp turmeric

Combine all the ingredients in an electric mixer and blend to a powder. Store in an airtight container or in a plastic bag in the freezer for up to 2 months.

Yemeni hilbeh

2 tbsp ground fenugreek seeds

1 large bunch coriander leaves and small stems

4 garlic cloves, crushed

sea salt and freshly ground black pepper

seeds of 3–4 cardamom pods, crushed

¼ tsp caraway seeds

2–4 green chillies, deseeded and chopped

juice of 1–2 lemons

Soak the ground fenugreek in plenty of hot water and leave overnight, or for at least 8 hours. It will separate into clear liquid at the top and a gelatinous mixture in the bottom of the bowl. Pour off the liquid; set aside.

Blend the coriander, garlic, and all the other ingredients with the juice of 1 lemon. Add the fenugreek and blend again. Taste and add more lemon juice or salt if necessary. A little water can be whizzed in to thin the mixture; it should be like a soft paste. The texture should be slightly frothy from the fenugreek, and the taste pungent and slightly bitter.

Hilbeh is stirred into stews at the end of cooking, or served at room temperature as a condiment to accompany dishes, or simply eaten with Middle Eastern flat bread. Chopped tomatoes are sometimes added; in the Jewish community in Calcutta, where it is popular, a little fresh ginger is used. Store covered in the refrigerator for up to a week.

Fenugreek seeds

Yemeni zhug

This paste is a combination of garlic and peppers, and whatever spices the cook chooses. It is popular in Israel, where it has spread beyond the cooking of Yemeni Jews. There are red versions, as this one, and green ones with more coriander leaf and also parsley instead of peppers.

2 small mild red peppers

2 red chillies

8 garlic cloves

2 tsp coriander seeds

1 tsp cumin seeds

seeds from 6 green cardamoms

handful of coriander leaves and young stems

Remove the seeds from the peppers and chillies and cut them into pieces. Chop the garlic roughly. Blend all the ingredients to a paste in a food processor. Store in a closed jar in the refrigerator for 1–2 weeks, covered by a layer of oil.

Zhug is used as a condiment, a sauce for grilled fish or meat, and is added to soups and stews just before serving. A spoonful or two of zhug can be added to hilbeh.

Aleppo blend

This mixture is used for grilled and roast chicken and lamb, and for preparing köfte and kibbeh.

1 tbsp black peppercorns

1 tbsp allspice

seeds of 5 green cardamoms

½ nutmeg

1 tsp coriander seeds

1 tsp cumin seeds

1 tbsp ground cinnamon

1 tbsp Turkish or Aleppo red pepper flakes (or paprika)

1 tsp sumac

Grind all the whole spices and blend with the cinnamon, red pepper, and sumac. Store in an airtight jar or in a plastic bag in the freezer for 2–3 months.

Cinnamon quills

Dukka

This Egyptian nut and spice blend varies from family to family. It is served at breakfast or as a snack later in the day. It has also become fashionable as a nibble with drinks and an appetizer and now can be found everywhere on bruschetta, roasted vegetables, and grilled fish. My favourite use for it is spread on a rack of lamb to be roasted.

120g (4oz) sesame seeds

90g (3oz) hazelnuts

60g (2oz) coriander seeds

30g (1oz) cumin seeds

salt to taste

olive oil, to serve

Dry roast all the ingredients separately until the sesame is golden, the hazelnuts are losing their skins, and the coriander and cumin darken and give off their aroma. For large quantities use a hot oven, 250°C (500°F/Gas 9). Allow to cool.

Remove loose skins from the hazelnuts. Put the ingredients into a food processor and grind to a coarse powder. Don't overwork or the oil from the nuts and sesame will be released and turn it into a paste. Store in an airtight container. Serve at room temperature with Middle Eastern bread and olive oil. Dip the bread into the oil and then into the dukka.

Ras el hanout

Ras el hanout is a Moroccan mixture of 20 or more spices. Many versions contain aphrodisiacs as well as herbs and spices. A typical blend could include allspice, ash berries, black and green cardamom, cassia, chufa nuts, cinnamon, cloves, cubebs, galangal, ginger, grains of paradise, lavender, mace, monk's pepper, nigella, nutmeg, orris root, black pepper, long pepper, rose buds, ground turmeric, and the potentially hazardous belladonna and cantharides (Spanish fly). Exported ready-ground blends tend to be less exotic. In Tunisia ras el hanout is a simpler blend of rosebuds, black pepper, cubebs, cloves, and cinnamon.

Ras el hanout is usually sold whole and ground as required. It is used with game, lamb, couscous, and rice.

Za'atar

Za'atar is a generic name for a number of herbs with a thyme-savory-oregano aroma (*p.98*). This mixture is popular in the Middle East, sprinkled on meatballs, kebabs, and vegetables, or used as a dip. Mixed to a paste with olive oil, it can be spread over bread before baking.

60g (2oz) sesame seeds

30g (1oz) ground sumac

30g (1oz) dried za'atar or thyme, powdered

Dry roast the sesame seeds for a few minutes, stirring frequently. Let them cool, then mix with the sumac and za'atar or thyme. Store in an airtight jar or in a plastic bag in the freezer for 2–3 months.

La kama

This Moroccan mixture is used for harira, the soup eaten to break the Ramadan fast, for stews, and as a seasoning for chicken.

1 tbsp freshly ground black pepper

1 tbsp ground ginger

1 tbsp turmeric

1 tsp grated nutmeg

2 tsp ground cumin

Combine all the spices and store in an airtight container or in a plastic bag in the freezer for 1–2 months.

Taklia

This mixture of garlic and coriander is used to flavour soups and stews just before they are served. Popular throughout the Arab world, it is widely used in Egypt with melokhia, a dish that is virtually the national soup.

3 garlic cloves

salt

2 tbsp sunflower oil

1 tbsp ground coriander

½ tsp cayenne

Crush the garlic with a little salt and fry in the oil until golden. Stir in the coriander and cayenne, mix to a paste and fry, stirring, for 2 minutes. Use at once.

Tunisian bharat

The simplest Tunisian mixture uses equal amounts of ground cinnamon and ground dried rosebuds or petals, sometimes with the addition of a little black pepper. It is used for fish, roast and grilled meat, couscous, and tagines.

Ground cinnamon

Qâlat daqqa

This blend of five spices is from Tunisia, where it is used primarily with lamb and vegetable dishes. It is particularly good with squash and pumpkin, aubergines, spinach, and with chickpeas and other legumes.

2 tsp black peppercorns

2 tsp cloves

1 tsp grains of paradise

1 tsp ground cinnamon

3 tsp grated nutmeg

Grind the whole spices to a powder and combine with the cinnamon and nutmeg. Store in an airtight jar or in a plastic bag in the freezer for 2–3 months.

Tabil

Tabil means coriander, and it is also the name of a spice blend found only in Tunisia, as far as I can discover.

3 tbsp coriander seeds

1 tbsp caraway seeds

1 tsp ground cumin

2 garlic cloves, peeled and crushed

2 tsp chilli flakes

Pound or grind all the ingredients together coarsely, then dry in the sun if you live in a hot place, or dry in a low oven, 130°C (250°F/Gas ½), for 30–45 minutes. When quite dry and cooled, grind to a fine powder.

Tabil is used for stews, sautéed and stuffed vegetables, and beef dishes. Store in an airtight container or in a plastic bag in the freezer for 1–2 months.

Africa

On the Horn of Africa and down the east coast, people have always looked eastwards for their flavourings. In West Africa chillies tend to dominate, together with local herbs and spices; in South Africa, Indian and Malay communities have influenced the cooking, with curries, sambals, and blatjangs.

West African pepper blend

Pepper blends are used as a seasoning for fish, meat, and vegetables. They may be used as a dry mixture or made into a paste with the addition of onion, garlic, tomatoes, sweet red peppers, dried shrimp, and palm oil.

2 tbsp black peppercorns

2 tbsp white peppercorns

1 tbsp cubebs

1 tbsp allspice

2 tsp grains of paradise

2 tsp ground ginger

1 tbsp chilli flakes

Grind the whole spices and combine with the ginger and chilli flakes. Store in an airtight container or in a plastic bag in the freezer for 2–3 months.

South African curry powder

This mixture comes from the Cape. It is used with a paste of ginger and garlic pounded with salt; 2 tsp turmeric may be added.

2 tsp fennel seeds

2 tsp coriander seeds

2 tsp cumin

small piece cinnamon

seeds of 5 cardamoms

Grind all the ingredients and store for 2–3 months in an airtight container or in a plastic bag in the freezer.

Cardamom

Berbere

Berbere is a fiery mixture used in Ethiopia and Eritrea. Rather like garam masala (*p.275*), it is a complex blend of spices made to suit the dish and the taste of the cook. It is used primarily to flavour stews (called wats) of meat, vegetables, or lentils, but also to coat foods to be fried or grilled, or served as an accompaniment. Ethiopian cardamom or korarima is different from the cardamoms used in Asia. If you can't find it, use black cardamom. The key spices are chillies, ginger, and cloves; others vary, and some are not found outside the region.

15–20 dried red chillies

1 tsp coriander seeds

seeds from 5 korarima or black cardamoms

12 allspice berries

1 tsp cumin seeds

1 tsp fenugreek seeds

8 cloves

½ cinnamon stick, broken

½ tsp ajowan

1 tsp black peppercorns

1 tsp ground ginger

Heat a large, heavy-based frying pan and dry roast the chillies for 2–3 minutes, turning and stirring. Add the other whole spices and roast for a further 5–6 minutes, stirring constantly, until all the spices have darkened.

Leave to cool, then grind, including the ginger, to a powder. Store in an airtight container or in a plastic bag in the freezer for 2–3 months.

Wat spices

This is a simple blend and quick to prepare.

3 long peppers

1 tbsp black peppercorns

1 tbsp cloves

½ nutmeg

2 tbsp chilli powder

2 tsp ground ginger

1 tsp ground cinnamon

Dry roast the peppers, peppercorns, cloves, and nutmeg, and grind them when cool. Stir in the chilli, ginger, and cinnamon. Add to a wat (stew) towards the end of cooking. The mixture will keep in an airtight jar or in a plastic bag in the freezer for 2–3 months.

Mitmita

1–2 tsp chilli flakes

½ tsp ground cloves

1 tsp ground cumin

1 tsp ground coriander

½ tsp ground allspice

1½ tsp ginger

1 tsp ground black pepper

¼ tsp turmeric

1 tsp salt

Combine all the ingredients and store in an airtight container. Use as Berbere.

Chilli

Europe

Early European food for the rich was spiced predominantly with pepper, cinnamon, cloves, and ginger, sweetened with honey, or later with sugar, and moistened with vinegar. By the 16th century the sweet element had diminished, and when, in the 17th and 18th centuries, spices became more widely available they were used less ostentatiously. Cookery books of the 19th century began to record curry powders (from recipes sent home by colonial administrators) and mixtures that were often called kitchen pepper. Today few European spice blends are still in use, although Europeans consume quantities of spiced foods from other parts of the world.

Quatre épices

The classic French blend is used primarily for charcuterie and other meat products. It is useful to flavour a glaze for baked ham and to season fresh pork before cooking.

6 tsp black or white peppercorns

1 tsp cloves

2 tsp grated nutmeg

1 tsp ground ginger

Grind the peppercorns and cloves finely, combine with the nutmeg and ginger and store in an airtight container or in a plastic bag in the freezer for 1–2 months.

Cinnamon sometimes replaces ginger, and I have also come across mixtures that use allspice instead of cloves, and mace instead of nutmeg.

Italian spice mixture

This blend is good sprinkled on chicken or pork chops to be grilled or baked, to flavour a loin of pork to be stuffed and roasted, and rubbed onto a shoulder of lamb to be slow-roasted, wrapped in foil with apricot leather or other dried fruits.

3 tsp white or black peppercorns

½ nutmeg

1 tsp juniper berries

¼ tsp cloves

Grind all the spices in an electric grinder – it may be easier if you crush the nutmeg first with a rolling pin. Store the powder in an airtight container or in a plastic bag in the freezer for 3–4 months.

Juniper berries

Baking or pudding spice

This English mixture, also sold as mixed spice, is used for biscuits, fruit cakes, mincemeat, and baked or steamed puddings. The selection and proportions of spices vary according to individual taste; some cooks add ginger to the blend, but I prefer this version.

½ stick cinnamon

1 tbsp allspice

1 tbsp coriander seeds

2 tsp cloves

4 blades mace

2 tsp grated nutmeg

Grind the whole spices to a fine powder and mix with the nutmeg. Store in an airtight container or in a plastic bag in the freezer for 2–3 months.

Pickling spice

An English mixture of whole spices used when pickling fruits and vegetables in vinegar.

2 tbsp pieces dried ginger

1½ tbsp yellow mustard seeds

2 tbsp blades of mace

3 tbsp allspice

2 tbsp black peppercorns

2½ tbsp cloves

2 tbsp coriander seeds

Combine all the spices and flavour the vinegar that is to be used in making the pickle. The spices can be added directly or put into a muslin bag for later removal.

Mace

The Americas

Many culinary influences can be traced in the Americas. In the US and Canada, English and French spice blends once predominated in the north, but now Mexican, Caribbean, and African ideas are widely popular. The Caribbean islands show a variety of colonial traditions (Spanish, French, and English) as well as immigrant influences – notably African, Indian, Sri Lankan, and Chinese – in the development of their cuisines. Mexico has maintained strong pre-Columbian food styles. Much of South America shows some vestiges of Spanish or Portuguese culinary traditions, combined with Indian food patterns in the Andes and with African traditions in Brazil.

Ají paste

Ají pastes are popular throughout the Andean countries and vary widely in flavour and heat depending on the chilli. Rocoto, mirasol, or amarillo would be used in the Andes, if you can't get these use chilaca or Spanish guindilla. This potent paste is from Bolivia, where it is used as the base flavouring for stews and thick soups. Fresh herbs – coriander or quillquiña, basil, oregano – are usually added just before the dish is served.

60g (2oz) dried chillies, deseeded

4 garlic cloves

½ tsp salt

3 tbsp sunflower or olive oil

Dry roast the chillies for 1–2 minutes and soak in 5–6 tbsp hot water for 30 minutes (*p.259*). Drain and tear into pieces. Crush the garlic with the salt.

Blend all the ingredients in the water to a smooth paste. Store for up to 2 weeks in the refrigerator under a layer of oil.

Chillies

Barbecue spice

This is a medium-hot spice blend to rub onto meat before grilling.

1 tsp black peppercorns

½ tsp cumin seeds

½ tsp dried thyme

½ tsp dried marjoram

½ tsp cayenne

2 tsp paprika

1 tsp mustard powder

½ tsp salt

1 tbsp soft brown sugar

Grind the peppercorns and cumin, crumble or grind the herbs if necessary, and combine all the ingredients. Spread the mixture over the meat and leave for 2–3 hours before cooking.

Cajun seasoning

The gumbos and jambalayas, blackened fish and grilled meats of the Cajun and Creole cooks of Louisiana are flavoured with aromatic herbs, chillies, and other spices. Commercial blends use dried garlic and onion, which I find have a synthetic taste, so I mix the dry ingredients and add fresh garlic and onion.

1 tsp paprika

½ tsp ground black pepper

1 tsp ground fennel seeds

½ tsp ground cumin

½ tsp mustard powder

1 tsp cayenne

1 tsp dried thyme

1 tsp dried oregano

½ tsp dried sage

½ tsp salt

1–2 garlic cloves

½ small onion

Combine all the dry ingredients. Crush the garlic and onion in a mortar and add to the dry ingredients.

Rub the mixture onto meat or fish, leave to marinate for up to 1 hour, then grill or fry to form a crisp crust. Alternatively stir some of the mixture into rice dishes or gumbos.

Virgin Islands spiced salt

The Virgin Islands were once an important stop for the Royal Navy, and salt-based curing and seasoning is still practised there, although the salt harvesting on nearby Salt Island is no longer undertaken.

3 tbsp sea salt

2 tsp black peppercorns

¼ tsp cloves

½ tsp grated nutmeg

¼ tsp dried thyme

2 garlic cloves, crushed

½ small onion, chopped

2 sprigs parsley

Grind all the ingredients in a mortar or food processor and store in the refrigerator. Use to rub on fish or steak before barbecuing, or over a chicken before roasting.

For a dry mix omit the garlic, onion, and parsley and add a crumbled, dried bay leaf and ¼ tsp dried rosemary to the blend. This will keep for 2–3 months in an airtight container.

Poudre de Colombo

Colombo is the name of a curry made on the French Caribbean islands, originally by indentured workers from Sri Lanka. The curry powder does not have the heat of those from some of the other islands, and is very similar to Sri Lankan curry powder (*p.278*).

1 tbsp raw rice

1 tbsp cumin seeds

1 tbsp coriander seeds

1 tsp black peppercorns

1 tsp fenugreek seeds

1 tsp black mustard seeds

4 cloves

1½ tbsp ground turmeric

Dry roast the rice until lightly browned, stirring frequently. Put it aside to cool and add the whole spices to the pan. Roast until they give off their aroma and darken in colour. Let them cool.

Grind the rice and spices to a powder in an electric grinder, then stir in the turmeric. Store in an airtight container or in a plastic bag in the freezer for 2–3 months.

West Indian masala

Just as labourers from Sri Lanka took Colombo powder to the French islands, Hindus from the subcontinent took their masalas with them to Trinidad and Tobago. This recipe comes from Trinidad.

3 tbsp coriander seeds

1 tsp anise

1 tsp cloves

1 tsp cumin seeds

1 tsp fenugreek seeds

1 tsp black peppercorns

1 tsp black mustard seeds

1 tsp ground turmeric

ground chilli to taste

3 garlic cloves, crushed

1 medium onion, chopped

Dry roast the whole spices and leave to cool. Grind them finely and combine with the turmeric and, if you wish, some ground chilli.

Pound together with the garlic and onion, or blend in a processor to a smooth paste. If necessary, add a little water, tamarind water, or lemon juice. Store in the refrigerator for 3–4 days.

Steak recado

Spice pastes, called recados, are essential to the cooking of the Yucatán peninsula in southern Mexico, which is itself firmly rooted in Mayan traditions. On market stalls bowls are piled high with red, black, and khaki pastes; similar pastes are found in Cuba. This is a khaki version.

8 garlic cloves

1 tsp allspice

1 tsp black peppercorns

¼ tsp cumin seeds

½ stick cinnamon

1 tsp coriander seeds

4 cloves

2 tsp dried oregano

½ tsp salt

1 tbsp cider or wine vinegar

Crush the garlic and combine all the ingredients in a food processor and blend to a paste. Store in the refrigerator; the flavours will develop if kept for a day before using, and the mixture will keep for several weeks.

The recado is used to rub on steaks for grilling or frying, but even more commonly in chicken and other dishes preserved in escabeche (a lightly spiced pickle).

Recado rojo: red annatto paste

1½ tbsp annatto seeds

½ tbsp coriander seeds

½ tbsp black peppercorns

½ tsp cumin seeds

3 cloves

2 tsp dried oregano

5 garlic cloves

1 tsp salt

1–2 tbsp wine vinegar or Seville orange juice

Grind the first 6 ingredients to a powder in an electric coffee or spice grinder. Annatto seeds are very hard, so it will take a little time. Crush the garlic with the salt in a mortar, then gradually work in the ground spices. A red chilli may be added; crush it with the garlic. Moisten with the vinegar or bitter orange juice so that you have a smooth paste.

Form the paste into small discs or balls and let them dry, or put the paste into an airtight jar. Whether dried or as a paste, the recado will keep for several months if refrigerated.

To use, mix with more Seville orange juice. The recado is essential to the local speciality, pollo pibil, chicken wrapped in banana leaves and steamed or baked. Fish and pork can be cooked in the same way, and the mixture gives depth to soups and stews.

Dried oregano

Sauces and condiments

Most regions of the world have developed their favourite sauces – as a dip, to accompany dishes, or as an integral part of the cooking process. In colonial times some became universally popular, and condiments and sauces based on herbs and spices were among the first foods to be manufactured commercially.

Salsa verde

2 handfuls of parsley sprigs, chopped

a few sprigs of mint or basil, chopped

1 garlic clove, crushed

1 tbsp capers, chopped

4 anchovy fillets, chopped

approx 150ml (5fl oz) extra virgin olive oil

salt and freshly ground black pepper

Blend the herbs, garlic, capers, and anchovy fillets to a coarse paste in a food processor. Scrape down the sides and trickle in enough oil through the feed tube to make a smooth sauce. Season to taste. Serve with poached or baked fish, grilled meats, or with artichokes, cauliflower, or broccoli.

Basil

Parsley and lemon sauce

1 tbsp Dijon mustard

juice of 1 lemon

150ml (5fl oz) extra virgin olive oil

salt and freshly ground black pepper

90g (3oz) parsley, finely chopped

2 shallots, finely chopped

Whisk the mustard into the lemon juice, add the oil, season, and stir in the parsley and shallots. Serve with grilled fish, seafood, or chicken.

Pesto

This Genoese sauce for pasta also goes well with vegetables and as a dip or a spread for bruschetta; a thin version makes a good sauce for fish.

4 handfuls basil leaves

1 large garlic clove, peeled and crushed

30g (1oz) pine nuts

30g (1oz) Parmesan or pecorino cheese, grated

5–6 tbsp extra virgin olive oil

Put all the ingredients except the olive oil into a food processor and blend. If you don't have a processor, put the basil and garlic in a large mortar and pound with a pestle. Scrape down the sides and add the oil slowly through the feed tube until you have a thick, green sauce. For a thinner sauce, add more olive oil. Add the pine nuts, a few at a time, then the cheese and oil alternately until you have a thick paste. Add more oil to obtain the consistency you want.

VARIATION
Coriander pesto
Replace the basil by coriander leaves and the pine nuts by walnuts.

Parsley pesto
Replace basil by parsley and use either pine nuts or blanched almonds.

Rocket pesto
Replace basil by rocket and use walnuts or pine nuts.

Rocket

Basil, mint, and red pepper sauce

3–4 sprigs mint

large handful of basil leaves

1 sweet red pepper

1 small garlic clove, finely chopped

salt and freshly ground black pepper

2 tbsp red wine vinegar

3 tbsp olive oil

Strip the leaves from the mint sprigs and chop them finely with the basil. Scorch the red pepper over a gas flame or under a grill until blackened all over. Put it into a plastic bag and leave until cool, then rub off the skin. Remove seeds and membrane, rinse, pat dry, and chop the flesh finely.

Mix the garlic and seasoning into the vinegar, then add the oil. Stir in the herbs and red pepper. The sauce goes well with cold fish, such as poached turbot or salmon.

Mint

Horseradish and apple sauce

This Austrian sauce (Apfelkren) makes a change from the standard horseradish cream. It goes well with beef, with smoked meats and sausages, and with smoked eel and trout. For a milder sauce, use more cream or add a few fresh breadcrumbs to the mixture.

2 tbsp lemon juice

60g (2oz) grated horseradish

1 large cooking apple

salt and caster sugar to taste

100ml (3½fl oz) double cream

Stir 1 tbsp lemon juice into the horseradish so that it doesn't discolour. Peel, core, and grate the apple and stir it into the horseradish with the remaining lemon juice. Season with a little salt and sugar and leave to stand for 15 minutes. Whisk the cream lightly and fold it into the horseradish mixture.

Tartare sauce

To 300ml (10fl oz) mayonnaise add 1 tsp each of chopped parsley, shallot, capers, gherkins, and green olives. The sauce is good with all fish and seafood, whether served hot or cold.

Remoulade sauce

Into 300ml (10fl oz) mayonnaise work 1 tsp Dijon mustard and 1 pounded anchovy, then stir in 2 tsp each of chopped parsley, chervil, tarragon, capers, and gherkins. The sauce goes well with lobster and other seafood.

Ravigote sauce

To 150ml (5fl oz) vinaigrette add 1 tbsp chopped capers, 1 tbsp chopped shallots, 2–3 tbsp chopped herbs (parsley, chives, chervil, and tarragon). The sauce is good with potato salad and grilled fish.

Sorrel sauce

Sorrel sauce can be made quickly to accompany fish and eggs. A thick version is also good with lamb chops.

200g (7oz) sorrel leaves

15g (½oz) butter

about 100ml (3½fl oz) crème fraîche or double cream

salt and freshly ground black pepper

Remove any thick stalks from the sorrel and cook the leaves gently in the butter. They will wilt quickly. Stir in the cream a little at a time; sorrel is acidic, so it is important to balance the sorrel and the cream. Taste and find the balance that suits you. Season with a little salt and pepper.

Romesco sauce

This famous Catalan sauce is particularly popular in Tarragona. Serve it with fish, chicken, and grilled vegetables.

2 ñora chillies

1 small hot dried chilli

2 tbsp blanched almonds

2 tbsp hazelnuts

6 tbsp olive oil

3 garlic cloves

1 slice white bread, crusts removed

2 piquillo peppers or 1 red bell pepper, roasted, peeled, and diced

2 tsp tomato purée

1 medium ripe tomato, peeled, deseeded, and chopped

2 tbsp white wine vinegar

salt and freshly ground black pepper

Break open the chillies, remove the seeds, and soak the flesh in hot water for 30 minutes.

Dry roast the almonds and then the hazelnuts. Rub the skins from the hazelnuts in a cloth.

Heat 2 tbsp oil and fry 2 of the whole garlic cloves until lightly coloured. Remove the garlic and fry the slice of bread in the same oil. Remove when lightly browned.

Put the drained chillies, all the garlic, bread, nuts, roasted pepper, and tomato purée into a food processor or blender. When you have a smooth sauce transfer it to a bowl and stir in the tomato, the remaining oil, and the vinegar. Taste and season. If the sauce is too thick add a little more olive oil or vinegar, or a little water. The sauce will keep for 2–3 days, covered, in the refrigerator.

Ñora chillies

Béarnaise sauce

This sauce is the classic French accompaniment to grilled steak.

150ml (5fl oz) dry white wine

3 tbsp white wine or tarragon vinegar

3 shallots, finely chopped

5 sprigs tarragon

freshly ground white pepper

180g (6oz) unsalted butter

3 egg yolks

salt

1 tbsp finely chopped tarragon leaves or a mixture of tarragon and chervil

Put the wine, vinegar, shallots, tarragon sprigs, and a good grinding of pepper into a small, heavy pan over low heat. Simmer, uncovered, until the liquid has reduced to 2–3 tbsp. Strain through a fine sieve, pressing the shallots and tarragon well to extract maximum flavour. Return the liquid to the pan. Melt the butter gently in another pan and set aside. When it has cooled to lukewarm, pour off the clear liquid to use later, and discard the white residue.

Set the pan with the wine and vinegar infusion over very low heat and whisk in the egg yolks and a little salt. Add the melted butter, a tbsp or so at a time, whisking continuously. Wait until each spoonful is absorbed before adding more butter. Remove the pan from the heat before adding the final spoonful; it will be hot enough to go on cooking the sauce. Stir in the tarragon and check that the seasoning is to taste.

The sauce can be kept warm for a short time in a bowl placed over a pan of hot, but not boiling, water.

VARIATION
Sauce paloise
Replace the tarragon with mint and serve the sauce with poached fish, grilled chicken, or lamb.

Bowles' mint

Green mojo

Green mojo is a dipping sauce from the Canary Islands, usually served with wrinkled potatoes (papas arrugadas).

Put new potatoes in their skins in a pan and almost cover with cold water. Add 100g (3½oz) salt per 500g (1lb 2oz) potatoes, bring to the boil, then reduce the heat; cook slowly until the potatoes are done, about 15 minutes. Drain, but leave the potatoes in the pan over a low heat, shaking them from time to time. They will be wrinkled and salty on the outside, but soft and tender inside.

Served with this mojo, they are decidedly moreish. The mojo is also good with fish, meat, and salads.

1 sweet green pepper

3 green chillies

10 garlic cloves

1 tsp coarse salt

leaves from a bunch of parsley

1 tsp ground cumin

4 tbsp wine vinegar

6 tbsp olive oil

Remove the seeds and veins from the pepper and chillies and chop coarsely. Crush the garlic with the salt. Blend all the ingredients in a blender or food processor, or pound in a mortar and pestle, until you have a smooth paste. Thin with water if you wish.

Covered with a layer of oil in a closed jar, the sauce keeps for 2 weeks in the refrigerator.

Harissa

This fiery chilli sauce is now widely available commercially, but it is quick and easy to make your own, and you will find it has more flavour than many on sale, which predominantly have a chilli bite, but little more. It is used throughout North Africa, but it is especially popular in Tunisia. It is usually made with dried chillies; the local chilli resembles the slender maroon guajillo of Mexico. If you prefer to use fresh chillies for a table sauce, substitute the same quantity as dried and omit the soaking. Harissa is used in cooking and as a condiment with eggs, couscous, and tagines.

100g (3½oz) dried chillies

2 garlic cloves, peeled

½ tsp salt

1 tsp ground cumin seeds

1 tsp ground caraway seeds

½ tsp ground coriander

olive oil

Break the chillies into pieces and discard the seeds. Soak the flesh in almost-boiling water for about 30 minutes, until soft. Meanwhile crush the garlic with the salt.

Drain the chillies and pound or process with the garlic and spices. Add 1–2 tbsp olive oil, or more, to loosen the mixture. Store in a jar under a layer of olive oil for 3–4 weeks.

Harissa is usually thinned with oil and lemon juice, water, or a few spoonfuls of hot stock from the dish with which it is to be served.

Chillies

Coriander

Preserved lemons

Preserved lemons are a speciality of Morocco, although they are used elsewhere in North Africa. Traditionally used as a flavouring for meat, fish, and vegetables, they have a distinctive, slightly salty taste that is also good in salads, salsas, and dressings.

10 unwaxed lemons

coarse sea salt

Cut 5 of the lemons lengthwise into quarters, but stop short of separating the quarters completely by leaving the lemons uncut at the stalk end. Gently pull the lemons open and sprinkle salt, about 1 tbsp per lemon, onto the exposed flesh; close up the lemons again and put them into a preserving jar. Press down well and put a weight (a clean, heavy stone will do) on top, then close the jar.

After 2–3 days the lemons will have released some of their juices. Pour over enough juice from the remaining 5 lemons to cover them completely and leave for 1 month. If a piece of lemon is exposed to the air it may develop a harmless white mould that can be washed off.

The lemons will keep for up to a year and the flavour mellows with keeping. Only the chopped skin is used; discard the flesh and pips when you take the pieces from the jar.

Nam prik

This sauce, which translates literally as chilli water, is popular throughout Thailand. Served with rice, fish, and raw or lightly cooked vegetables, it includes dried shrimps, shrimp paste, chillies, and garlic pounded with palm sugar, fish sauce, and lime juice. Shallots, peanuts, small aubergines, and unripe fruits are also used. Nam prik is made in minutes, to individual taste.

4 fresh red chillies, deseeded and chopped

4 garlic cloves, chopped

2 tbsp dried shrimps

1 tbsp palm or granulated sugar

2 tbsp fish sauce

lime juice

Pound the chillies, garlic, dried shrimps, and sugar in a mortar and pestle or blend in a food processor with 1 tbsp water. Gradually add the fish sauce and enough lime juice, probably 3–4 tbsp, to give a well-blended consistency. Taste. In a closed jar the sauce will keep for 1–2 weeks in the refrigerator.

Thai chilli jam

This relish, called nam prik pad in Thai, is similar to Indonesian sambals. It is served as a condiment or stirred into soups, stir-fries, and rice dishes.

1 tsp shrimp paste (kapi)

8 large red chillies, fresh or dried

8 garlic cloves, cut in half

8 shallots, cut in half

4 tbsp dried shrimps

3 tbsp sunflower oil

1 tbsp fish sauce

2 tbsp palm sugar

2 tbsp tamarind water (*p.157*)

Wrap the shrimp paste in foil and dry roast in a pan or in a preheated oven, 200°C (400°F/Gas 6), for a few minutes.

Remove stalks and, if you wish, seeds from the chillies. Dry roast the chillies, garlic, and shallots separately in a heavy pan or on a tray in the preheated oven. Do not let them burn. When the chillies, garlic, and shallots are soft, put them into a food processor with the shrimp paste and blend, scraping down the sides if necessary. Pound the shrimps and add them to the mixture.

Heat the oil and fry the paste until it smells fragrant, then add the fish sauce, sugar, and tamarind water and cook until all is well mixed and slightly reduced. Cool, then store in a jar in the refrigerator for 2–3 weeks.

Roasted nam prik

1 tsp tamarind concentrate

2 tbsp peanuts

5 garlic cloves, unpeeled

5 shallots, unpeeled

5 fresh red chillies

thin slice of shrimp paste (kapi)

1 tbsp palm or granulated sugar

Dissolve the tamarind in 2 tbsp hot water. Heat a heavy frying pan and quickly dry roast the peanuts. Set them aside. Dry roast the garlic and shallots until the skins are dark brown and the insides soft. Wrap the chillies in foil and dry roast until they soften. At the same time wrap the shrimp paste in a tightly closed foil parcel and dry roast for 1–2 minutes on each side, or until it darkens.

Peel the garlic and shallots, remove the seeds from the chillies, if you wish, and chop the flesh. Pound or process everything (including the sugar) to a paste. Store for 1–2 weeks in a closed jar in the refrigerator.

Sweet chilli sauce

This easy sauce is good with fried or grilled fish and seafood or spring rolls.

6 tbsp sugar

4 medium red chillies, deseeded and finely sliced

2 garlic cloves, finely chopped

small piece of ginger, cut into fine strips

5 tbsp rice or cider vinegar

1 tbsp fish sauce

3–4 tbsp chopped coriander

Heat 120ml (4fl oz) water and sugar together to make a syrup, let it thicken a little, then stir in all the ingredients except the coriander. Bring to the boil and simmer for 3 minutes.

Pour the sauce into a bowl and leave to cool, then stir in the coriander. Taste for seasoning and add a little salt if necessary; I find that the fish sauce makes it salty enough.

Mint dipping sauce

This Vietnamese sauce is good with spring rolls and with grilled prawns combined with vegetables and herbs from the herb platter (p.270) and wrapped in a lettuce leaf.

A handful of mint leaves

2 garlic cloves, chopped

1 bird chilli, deseeded and chopped

2 tbsp rice vinegar

3 tbsp lime juice

2 tbsp fish sauce

2 tbsp palm sugar or brown sugar

Blend the mint, garlic, and chilli to a paste in a food processor. Combine the other ingredients with 2–3 tbsp water and stir until the sugar has dissolved. Then add the paste.

Nuoc cham

Nuoc cham is the dipping sauce served with every Vietnamese meal. There are different styles according to the region: in the north the sauce is often a simple one of fish sauce (nuoc mam) and water with chopped chillies, whereas in the south, garlic, sugar, and lime juice are added. Bird chillies are best, but if you can't find them substitute other fresh chillies.

2 tbsp lime juice

3 tbsp fish sauce

2 tbsp sugar

1 bird chilli, deseeded and finely chopped

1 garlic clove, finely chopped

Combine the liquids, sugar, and 3 tbsp water, stirring until the sugar has dissolved. Add the chilli and garlic.

VARIATIONS
Peel and finely chop a small piece of fresh ginger and add to the sauce.

Replace the fish sauce by soy sauce and reduce the sugar to 1 tbsp.

Black peppermint

Sambals

Unlike curry pastes or masalas, Indonesian bumbus, or spice mixtures, are an integral part of each dish. They usually have a base of onion and garlic with coriander and cumin, soy sauce, and tamarind or lime juice. The other spices and herbs vary according to the dish. Indonesians also make aromatic, chilli-based table sauces called sambals; some of them are very hot.

Sambal bajak

This sambal is made with large chillies and is fairly mild and quite sweet because of the addition of shallots, garlic, and coconut milk. It goes well with rice dishes such as nasi goreng.

10 large red chillies

8 shallots, chopped

5 garlic cloves, chopped

1 tsp shrimp paste (trassi)

5 candlenuts

1 tsp tamarind concentrate

½ tsp powdered galangal

2 makrut lime leaves, shredded

2 tbsp sunflower oil

1 tsp salt

2 tsp palm sugar

250ml (9fl oz) coconut milk

Discard the stalks and, if you wish, the seeds of the chillies before chopping them coarsely. Process the chillies, shallots, garlic, shrimp paste, candlenuts, tamarind, galangal, and lime leaves to a paste.

Heat the oil and fry the paste for 10 minutes. Add the remaining ingredients and cook gently for 20–25 minutes, until the mixture thickens and has a visible layer of oil. Stir the oil into the sambal, cool, and then store in jars in the refrigerator for 2–3 weeks.

Lime leaves

Sambal ulek

The chillies used in this simple sambal are lomboks, but other fresh red chillies can be substituted. A large quantity can be made; it will keep in the refrigerator for 2–3 weeks in a closed jar, or can be frozen in small pots.

500g (1lb 2oz) red chillies

2 tsp salt

1 tbsp lemon juice

Discard the stalks and dry roast the chillies briefly until they soften. Do not let them burn. Cool, then remove seeds if you wish. Transfer the chillies to a food processor with the salt and lemon juice and process to a paste.

VARIATION
Sambal kemiri
Make half the quantity of sambal ulek. Dry roast and grind 10 candlenuts and add when processing.

Sambal manis
Add 2 tsp palm sugar to half the quantity of sambal ulek.

Korean dipping sauces

Koreans have a number of dipping sauces based on combinations of sesame, chilli, vinegar, and soy sauce. They are served with dumplings and pancakes, with raw fish, vegetables, and grilled meats.

Jon Dip

1 tsp sugar

4 tbsp soy sauce

2 tsp rice or cider vinegar

1 tsp sesame oil

2 tsp toasted sesame seeds

1 spring onion, very finely sliced

½ tsp hot chilli powder

Stir the sugar into the soy sauce and vinegar. When it has dissolved, add all the other ingredients. The sauce will keep in the refrigerator for several days.

Kochujang red pepper sauce

This recipe comes from *Flavours of Korea* by Marc and Kim Millon. Kochujang, a staple of the Korean kitchen, is a fermented paste made by pounding chillies into glutinous rice. It can be bought in Asian shops and some supermarkets. The Millons use kochujang as the basis of a livelier, more vibrant sauce.

2 tbsp kochujang

2 garlic cloves, crushed and finely chopped

1 tbsp rice or cider vinegar

1 tbsp soy sauce

1 tsp sesame oil

2 tsp toasted sesame seeds

2 spring onions, shredded finely on the diagonal

2 tsp sugar

Mix all the ingredients together and serve in saucers as a dip, with grilled meats, raw fish, or vegetables.

Yuzukosho

The name means yuzu chilli paste and this Japanese seasoning is from Kyushu, where much of the yuzu crop comes from. It is a blend of yuzu zest, chillies (usually green) and salt that is left to ferment. Originally made in domestic kitchens it is now produced commercially. If you can find yuzus in season, you will need 4, along with 2 hot chillies and ½–1 tsp salt. Grate the zest, deseed the chillies, and chop finely, then combine both in a mortar with the salt and pound to a paste. Refrigerate for up to 2 weeks.

Traditionally served with nabemono (simmered dishes), it is now served with ramen and udon noodles, sashimi, tempura, grilled chicken, and as a salad dressing or a sauce for spaghetti.

Ponzu

This sauce is widely used in the Japanese kitchen. It is made by simmering rice vinegar, mirin, soy sauce, dried bonito flakes, and kombu (kelp); the liquid is strained and cooled, then yuzu or bitter orange juice is added to taste. The consistency is thin but the sauce may have a sediment. If you want to make your own, the proportions are 2½ tbsp rice vinegar, 3 tbsp mirin, 1 tbsp soy, 1½ tbsp bonito flakes plus citrus juice to taste once strained and cooled.

Ponzu is served as a dip with nabemono (simmered dishes), grilled fish, and sashimi.

Ginger-soy dipping sauce

This Chinese sauce is served with dumplings and fried seafood and also goes well with barbequed chicken. You could add a little chilli sauce if you wish.

3 tbsp light soy sauce

3 tbsp rice vinegar

1 tsp grated ginger

1 spring onion, finely sliced

a few sprigs of coriander, chopped

Combine the soy sauce and vinegar and stir in the other ingredients.

Ginger juice

Lime and chilli sauce

There are different versions of this sauce throughout the Caribbean. This one is from Guadeloupe.

2 fresh red chillies

1 tbsp sea salt

250ml (9fl oz) lime juice

Remove the seeds from the chillies and slice finely. Dissolve the salt in the lime juice, pack the chillies into a jar, and pour over the lime juice. It is best after 2–3 days, but will keep for up to 1 month. Serve with fish or grilled vegetables.

Ajilimójili

This Puerto Rican sauce is made with mild chillies called ají dulce. It is served with tostones (fried green plantains), but also goes well with fried or grilled fish or meat. This version is from *The Complete Book of Caribbean Cooking* by Elisabeth Lambert Ortiz.

3 fresh red chillies

3 sweet red peppers

4 peppercorns

4 garlic cloves, crushed

2 tsp salt

150ml (5fl oz) lime juice

150ml (5fl oz) olive oil

Remove the seeds and veins from the chillies and peppers and chop them roughly. Reduce them to a coarse purée in a processor with the peppercorns, garlic, and salt.

Add the lime juice and olive oil and whizz until smooth. Store in the refrigerator in a closed jar for 3–4 weeks.

Mole verde

Moles are Mexican cooked sauces, flavoured with chillies and herbs. Green mole is good with poached chicken breast and sautéed duck breast.

100g (3½oz) pumpkin seeds

6 tomatillos, fresh or canned

4 serrano chillies, deseeded and chopped

2 garlic cloves, crushed

1 small onion, chopped

10 cos lettuce leaves, torn

3 tbsp chopped coriander

leaves from 3 sprigs fresh epazote, or 1 tbsp dried

¼ tsp ground cumin

2 tbsp sunflower oil

250ml (9fl oz) chicken stock

Dry roast the pumpkin seeds, stirring to prevent burning. Cool, then grind. Blend the tomatillos – if they are fresh, first remove the husks and chop the flesh – with the vegetables, herbs, and spices. Heat the oil in a pan and cook the sauce, stirring constantly, over high heat so that it thickens – about 5 minutes. Set aside.

Stir the pumpkin seeds into the stock and add to the sauce. Very gently heat it, avoiding boiling or it will lose its colour. Let it barely simmer for 15 minutes, stirring regularly.

Salsa fresca

This is the standard salsa found throughout Mexico.

4 tomatoes, peeled, deseeded, and chopped

1 red onion, finely chopped

4 jalapeño chillies, deseeded and sliced in thin rings

5 tbsp chopped coriander leaves

5 tbsp lime juice or sherry vinegar

salt

Combine all the ingredients and leave to stand at least 30 minutes before using.

Jalapeño chillies

Cuban mojo

A mojo is a table sauce, akin to a Mexican salsa. Seville (bitter) orange juice is most often used; lime juice on its own or with a little sweet orange juice can be substituted.

4 tbsp olive oil

2 garlic cloves, finely chopped

1 shallot, finely chopped

½ tsp salt

1 tsp dried oregano

1 tsp ground cumin

100ml (3½fl oz) Seville orange juice or one-third sweet orange juice and two-thirds lime juice

3 tbsp chopped coriander leaves

Heat the oil and gently fry the garlic and shallot until lightly browned. Remove from the heat and add the salt, oregano, cumin, and orange juice. Stir well and leave to cool.

Transfer to a bowl and stir in the coriander. The mojo will keep in a bottle or jar in the refrigerator for 2–3 weeks, but it tastes best when fresh. Good with steak, chicken, and vegetables.

Whole cumin seeds

Mango and papaya mojo

1 ripe mango

1 ripe papaya

2 spring onions, finely sliced

small piece of fresh ginger, finely chopped

2 tbsp chopped mint leaves

100ml (3½fl oz) lime juice

Cut the flesh of the mango and the papaya into small cubes and combine with the other ingredients. Serve with grilled fish, seafood, or chicken.

Xni-pec

This explosively hot salsa comes from the Yucatán in southern Mexico.

2–3 habanero chillies

4 large ripe tomatoes, chopped

1 onion, finely chopped

large handful of coriander leaves, chopped

4 tbsp bitter orange juice or lime juice

salt to taste

Roast the habaneros (*see p.244*), peel, and deseed them. Chop the flesh and mix with the chopped tomatoes and onion. Stir in the coriander and pour over the orange juice. If Seville oranges aren't in season, lime juice can be used. Season with salt to taste. Let the salsa marinate for an hour at room temperature.

In the Yucatán it is regularly on the table and is served with grilled meats, fish, and seafood. Corn chips are good to dip in it too. It is best eaten fresh.

Pebre

This is a popular sauce throughout Chile and recipes change from region to region and cook to cook.

1 onion, finely chopped

1–2 garlic cloves, finely chopped

large bunch of coriander

3 ripe tomatoes, deseeded and chopped (optional)

1–2 tbsp ají paste (*see p.286*) or 1–2 fresh chillies

2 tbsp red wine vinegar or to taste

3 tbsp olive oil or to taste

salt

Combine the onion and garlic in a bowl. Chop the coriander leaves and small stalks finely. If you use a food processor don't let them become a purée. Add to the onion and garlic. If you are using tomatoes add them now. Stir in the ají paste or if you are using fresh chillies, deseed and chop before adding to the other ingredients. Stir in the vinegar and olive oil, taste as you go along to get a balance that pleases you. Season lightly with salt.

Leave to stand for 3–4 hours before serving with cold meats, seafood, or roasted vegetables.

Argentine salsa criolla

This is an excellent accompaniment to barbecued meats.

1 red onion, finely chopped

1 red pepper, finely chopped

2 tomatoes, deseeded and chopped

1 garlic clove, finely chopped

small handful of parsley leaves, chopped

juice of 1 lime

2 tbsp light olive oil

salt and freshly ground black pepper

Combine all the ingredients in a bowl, cover and leave to rest for 1–2 hours so that the flavours blend. Use as a condiment with fish, meat, and poultry.

Peruvian salsa criolla

If you can't get ají Amarillo use a Scotch bonnet, or for a milder bite, a jalapeño.

1 red onion, sliced very thinly

1 ají Amarillo, deseeded and finely chopped

small handful of coriander leaves, chopped

2 tomatoes, deseeded and diced (optional)

3 tbsp lime juice

2 tbsp light olive oil

salt

Put the onion into a bowl of cold water and leave to soak for 15 minutes. Drain thoroughly and mix with the other ingredients. Let the salsa stand for an hour or two and the flavours will blend.

Use as a condiment with fish, meat, and poultry.

Chimichurri

This Argentinian herb sauce is served with grilled meats. It goes well with pies, vegetables, or stirred into soups.

4 garlic cloves, finely chopped

1 tsp freshly ground black pepper

½ tsp chilli flakes

1 tsp paprika

2 tsp oregano leaves, finely chopped

large handful parsley leaves and sprigs, finely chopped

100ml (3½fl oz) olive oil

5 tbsp red wine vinegar

salt to taste

Mix all the ingredients together in a jar and shake well. Leave for 3–4 hours before using.

Peruvian parsley salsa

This salsa is served with corn, potatoes, and meat dishes.

1 small onion, finely chopped

1 tsp oregano

salt and freshly ground black pepper

wine vinegar

3 handfuls of parsley leaves

1 tomato

Put the onion and oregano into a bowl, season, and add vinegar to cover. Leave to marinate for at least 30 minutes, then drain off the vinegar. Chop the parsley leaves to a paste in a food processor and add it to the onion and oregano.

Dip the tomato in boiling water, remove the skin, and grate the flesh into the salsa, or chop very finely and then add it. Stir well to combine all the ingredients.

Paprika

Oregano

Green mango relish

1 large green mango, about 500g (1lb 2oz)

1 garlic clove, finely chopped

1 small green chilli, finely chopped

½ tsp salt

1 tbsp olive oil

handful of parsley or mint leaves, chopped

Chop the mango finely and mix with the other ingredients. It will keep for 2–3 days if you put it in a closed jar with a layer of oil over the top and store in the refrigerator.

Nepali mint chutney

large handful of mint leaves, finely chopped

2 garlic cloves, finely chopped

¼ tsp chilli powder

½ tsp salt

juice of 1 lemon

2 tbsp mustard or sunflower oil

½ tsp fenugreek seeds

½ tsp ground turmeric

Combine the mint, garlic, chilli powder, salt, and lemon juice; set aside. Heat the oil and fry the fenugreek seeds until they are very dark; add the turmeric and stir for a moment. Allow to cool, then stir into the mint mixture. Serve with rice or bread, or pakoras.

Apple mint

Mint relish

100g (3½oz) fresh mint leaves

1 garlic clove, finely chopped

2–4 small fresh green chillies, deseeded and diced

½ tsp salt

juice of 1 lime

1–2 tbsp vegetable oil

pinch of white sugar (optional)

90ml (3fl oz) yogurt (optional)

Combine the mint leaves, garlic, chilli, salt, and lime juice in a food processor and blend, drizzling in oil as needed. Add sugar if too tart. This goes well with all grilled meats. Add yogurt if accompanying rice.

Fresh tomato chutney

This recipe and the previous one come from Myanmar (Burma) and are based on recipes in *The Burma Cookbook* by Robert Carmack and Morrison Polkinghorne. They can be served to accompany a curry or with meat or chicken grilled on your barbecue. Chillies in Myanmar are mild compared to those eaten in other parts of Asia, so use paprika or mild chilli flakes for a more authentic taste.

This tomato chutney is quickly made and should be eaten on the day. It can be made with green or ripe tomatoes, but if you use green, don't peel or deseed them and adjust the sugar.

500g (1lb 2oz) tomatoes, peeled, deseeded, and coarsely chopped

1 small onion, finely chopped

1 tsp hot paprika or chilli flakes

2 tsp white sugar or to taste

1 tbsp rice vinegar

½ tsp salt

Combine all the ingredients and stir lightly. Refrigerate until ready to serve.

Cucumber sambal

Sambals with hot, sweet, and sour flavours are popular condiments in Indonesia and Malaysia. This one goes well with chicken satay, grilled fish, or vegetables.

1 cucumber

1 tbsp finely chopped onion

1 small red chilli, deseeded and cut in shreds

1 tbsp chopped parsley or coriander

½ tsp ground fennel seeds

1 tsp sugar

salt and freshly ground black pepper

2–3 tbsp lemon juice

2 tbsp sunflower oil

Remove the seeds from the cucumber and cut the flesh into short, thin strips. Mix with the onion, chilli, and parsley or coriander. Mix the rest of the seasonings with the lemon juice, then stir in the oil and toss the cucumber in the mixture.

Tomato sambal

4 shallots, sliced

3 chillies, deseeded and sliced

3 large tomatoes, chopped

3 tbsp chopped mint or basil

juice of 1 lime or lemon

salt to taste

Combine all the ingredients and serve at room temperature. Good with chicken or pork satay.

Kachumbar

This relish is a pleasant complement to many Indian dishes. The chillies can be omitted, or the number reduced if you prefer a milder version.

salt

2 onions, finely chopped

1 tbsp palm sugar or brown sugar

1 tbsp tamarind paste

4 tomatoes, diced

1 small cucumber, halved, deseeded, and cut in thick slices

2–3 red or green chillies, deseeded and thinly sliced

1 tbsp finely shredded ginger

mint leaves to garnish

Sprinkle the salt over the onions and leave for an hour. Drain, rinse, and press out all the liquid. Loosen the tamarind paste with water and stir in the sugar. Add more water if it is too thick. Add the vegetables, chillies, and ginger and mix well. Chill and serve garnished with mint leaves.

Pili pili sauce

This table condiment is popular in West Africa.

250g (9oz) fresh red chillies

1 small onion

1 garlic clove

juice of 1 lemon

Remove stalks, and seeds if you wish, from the chillies and blend all the ingredients.

Coriander chutney

This chutney goes well with kebabs, samosas, pakoras, and fried or grilled vegetables. Vary the number of chillies to suit your taste.

60g (2oz) sesame seeds

1 tsp cumin seeds

250g (9oz) coriander leaves and young stalks

2–6 green chillies, deseeded and chopped

1 tbsp chopped fresh ginger

salt

juice of 1 lemon

Dry roast the sesame seeds and cumin seeds separately. Put all the ingredients except the salt and lemon juice into a food processor and blend to a paste.

Scrape down the sides of the bowl if necessary. Add salt to taste and enough lemon juice to loosen the paste a little; it should remain quite thick. In a closed jar the chutney will keep for a week in the refrigerator.

Garlic purée

250g (9oz) fresh red chillies

1 small onion

1 garlic clove

juice of 1 lemon

Put 6 heads of young garlic in a pan and cover with boiling water. Simmer for 15–20 minutes until soft. Drain and leave to cool, then skin and blend in a food processor with a little salt.

Mix in 4–6 tbsp fruity olive oil and transfer to a jar. Cover with a layer of olive oil, then the lid, and refrigerate. Top up the oil each time you use the purée. It will keep for up to 2 weeks.

Chillies

Marinades

Marinades tenderize and enhance flavour, and they also preserve food. They are useful in preparing fish, meat, and poultry to be grilled, roasted, or fried. Mix the ingredients in a container that will not react with acid (glass or ceramic, for example). Immerse the food in the marinade, turning it periodically. Keep in the refrigerator, but bring to room temperature before cooking. Marinate fish for 1–2 hours, shellfish for up to 1 hour; allow 3–4 hours for pieces of meat or chicken; large pieces of meat or a whole chicken can be left overnight. A marinade can be used to baste food while it is cooking, but never keep it for re-use. Some of the other mixtures can also be used as marinades – see Cuban adobo and Chilean aliño (*p.267*), Seasoning (*p.269*), Masala for fish (*p.276*), and the Barbecue and Cajun mixtures (*p.287*).

Ginger and lime marinade

Use for salmon and firm, meaty fish such as swordfish.

small piece of ginger, finely chopped

2 garlic cloves, crushed

grated rind of 1 unwaxed lime

4 tbsp lime juice

2 tbsp soy sauce

1 tbsp sesame oil

1 tbsp dry sherry

Yogurt marinade

Use for lamb or chicken.

200ml (7fl oz) plain yogurt

1 garlic clove, crushed

2 tbsp mint, chopped

2–3 tsp tandoori masala (*p.276*) or massalé (*p.277*).

Pernod marinade

Use for fish and seafood.

3 tbsp lemon juice

1 tbsp fennel seeds or a handful of fresh fennel leaves

4 tsp olive oil

small glass dry white wine

3 tbsp Pernod or other anise-based drink

Red wine marinade

Use for large cuts of beef and venison and for hare.

½ bottle red wine

2 tbsp olive or sunflower oil

1 onion, sliced

1 stalk celery, sliced

2 bay leaves

sprig rosemary

2 sprigs thyme

8 crushed black peppercorns

4 crushed allspice berries

Bay leaves

Barbecue marinade

Use for steaks, pork chops, and spare ribs.

2 shallots, chopped

¼ tsp ground cloves

¼ tsp ground allspice

3 tbsp sunflower oil

1 tbsp honey

2 tbsp soy sauce

3 tbsp dry sherry

Oriental marinade

Use for spare ribs, poultry, or fish.

2 shallots, peeled and chopped

small piece of ginger, chopped

1 chilli, sliced

2 tsp sugar

4 tbsp chopped coriander – root, leaf, and stalk

4 tbsp lime juice

2 tbsp fish sauce

5 tbsp rice vinegar

Adobo for pork

This marinade for a loin of pork is from Chile. The meat can be left as a rack or boned, stuffed, and rolled before cooking. The adobo is rubbed over all the surfaces and it is marinated overnight.

3–4 tbsp wine vinegar

3–4 tbsp olive or sunflower oil

2 tsp crushed oregano

1 tsp ground cumin

1 tbsp (or to taste) ají paste (p.286)

4 tsp Spanish paprika

½ tsp salt

Dry adobo

Dry rubs of this kind are common in the Spanish-speaking Caribbean islands.

2 tbsp cumin seeds

4 tbsp coarse sea salt

1 tbsp fennel seeds

½ tbsp black peppercorns

2 tbsp chilli flakes

1 tbsp dried oregano

Dry roast the cumin until lightly coloured. Cool, and grind with the salt, fennel, and peppercorns, then combine with the chilli and oregano.

Lightly coat meat or poultry to be grilled with the mixture. The adobo will keep in an airtight jar for 3–4 months.

Mexican marinade

Use this marinade for meat that is to be barbecued or grilled.

3 pasilla chillies

½ tsp ground cumin

3 tsp dried oregano

3 tsp dried thyme

juice of 1 lime and ½ orange

½ small onion, sliced

2 garlic cloves

4 tbsp olive oil

Discard stalks and seeds from the chillies. Toast the chillies in a preheated, heavy-based frying pan for 1–2 minutes. Transfer them to a bowl and just cover with boiling water; soak for 30 minutes. Blend the other ingredients in a food processor, add the chillies, and blend with enough of their soaking liquid to make a marinade of pouring consistency.

Juniper and wine marinade

Use for duck and game birds.

10 juniper berries, lightly crushed

10 black peppercorns, crushed

sprig of rosemary

250ml (9fl oz) red or white wine

3 tbsp brandy

3 tbsp olive oil

Mediterranean marinade

Use for lamb, chicken, or pork. You could substitute 1 tbsp herbes de Provence (p.267) for the sprigs of herbs, and 1 tsp Italian spice mixture (p.285) could be used instead of the black pepper.

1 garlic clove, crushed

2–3 sprigs thyme or lemon thyme

3–4 sprigs lavender or rosemary

1 tsp crushed black peppercorns

juice of 2 oranges

juice of 1 lemon

Lemon-scented thyme

Soups, small plates, and salads

Spiced pumpkin soup

Once you've cleaned the pumpkin, this soup is fast to make. Pumpkin's mild, sweet taste combines well with coconut milk and both are enhanced by the spices. In this soup, the citrus flavours of lemon grass and coriander set off the bite of ginger and chillies, with a background note of earthy turmeric.

SERVES 4–6

2 tbsp sunflower oil

½ tsp coriander seeds

½ tsp fennel seeds

1 tsp turmeric

1 large onion, chopped

2cm (1in) piece of fresh root ginger, chopped

2 garlic cloves, chopped

1 kg (2¼lb) pumpkin, peeled, deseeded, and cubed

2 dried chillies

2 stalks lemon grass, bruised

salt to taste

600ml (1 pint) vegetable stock

400ml (14 fl oz) coconut milk

lime juice (optional)

Heat the oil in a large, heavy-based saucepan and fry the coriander, fennel, and turmeric until their aromas are released. Stir in the onion, ginger, and garlic, and fry for a few minutes more. Then add the pumpkin, chillies, and lemon grass. Stir well, season with a little salt, and pour over the stock. Cover the pan and simmer until the pumpkin softens, then stir in the coconut milk. Don't cover the pan now or the coconut milk may curdle.

Bring the soup back to a simmer and cook until the pumpkin is soft enough to crush with a wooden spoon. Discard the chillies and lemon grass, and blend and strain the soup. Taste, and if you wish to sharpen the flavour, stir in a little lime juice. Serve with country bread.

Fennel

Hot and sour soup

Hot and sour soups are found throughout southeast Asia. The soup has satisfying, mellow flavours from the tingling warmth of the chilli balanced by the sour note of the vinegar. You could replace the pork with slivered chicken breast or replace the meat with more vegetables for a vegetarian soup. If you have it, Chinese black vinegar is good in this soup.

SERVES 4

4 dried shiitake mushrooms or a handful of fresh, sliced

750ml (1¼ pints) chicken or vegetable stock

a small piece of ginger, finely sliced

1–2 red chillies, deseeded and cut in slivers

100g (3½oz) bamboo shoots, cut in matchsticks

100g (3½oz) lean pork, cut in slivers

100g (3½oz) firm tofu, shredded or diced

1 tbsp soy sauce

salt to taste

1–2 tbsp rice vinegar

1 tbsp cornflour

1 egg

1 tsp sesame oil

2 spring onions, finely sliced

Soak the dried shiitake in warm water for about 30 minutes. Drain, remove the stalks, and slice the caps finely. Bring the stock to a simmer in a large saucepan, add the ginger, chilli, mushrooms, bamboo shoots, and pork. Cover and simmer for 10 minutes. Add the tofu, soy sauce, salt, and vinegar. Taste to ensure a good balance between the chilli heat and the vinegar.

Mix the cornflour to a paste with 2 tbsp water, and when the soup starts to bubble again stir half of it in. Simmer the soup over very low heat. It should thicken slightly. Add more cornflour as needed, but don't let it become gluey. Beat the egg lightly and pour it into the soup through a strainer or the tines of a fork so that it sets in light strands. Stir in the sesame oil and spring onions, and serve at once.

Pomegranate and herb soup

This Iranian recipe uses pomegranate molasses to give a fruity, sweet-sour flavour to this deep green winter soup. Small meatballs may be added for a more substantial soup.

SERVES 6

120g (4oz) yellow split peas

120g (4oz) rice

3 tbsp sunflower oil

2 onions, sliced

½ tsp turmeric

½ tsp cinnamon

meatballs (optional)

150g (5½oz) flat-leaf parsley

150g (5½oz) coriander

100g (3½oz) mint

100g (3½oz) spring onions

salt and freshly ground black pepper

3 tbsp pomegranate molasses

lemon juice (optional)

1 tsp dried mint

Soak the split peas and rice separately in plenty of water for at least 4 hours. Heat 2 tbsp oil in a large saucepan and gently sauté the onions until soft and lightly coloured. Stir in the spices. Drain the split peas and rice and add them to the pan with 1.5 litres (2¾ pints) water. Bring to the boil, cover, and simmer for about 1 hour. Stir from time to time to ensure nothing sticks to the bottom of the pan. If you want to add meatballs put them in now.

Remove large stalks from the herbs, and the outer skins of the spring onions, and chop together in a food processor. Stir them into the soup and cook for a further 30 minutes. Add more water if necessary and stir occasionally to make sure all the ingredients are well combined. Season with salt and pepper. Stir in the pomegranate molasses, taste and add more if needed, or a little lemon juice if the soup lacks sharpness.

Fry the dried mint in the remaining oil and pour over. Serve at once.

Molasses

Coriander soup

This soup is based on the recipe given to me by the chef at the Visalam Hotel in Karaikudi, one of the extraordinary Chettinad towns in Tamil Nadu. We enjoyed the soup very much and I've been making versions of it since that visit.

SERVES 4–6

80g (3oz) fresh coriander leaves and small stalks

2 tbsp groundnut or sunflower oil

1 tbsp cumin seeds

½ tsp black mustard seeds

½ tsp turmeric

1 onion, chopped

5 garlic cloves, chopped

1 green chilli, deseeded and sliced

4–5 tbsp coconut milk

1 tsp salt

Chop the coriander. Heat the oil in a large saucepan and temper the cumin and mustard seeds, shaking the pan until the mustard seeds begin to pop. Add the turmeric, onion, and garlic and fry gently, stirring to ensure they colour but don't burn. Put in the chopped coriander and the chilli, stir well to mix, and continue to fry until everything is soft. Cool, then blend to a smooth paste with the coconut milk.

Wipe the pan, place the coriander mixture back in, and add about 1 litre (1¾ pints) water. Bring to the boil, taste for salt, stir well, and serve with bread.

Mustard seeds

Chilled beetroot and yogurt soup

This fresh-tasting, rich purple soup is perfect for summer and quick and easy to make.

SERVES 4–6

500g (1lb 2oz) small beetroots

1 cucumber, peeled

handful of dill, stalks removed

1 garlic clove, chopped

1 tsp ground cumin

500ml (16 fl oz) full-fat yogurt

salt and freshly ground black pepper

lemon juice (optional)

Top and tail the beetroots, place in a saucepan, cover with water, and bring to the boil. Simmer until you can push a knife tip into the beets, about 30–40 minutes, depending on size and age of the beets. Drain, rinse well in cold water, and leave to cool. Peel and chop them. Cut the cucumber across in half, then split each half vertically and remove the seeds. Chop half into medium cubes and the rest into small cubes.

Place the beetroots in a food processor and add the dill, setting aside some small sprigs for later. Then, add the medium pieces of cucumber, garlic, cumin, yogurt, and season well with salt and pepper. Whizz to a purée and stir in the small cubes of cucumber. Taste and adjust seasoning, adding a little lemon juice if you prefer a sharper flavour.

Chill the soup in the refrigerator for at least 1 hour. To serve, finely chop the remaining dill leaves and scatter over the top.

Dried cloves

Sassoun

This is an old country recipe from Roquebrune in Provence. Old Provençal books call it a sauce, but it is more like a thick mayonnaise and makes an original, fresh-tasting topping for bruschetta or spread on slices of sourdough bread for a snack lunch.

SERVES 4

5–6 anchovy fillets

100g (3½oz) blanched almonds

a sprig of fennel

4 mint leaves

3–4 tbsp olive oil

salt

lemon juice (optional)

Rinse the anchovies to remove excess salt and set aside. Put the almonds into a food processor, or use a pestle and mortar, and grind them to rough pieces. Add the anchovies, fennel, and mint leaves and grind to a rough paste. Slowly add enough oil and 4–6 tbsp water to make a smooth, thick mass. Taste and add a little salt, and, if needed a drop of lemon juice.

Tapenade

Tapenade is usually made with black olives, but green olives, such as picholine, make a fine alternative.

SERVES 6–8

1 garlic clove

salt

250g (9oz) large black olives, pitted

4 anchovy fillets

2 tbsp capers

1 tsp chopped fresh savory leaves or a pinch of dried

pinch of cayenne or piment d'Espelette

3–4 tbsp olive oil

Crush the garlic to a paste with a little salt. Put all the ingredients except the oil into a food processor and pulse to a coarse purée. Add the olive oil, a little at a time, and pulse until the mixture is well blended. Store in a covered container in the refrigerator and serve on croûtons, as a dip, or to accompany a grilled fish.

Grilled, sliced aubergines with ricotta, mint, and pine nuts

Grilled aubergines are easy to prepare and combine well with many flavours.

SERVES 3–4

2 large aubergines, peeled and sliced about 1cm (½in) thick

2–3 tbsp olive oil

100g (3½oz) ricotta cheese

2 tbsp chopped mint

3 tbsp dry-roasted pine nuts

salt and freshly ground black pepper

Brush the aubergine slices with oil and grill on a barbecue or a griddle plate, about 4 minutes on each side, until soft and lightly browned. Crumble the ricotta and mix it with most of the mint and pine nuts. Season well. Put a spoonful on each aubergine slice and scatter over the remaining mint and nuts.

VARIATIONS

For the topping:

Combine 3 tbsp pomegranate molasses with 1 tbsp red wine vinegar, ¼ tsp ground chilli and 80g (3oz) finely chopped walnuts.

Chop coriander leaves, green chilli, and fresh ginger into thick natural yogurt.

Mix grilled red pepper with chopped anchovy, parsley, and black olives.

Lahmacun

Lahmacun (pronounced lah-ma-joon) is a popular snack in Turkey. Lahmacun are flat breads baked with a topping, somewhat in the style of a pizza. Toppings vary according to season and to suit what is in the house. Tomatoes and red peppers make one popular mixture, another uses lamb, walnuts, and pomegranate molasses, a third uses meat, walnuts, and green olives. Parsley and red pepper flakes are common to all.

MAKES 10 PIECES

FOR THE DOUGH

500g (1lb 2oz) strong white bread flour, plus extra for dusting

7g (¼oz) instant yeast

1 tsp sugar

½ tsp salt

1 tbsp olive oil

FOR THE TOPPING

250g (9oz) minced lamb

1 tbsp olive oil

1 onion, finely chopped

2 garlic cloves, finely chopped

1 large bunch flat-leaf parsley, big stalks removed

2 large plum tomatoes, peeled, deseeded, and diced

1 tbsp tomato paste

1 tsp pepper paste (optional)

1 tsp salt

1 tsp red pepper flakes

sumac

To make the dough, dissolve the salt in about 300ml (10fl oz) warm water. Put the flour into a large bowl, stir in the yeast and sugar, make a well in the centre, and pour in the water. Stir well to mix all together, add the olive oil, and use your hands to turn the dough into a ball. Leave the dough in a bowl, covered, for 10–15 minutes. Then, place it on a lightly floured surface and knead until it loses its stickiness and is smooth and elastic. Rinse out the bowl and put the dough back in it, cover with cling film or a cloth, and leave for 1 hour, until it has doubled in size.

For the topping, chop the lamb if it is coarsely minced. Heat the oil in a small frying pan and lightly fry the onion for a few minutes, add the garlic, and continue to fry until they are soft and lightly coloured. Set aside. Chop the parsley, turn all the topping ingredients into a large bowl and mix well. It should almost have a coarse paste-like consistency.

Heat the oven to 220°C (425°F/Gas 7). Lightly dust a work surface with flour, punch down the dough and form it into a long roll. Cut it into 10 equal pieces. Roll each one out as thinly as possible into an oval, and spread the topping evenly over the top, including the edges. Transfer the Lahmacun to a couple of baking trays and bake in the oven for 6–8 minutes. Serve warm sprinkled with sumac and a bowl of thick yogurt and a salad, if you wish.

Crab with avocado and ginger

Crab and avocado are natural partners and both respond well to the delicate flavour of Japanese lightly pickled ginger.

FOR 2 AS A LIGHT DISH OR FOR 4 WITH OTHER DISHES

250g (9oz) white crab meat, shredded and all bits of shell removed

2 tbsp pickled ginger, drained and shredded

zest of ½ lime

juice of ½–1 lime

1 avocado

a handful of rocket leaves or watercress sprigs

extra virgin olive oil

ground sansho (*p.220*)

Marinate the crab with the ginger, lime zest, and most of the juice for 30 minutes. Slice the avocado and brush it with the remaining juice to prevent it discolouring. Make a bed of rocket or watercress, arrange the avocado slices on one side, and the crab and ginger on the other. Pour a little olive oil over and sprinkle with sansho.

Pomegranate, olive, and walnut salad

This salad comes from Gaziantep in southeastern Turkey, where all the ingredients grow on the hills around the town.

SERVES 4

2 pomegranates

125g (4½oz) green olives, pitted and coarsely chopped

bunch of coriander leaves, chopped

2–3 shallots, chopped

125g (4½oz) walnuts, coarsely chopped

4 tsp lemon juice

3 tbsp olive oil

½ tsp red pepper flakes

salt

Cut the pomegranate round the middle, hold each piece upside down in your open hand and tap the skin with a wooden spoon so that the seeds drop into a bowl. Discard any pith and strain the juices into a cup and set aside. Add the olives, coriander, shallots, and walnuts to the bowl.

Make a piquant dressing with the remaining ingredients and add the pomegranate juice. Pour this over the salad, toss, and serve with bread. If you have any left over, it will keep for a day or two in the refrigerator.

Salad of cooked peppers and tomatoes

This richly flavoured salad from the Mahgreb makes an excellent first course. It also goes well with grilled chicken or fish.

SERVES 4–6

2 kg (4½lb) ripe tomatoes

6 tbsp olive oil

salt and freshly ground black pepper

1 tsp paprika

5–6 red peppers

5–6 garlic cloves, unpeeled

1 preserved lemon (*p.172*)

4 tbsp chopped parsley

Heat the grill. Peel, deseed, and chop the tomatoes and cook them gently in the olive oil with salt, pepper, and paprika. Keep the heat low, stir from time to time, and cook until all the water has evaporated and you have a thick sauce that begins to fry in the oil. This can take up to 30 minutes if the tomatoes are watery. Remove from the heat.

While the tomatoes are cooking put the peppers and garlic under the grill, turning until the skins of the peppers are blackened on all sides and the garlic skins are crisp. The garlic will be ready before the peppers. Leave the garlic to cool, then squeeze it between your fingers and the cooked puree will pop out. Stir it into the tomatoes. Place the peppers in a plastic bag and leave to cool.

Peel the peppers, discard the seeds and white ribs, and dice the flesh. Add the peppers, lemon, and parsley to the pan and put this back over very low heat for 10–15 minutes, stirring frequently to prevent sticking. Leave to cool before serving.

Thai chillies

Fattoush

The essential ingredients in this Lebanese salad are sumac, fresh herbs, and bread. Use watercress or more mint and parsley if you haven't got purslane.

SERVES 6

1 pitta bread

1 cucumber

3 tomatoes, cut in chunks

handful of radishes, cut in half

6 spring onions, sliced

a few lettuce leaves, torn if large

large handful flat-leaf parsley, coarsely chopped

large handful mint, coarsely chopped

sprigs and leaves from a small bunch of purslane

1 tbsp sumac

salt and freshly ground black pepper

6 tbsp lemon juice

6 tbsp olive oil

Split open the pitta bread and toast with the open side to the grill until lightly golden and crisp. Break it into small pieces.

Cut the cucumber into four lengthways, and then into pieces. Put all the vegetables and herbs into a bowl and scatter the bread over the top.

Whisk the sumac, salt, and pepper into the lemon juice, then whisk in the oil. Pour the dressing over the salad, toss, and serve at once or the bread may get soggy.

Figs with walnuts and goat's cheese

This salad depends on having perfectly ripe figs, fresh goat's cheese, the best olive oil, and balsamic vinegar. Use burrata or mozzarella instead of goat's cheese.

SERVES 4

6 large ripe figs

a handful of walnuts

250–300g (9–10oz) young goat's cheese

a handful or two of small salad leaves (optional)

salt and freshly ground black pepper

1 tbsp balsamic vinegar

2–3 tbsp extra virgin olive oil

young mint and basil leaves

Cut the figs in four or in six pieces. Break or chop the walnuts into largish pieces. Cut or crumble the goat cheese into pieces. If you are using the salad leaves spread them on a platter; if not arrange the figs straight onto the platter and arrange the walnuts and cheese around them.

Season lightly with salt and pepper, drizzle the vinegar and olive oil over, and scatter over the mint and basil leaves.

Spinach with sesame dressing

This fresh-tasting Japanese salad is quick to make.

SERVES 2–4

500g (1lb 2oz) spinach

2 tbsp sesame seeds

2 tsp mirin (or caster sugar)

2 tsp rice vinegar

2–3 tbsp soy sauce

Remove any large stalks from the spinach, wash and transfer the leaves to a large pan with the water from washing still clinging to them. Cook, stirring until all are wilted, then rinse under cold water to stop the cooking. Squeeze to remove all the water then chop coarsely.

Heat a heavy frying pan and dry roast the sesame seeds until just starting to brown. Crush with a pestle and mortar until quite finely ground, though it's all right to have a few larger bits. Don't be tempted to grind in a processor because the seeds might become paste-like. Turn the sesame into a serving bowl, add the mirin, rice vinegar, and soy sauce, stirring well to make a dressing. Toss the spinach in the dressing and serve at room temperature or chilled.

Fish

Salt and pepper squid

Cleaned baby squid are widely available at fishmongers and fish counters in supermarkets. Boxes of frozen squid are on sale too, but fresh taste better. Cucumber sambal (*p.300*) makes a good dipping sauce.

SERVES 2

400g (14oz) baby squid, cleaned

½ tsp Sichuan pepper

1 tsp sea salt

freshly ground black pepper

4 tbsp potato flour

sunflower oil, for deep-frying

2 spring onions, finely sliced

1 red chilli, deseeded and finely sliced

1 garlic clove, finely sliced

1 tbsp dark soy sauce

2 limes

fresh coriander sprigs

Remove the tentacles from the squid, cut in short lengths if necessary, and set aside. Cut along one side of the squid's body to open it out and score the inside in a diamond pattern, making sure not to cut all the way through the flesh. Cut the squid into smaller pieces, diamond shapes look best. Dry the squid on kitchen paper.

Heat a small frying pan and toast the Sichuan pepper for a minute or so, until the aroma rises. Tip into a mortar, add the salt, and crush to a powder or use a spice grinder. Stir in a few grindings of black pepper. Put the potato flour into a wide bowl and stir in the salt and pepper mixture.

Pour oil into a wok or wide pan, enough to cover the squid, and heat it to 170°C (350°F) or until a small piece of bread browns rapidly, when added.

Dip the squid in the seasoned flour until evenly coated. Fry, in batches if necessary, until golden-brown. Stir gently or they might stick to the sides or bottom. Lift them out with tongs or a slotted spoon onto kitchen paper.

Drain all but a tablespoon of oil from the wok. Add the spring onions, chilli, and garlic, and fry. Put in the squid and toss all together. Stir in the soy sauce and a little lime juice.

Turn the squid onto a serving plate, and serve with a few coriander sprigs and wedges of lime.

Ceviche

Ceviche, the national dish of Peru, dates back some 2000 years to the Moche tribe who lived on the coast of northern Peru. They preserved fish by marinating it in the juice of the tumbo, a long fruit related to passionfruit.

Ceviche evolved after the arrival of the Spaniards who brought new ingredients, including citrus fruits, and their juice replaced tumbo juice. All coastal Andean countries have their version of ceviche. Peruvian ceviche is made with a marinade called leche de tigre, or tiger's milk. It is traditionally served with cobs of Peruvian choclo (white corn) and sweet potato.

SERVES 4

FOR THE TIGER'S MILK

juice of 6 limes

¼ tsp salt

1 garlic clove, crushed

1 small red onion, finely sliced

small handful of coriander leaves, chopped

1–2 chillies, deseeded and sliced, or 2 tsp chilli paste

FOR THE FISH

600g (1lb 5oz) very fresh firm fish fillets such as bream, sea bass, or John Dory

1 avocado, diced

2 corn cobs, cooked and cut in half (optional)

1 sweet potato, baked and sliced (optional)

Combine all the ingredients for the tiger's milk in a large non-metallic bowl. Dice the fish and add it to the marinade. Refrigerate and leave for 10 minutes.

Add the avocado pieces to the fish, mix together gently, and serve with the corn and sweet potato if you wish.

Mirasol

Salmon cured with gin, juniper, and elderflower

This dish is made in the same way as gravad lax; the powerful flavouring of juniper is balanced by the more subtle elderflower.

SERVES 4–6

500g (1lb 2oz) centre piece of salmon fillet

50g (1¾oz) coarse sea salt

10g (¼oz) caster sugar

1 tsp white peppercorns

¾ tsp juniper berries

¾ tsp coriander seeds

4 tbsp gin

4 tbsp elderflower cordial

sprigs of dill

Remove any pin bones from the salmon with a pair of tweezers. Grind together the salt, sugar, peppercorns, juniper, and coriander. Rub half of the mixture into the salmon on both sides. Mix together the gin and elderflower cordial and stir in the remaining spices. Pour half of this into a shallow bowl that will just hold the salmon and put it in, skin side down. Pour over the remainder of the gin and elderflower. Cover with a large piece of cling film that hangs over the bowl, and place a weighted board on the fish. Keep in the fridge for 48 hours, turning the salmon two or three times until it feels firm.

Remove the salmon from the bowl, rinse lightly to remove the spices, and dry with kitchen paper. Slice very thinly on the slant with a long sharp knife. Serve garnished with sprigs of dill and rye bread. The salmon will keep in the refrigerator, tightly wrapped in cling film, for 4–5 days.

John Dory baked in a coriander and walnut sauce

This dish of Lebanese origin can be made with any firm white fish such as cod, hake, bream, or snapper.

SERVES 4

125g (4½oz) walnuts

juice of 1 lemon

salt

½ tsp red pepper flakes

200g (7oz) coriander leaves

3 garlic cloves

1 small onion

2 tbsp olive oil

4 fillets of John Dory

Grind the walnuts coarsely in a food processor. Add 6 tbsp water and the lemon juice, and blend briefly with a pinch of salt and the pepper flakes. The sauce should have a crunchy texture. Heat the oven to 180°C (350°F/Gas 4).

Chop together the coriander, garlic, and onion - this can also be done in a food processor. Heat the oil and fry the coriander mixture for a few minutes, then stir in the sauce. Simmer for 2–3 minutes and check the seasoning.

Spread a little of the sauce on the bottom of an ovenproof dish, just big enough to place the fillets in a single layer.

Place the fillets in the dish and pour over the remainder of the sauce. Bake for 20–25 minutes, then leave to cool to room temperature before serving.

Lemons

Baked sea bass with star anise

SERVES 4

1 sea bass, about 1.5kg (3lb 3oz)

1 tbsp fresh ginger, chopped

2 tbsp rice wine or dry sherry

1 tsp five spice powder (p.272)

4 green onions or spring onions, finely chopped

1 tbsp soy sauce

1 tsp sesame oil, plus extra for greasing

salt

3 star anise

Make two diagonal slits in each side of the bass. Combine the ginger, rice wine, and five spice powder and rub the fish with the mixture. Marinate for 1 hour. Heat the oven to 220ºC (425ºF/Gas 7). Mix together the onions, soy sauce, and sesame oil with a little salt, and stuff the fish with the mixture and the star anise.

Spread a piece of foil big enough to wrap the fish on a baking tray and oil it lightly. Lift the sides and wrap the fish, folding the edges at least twice, and pinch them closed.

Bake the sea bass for about 35 minutes. Open the parcel. If the flesh flakes when a knife is inserted near the bone, it is ready. Serve with the juices.

Snapper with chermoula

SERVES 4

3 garlic cloves

1 tsp salt

1 small onion, finely chopped

small bunch of coriander, chopped

small bunch of parsley, chopped

1 tsp paprika

½ tsp chilli powder

½ tsp ground cumin

6 tbsp olive oil

juice of 1 lemon

2 snappers, each weighing about 800g (1¾lb)

800g (1¾lb) ripe tomatoes

150g (5½ oz) cracked green olives

Chermoula is a Moroccan seasoning for fish. To make the chermoula, crush the garlic with the salt and combine with the onion, herbs, and spices. Then, add the olive oil and lemon juice to make a paste.

Slash the sides of the fish in two or three places and rub the fish well with the chermoula, putting some into the slashes and the cavity. Place the fish into a dish, cover, and refrigerate for at least 2 hours, or even overnight, to allow the flavours to develop. Take out the fish 30 minutes before it is to be cooked and place it in an ovenproof dish. Heat the oven to 190°C (375°F/Gas 5). Slice the tomatoes and put them over the fish. Add a little salt, scatter over the olives, and spoon over any remaining chermoula.

Cover with foil and bake the fish for 35–45 minutes, depending on its thickness. The fish is cooked if the flesh flakes when a knife is inserted near the backbone. Serve directly from the dish.

Sea bass baked in a salt crust

No dish could be simpler than this. All you need is a handsome fish and a lot of coarse sea salt. A bass would be my first choice, but bream and snapper can also be used. For an Asian flavour, put 3–4 makrut lime leaves or 2–3 crushed lemon grass stems into the cavity before baking the fish and serve with olive oil and lime quarters.

SERVES 4

1 sea bass, about 1–1.5kg (2¼lb–3lb 3oz)

1.5kg (3lb 3oz) coarse sea salt

3–4 makrut lime leaves (optional)

2–3 stems lemon grass (optional)

Heat the oven to 220°C (425°F/Gas 7). Have the fish gutted and trimmed but not scaled. The scales are necessary to ensure that the salt doesn't penetrate the skin too much. Put an even layer of salt, about 1cm (½in) thick, in a baking dish just big enough to hold the fish. Place the fish on it.

Cover the fish entirely with salt until you have a mound of salt and no sign of the fish. Bake for 25 minutes for a fish weighing 1kg (2¼lb), 35 minutes for one weighing 1.5kg (3lb 3oz), and 40 minutes for one weighing 2kg (4½lb).

For a fish weighing less than 1kg (2¼lb) bake for 20 minutes. Remove from the oven, break and carefully lift off the salt crust, and then remove the skin. Lift off the top fillets, take out the backbone and remove the lower fillets.

Serve with olive oil, lemon quarters, and black pepper or with salsa verde (*p.289*).

Lemon grass

Mussels with lemon grass and ginger

SERVES 4

2 kg (4½lb) mussels

2 stalks lemon grass, lower third only, finely sliced

2 cloves garlic, peeled and chopped

4 makrut lime leaves

small piece of ginger, peeled and chopped

freshly ground black pepper

200ml (7fl oz) coconut milk

3 tbsp chopped coriander

Scrub the mussels, pull out the beards, and discard any that are broken or remain open when tapped firmly. Put them into a large pan (you may need to cook them in batches) with 6 tbsp water, lemon grass, garlic, lime leaves, ginger, and pepper. Cover and cook over high heat, shaking the pan now and then until the mussels open, about 2–3 minutes.

Lift out the mussels and put them into a warmed serving bowl. Boil the cooking liquid to reduce by half, pour in the coconut milk, bring to the boil to thicken it slightly, and pour over the mussels. Remove the lime leaves, stir in the coriander, and serve.

Seychelles fish curry

SERVES 4

1kg (2¼lb) snapper or monkfish fillet

salt and freshly ground black pepper

3 tbsp sunflower oil

2 onions, chopped

2 tbsp massalé (*p.277*)

½ tsp ground turmeric

2 cloves garlic, chopped

small piece ginger, chopped

3 tbsp tamarind water (*p.157*)

leaves from 2 sprigs thyme

½ tsp anise

450ml (15fl oz) fish stock or water

Cut the fish into bite-sized pieces, season with salt and pepper, and set aside.

Heat the oil in a heavy pan and fry the onion until golden. Stir in the massalé and turmeric and fry lightly. Put in the pieces of fish, and all the other ingredients. Bring to a simmer and cook for about 10 minutes until the fish is ready. Serve with rice.

Prawn and coconut curry

SERVES 3–4

500g (1lb 2oz) medium or large raw prawns, shelled

salt

½ tsp mustard seeds

½ tsp ground turmeric or zedoary

2 tsp ground coriander

1 tsp ground anise

3 tbsp sunflower oil

2 tbsp green masala (*p.268*)

2 onions, thinly sliced

400ml (14fl oz) coconut milk

Remove the black intestine from the prawns, rub with salt, and set aside. Dry roast the mustard seeds quickly, then add the other spices. Stir and shake the pan; when the aroma rises, remove the spices from the pan and leave to cool.

Heat the oil in a heavy pan and fry the green masala paste for 2–3 minutes, add the onion, and stir for a few minutes more. Add the spices and the coconut milk.

Simmer, uncovered, for 8–10 minutes, stirring frequently. Put in the prawns and simmer for 4–6 minutes, until the prawns are cooked through. Do not overcook or they will be tough. Serve with rice.

Anise

Meat

Lamb korma

In this Moghul dish the lamb is cooked in a spiced yogurt sauce thickened with poppy seeds and almonds.

SERVES 6–8

450ml (15fl oz) thick yogurt

small piece ginger, chopped

4 green chillies, deseeded and chopped

4 garlic cloves, chopped

2 tbsp blanched almonds

2 tbsp poppy seeds

small piece cinnamon

3 blades mace

½ tsp cumin or black cumin seeds

4 cloves

seeds of 4 brown cardamoms

10 black peppercorns

3 tbsp sunflower oil or ghee

1 large onion, sliced

1 kg (2¼lb) lean lamb, cubed

¼ tsp powdered saffron soaked in 1 tbsp water

salt

3 tbsp chopped coriander leaves

Set a fine strainer over a bowl and strain the yogurt in it for 1 hour. Discard the whey in the bowl. Blend the ginger, chillies, garlic, and 3 tbsp water to a paste. Grind together the almonds and all the spices.

Heat the oil or ghee in a large, heavy pan and fry the onion until golden. Stir in the ginger paste and the ground almonds and spices, and fry for 2–3 minutes more. Add the meat and stir well to coat it with the spices. Add the yogurt and saffron, season with salt, and cover the pan.

Simmer over very low heat for 1½–2 hours, until the lamb is tender. Stir frequently to make sure it is not sticking; if necessary, add a little water. Garnish with the coriander.

Roast rack of lamb with dukka

Dukka is most often served as a dip for pieces of warm pitta bread dunked in olive oil. It is also good sprinkled over rice or soup and makes an excellent crust for lamb.

SERVES 2

2–3 tbsp dukka (p.282)

1 rack of lamb

olive oil

Heat the oven to 220°C (425°F/Gas 7). Rub the lamb with olive oil and press 2–3 tbsp dukka into the fat side. Roast for 20 minutes if you like your lamb rare or a few minutes longer for medium rare. Serve with Spiced lentils (p.319) and Glazed carrots with marjoram (p.320).

Spiced lamb shanks

Lamb shanks are quick to prepare and can be left to simmer for a couple of hours to produce a rich, succulent sauce.

SERVES 4

4 lamb shanks, excess fat trimmed

2 tbsp olive oil

¾ tsp cinnamon

¾ tsp ginger

½ tsp cumin seeds

¼ tsp allspice

¼ tsp nutmeg

1 large onion, chopped

400g can tomatoes

salt to taste

250ml (9fl oz) stock

Brown the shanks in the oil in a large pan. Remove them and set aside while you fry the spices lightly in the oil. Put in the onion and fry with the spices for 3–4 minutes, then put back the shanks. Add the tomatoes, a little salt, and enough stock or water to almost cover the lamb shanks. Bring to the boil, cover, and simmer on a heat diffuser or in the oven pre-heated to 150°C (300°F/Gas 2). It will take 2–3½ hours.

Check from time to time to see that the shanks are immersed in the liquid and that they are not cooking too quickly. Lift out the shanks carefully; the flesh will be loose on the bone. Put them into a warm bowl and cover it while you boil the cooking liquid to reduce it slightly, and then blend it to make a sauce. Strain it into the rinsed out pan, put back the lamb shanks, and reheat gently if necessary.

Serve with rice, soft polenta, or couscous and a bowl of harissa.

Cumin seeds

Pork chops with fennel and potatoes

This is a substantial, rustic dish for a winter meal, quickly prepared and left to cook slowly in the oven.

SERVES 4

4 pork chops

700g (1lb 10oz) potatoes

1 onion, finely sliced

1 tsp fennel seeds, lightly crushed

1 tbsp light olive oil

4 small or 2 large garlic cloves, crushed

salt and freshly ground black pepper

100g (3½oz) streaky bacon

1 glass white wine

Heat the oven to 170°C (338°F/Gas 3½). Trim excess fat from the chops. Slice the potatoes and onion very thinly. Arrange half of the potatoes and onion in an ovenproof dish that will hold the chops in one layer and season them.

Rub the fennel seeds into the chops on both sides, brown them in the oil, and put them on top of the potatoes. Stuff some of the garlic near the bone of each chop. Cover with the remaining potatoes and onion, season, and spread the bacon over the top. Pour over the wine. Put 2 layers of foil or greaseproof paper over the top before putting on the lid. Bake in the oven for about 3 hours. There will be a large amount of fat so it would be best to drain this off before serving.

A salad of finely sliced fennel dressed with oil and lemon juice would be a good accompaniment.

VARIATION
Use 2 sage leaves for each chop instead of fennel seeds and press them onto each side of the meat after browning. Serve with a watercress salad.

Fennel

Slow roast pork belly with juniper

Pork belly is quick and easy to prepare and then is left in a low oven to cook for several hours. The refreshing bittersweet taste of juniper marries well with pork; most often used in pâtés and terrines, its sharpness also cuts through the fat of pork belly.

SERVES 4

sea salt and freshly ground black pepper

1 kg (2¼lb) pork belly, rind scored

6 ripe plum tomatoes, cut in half

10 garlic cloves, crushed

2 tsp juniper berries, crushed

2–3 bay leaves

small handful of thyme sprigs

Rub a handful of salt over the rind and leave the meat in the refrigerator for up to 2 hours. Heat the oven to 150°C (300°F/Gas 2) and put in a small roasting tin. Let it heat through for a few minutes.

Gently rinse the salt off the pork and dry with kitchen paper. Take out the tin, put in the tomatoes, and season them with salt and pepper. Scatter the garlic, juniper berries, myrtle or bay leaves, and thyme over and between them. Put the pork on top, skin side up. Return the pan to the oven and cook slowly for 3–3½ hours.

Heat an overhead grill, take the pork from the oven, and put it under the grill for 5–6 minutes to crisp the skin. Cover the pork with a piece of foil or a lid and leave to rest for 10 minutes. Lift out the pork to carve. Scoop up the tomatoes and garlic, leaving behind the fat in the pan.

Serve the pork with the garlic and tomato "sauce" and boiled or mashed potatoes.

Malaysian rendang

SERVES 8

8 shallots, chopped

4 garlic cloves, crushed

5 red chillies, deseeded and sliced

small piece of fresh galangal, chopped

1 litre (1¾ pints) coconut milk

1 kg (2¼lb) chuck steak, cubed

1 salam leaf or a spray of curry leaves

2 tbsp ground coriander

1 tsp ground cumin

1 tsp ground turmeric, or 1 tbsp fresh, chopped

1 stalk lemon grass, bottom third only, crushed

2 tsp sugar

1 tsp tamarind concentrate, soaked in warm water

First prepare the spice paste: blend the shallots, garlic, chillies, and galangal to a smooth paste with 2–3 tbsp coconut milk. Turn it into a wok, add the beef, and stir well to coat it with the mixture.

Add the remaining spices and the rest of the coconut milk. Stir well, bring to the boil, then simmer uncovered over gentle heat for about 1½ hours, until most of the liquid has evaporated and the meat is tender.

When the oil from the coconut starts to separate out, stir constantly until it is absorbed by the meat. Stir in the sugar and tamarind and remove the pan from the heat.

Rendang has little liquid and is served with rice. Like most stews it improves if made a day in advance and reheated.

Thai beef curry

SERVES 4

2 tbsp sunflower oil

2 tbsp red curry paste (*p.272*)

750g (1lb 10oz) sirloin or rump steak, cut in strips

750ml (1¼ pints) coconut milk

2 tbsp fish sauce

4 makrut lime leaves

2 red chillies, deseeded and sliced

1 tbsp palm or brown sugar

4 tbsp roasted peanuts, crushed

2 tbsp chopped coriander leaves

Heat a wok, add the oil, stir in the curry paste, and fry until it is fragrant. Add the beef, and toss until it browns. Pour over the coconut milk, fish sauce, lime leaves, and chillies, bring to the boil, and simmer for about 20 minutes, until the beef is tender.

Stir in the sugar and peanuts, turn into a serving dish, and scatter over the coriander. Serve with jasmine rice.

Massaman curry paste (*p.273*), with its flavours of Indian spices, could be used instead of red curry paste.

Chicken wat

Ethiopian wats are well-spiced stews, usually served with flat bread, but rice or couscous make a good alternative.

SERVES 6

1.5–1.8 kg (3 lb 3oz–4lb) chicken pieces, skinned

60g (2oz) butter

4 large onions, chopped

3 garlic cloves, finely chopped

1 heaped tbsp berbere (*p.284*) or wat spices (*p.285*)

400g can tomatoes, chopped

salt

Lightly score each piece of chicken with a sharp knife to allow the flavours of the sauce to penetrate. Heat the butter in a large, heavy-based pan and fry the onions until golden. Add the garlic and fry for a minute or two longer. Add the spice mix and stir it into the onions, then add the tomatoes.

Cover and simmer for 15 minutes until you have a thick sauce. Put in the chicken pieces, bring back to a simmer; add a little water if necessary. Cover and cook for 40–45 minutes, until the chicken is tender. Taste and season, if needed.

Chicken tikka

SERVES 4

600g (1lb 5oz) boned chicken

200ml (7fl oz) yogurt

1 tbsp tandoori masala (*p.276*)

2 tbsp sunflower oil

2 lemons

small handful coriander or mint

Cut the chicken into 5cm (2in) cubes. Whisk the yogurt and stir in the masala and the oil. Marinate the chicken in the yogurt for at least 2 hours. When you are ready to cook, heat the oven to 220°C (425°F/Gas 7) or heat the grill or barbecue. Thread the chicken pieces onto skewers and put the skewers on an oiled grill rack, standing in its tray if they are to be cooked indoors.

Bake the chicken for about 12 minutes or grill for about 10 minutes, turning the skewers once. Allow 10–12 minutes for barbecuing; the skewers should be turned at regular intervals. Serve with lemon wedges and chopped coriander or mint. Coriander chutney (*p.301*) goes well with chicken tikka.

Caribbean chicken Colombo

This curry from the French Caribbean islands is made with kid, lamb, beef, or pork as well as chicken.

SERVES 6–8

1.5kg (3lb 3oz) chicken pieces, skinned

3 tbsp sunflower oil

2 onions, chopped

4 garlic cloves, chopped

small piece of fresh ginger, chopped

2 tbsp poudre de Colombo (*p.287*)

2 tbsp tamarind water (*p.157*)

300g (10oz) pumpkin flesh, cut in chunks

300g (10oz) sweet potatoes, peeled and cut in chunks

1 chayote or 1 aubergine, peeled and cut in chunks

600ml (1 pint) chicken stock

salt

1 tbsp lime juice

bunch of chives or 3 spring onions, chopped

Sauté the chicken pieces in the oil in a large, heavy-based saucepan until they are lightly coloured on both sides. Remove them to a plate. In the oil remaining in the pan, sauté the onions until golden, add the garlic, ginger, and poudre de Colombo and stir for 3–4 minutes until the aromas rise from the spices. Return the chicken to the pan, add the tamarind, vegetables, and stock, and season with salt.

Cover, bring to the boil, then simmer gently until the chicken and vegetables are tender, about 45 minutes. Just before you serve, stir in the lime juice and scatter over the chives or spring onions. Serve with rice.

The Colombo can be made in advance and reheated, but wait to add the lime juice and garnish.

Chives

Pot-roasted chicken with Indian spices

SERVES 4

1.5kg (3lb 3oz) chicken

4 tsp aromatic garam masala (*p.275*)

thick slice of fresh ginger, finely chopped

1 garlic clove, crushed

½ tsp salt

30g (1oz) butter

3 tbsp sunflower oil or clarified butter

Prepare the chicken 2–3 hours before you want to cook it. Mix the garam masala, ginger, garlic, and salt, then work the mixture into the butter to make a paste.

Work your fingers under the skin of the chicken, loosening but not breaking the skin over the breast and then the legs. Push the spice paste under the skin, rubbing it into the flesh. Leave for 2–3 hours for the flavours to penetrate the meat. Heat the oven to 190°C (375°F/Gas 5).

Heat the oil in a heavy, ovenproof casserole that just holds the chicken. Put in the chicken on its side, cover tightly, and bake for 30–35 minutes, then turn the chicken over and bake for another 30 minutes or so. Finally turn it breast uppermost, baste with the pan juices, and return the casserole to the oven, uncovered, for 10–15 minutes to allow it to brown. Pierce the thickest part of the thigh with a skewer; if the juices flow clear, it is ready. Spoon the juices from the casserole over the chicken when it is carved. Serve with lemon wedges, a chutney or yogurt and herb dressing, and a bowl of rice.

Fresh garlic

Vegetables

Peas in saffron cream

The dish is best made with newly podded peas, but if you can't get them frozen petits pois could be used.

SERVES 6

60g (2oz) butter

2.25kg (5lb) peas, about 600g (1lb 5oz) shelled

1 tsp sugar

salt and freshly ground black pepper

10 saffron threads, crushed

150ml (5fl oz) double cream

½ tsp flour

1 tbsp chopped dill or chives

Bring the butter and 100ml (3½fl oz) water to the boil. Add the peas and sugar, season, and simmer, covered, over a low heat for 8–10 minutes, until the peas are nearly tender. If there are more than a few spoonfuls of liquid in the pan, leave uncovered for the moisture to evaporate.

Blend the saffron with 1 tbsp warm water and stir it into the cream with the flour. Pour the cream mixture over the peas, and, as soon as it comes to the boil, stir in the dill or chives and serve.

Spiced lentils

SERVES 4

250g (9oz) Puy lentils

2 bay leaves

1 tsp ground coriander

¾ tsp ground cumin

seeds of 2 cardamom pods, crushed

1 medium onion

salt

4 tbsp double cream or extra virgin olive oil

1 garlic clove, crushed with a little salt

1 tbsp chopped mint

1 tbsp chopped basil, preferably Thai or anise basil

Put the lentils into a large saucepan with the bay leaves, spices, and whole onion. Add 900ml (1½ pints) water, bring to the boil, then simmer, partly covered, until the lentils are tender, about 20 minutes. Add salt to taste in the last 5 minutes of cooking.

Drain thoroughly and discard the bay leaves and onion. Heat the cream or olive oil, stir in the garlic, and pour over the lentils, turning to coat them well. Stir in the herbs, and serve.

Dried bay

Green beans with a miso and sesame sauce

This dish can be made with fine, young green beans or with flat helda beans, although in both cases when topping and tailing I would also run a knife along the sides to ensure there are no strings. Dashi soup stock can be bought in sachets in the same part of a supermarket as mirin, or in health food shops.

SERVES 4

2 tbsp white miso paste

2 tbsp oriental sesame paste

a small piece of ginger, chopped very finely

1 tbsp mirin

2–3 tbsp dashi

350g (12oz) young green beans or helda beans

2 tsp sesame seeds, toasted

Blend together the miso and sesame pastes with the ginger and mirin. Add the dashi, a little at a time, to thin the mixture to a thick cream.

Blanch the beans in boiling water for 1 minute if using thin green beans, or for 2 minutes for flat helda beans. Drain, refresh under cold water, and leave to cool. Cut them on the diagonal into 2 cm (¾in) lengths. Toss the beans in the sauce, scatter over the sesame seeds, and serve at room temperature.

Braised fennel with star anise

SERVES 4

4 heads fennel

2 garlic cloves, sliced

2 star anise

4 tbsp olive oil

300ml (10fl oz) vegetable stock

salt and freshly ground black pepper

1 tbsp chopped chives

Trim the fennel tops and bottoms and peel the outer leaves. Put them into a heavy-based saucepan, side by side, with the garlic and star anise. Pour over the olive oil and stock, or equal quantity of water, if preferred. Season with salt and pepper.

Cover and bring to the boil, then reduce the heat and braise slowly for 30–40 minutes, turning the fennel once. It is ready when it can be pierced with a knife, but don't overcook it – fennel tastes better with a slight bite. Remove the fennel from the pan and cut in half. Spoon over a little of the cooking liquid and sprinkle over the chives.

Glazed carrots with marjoram

SERVES 4

500g (1lb 2oz) carrots, thinly sliced

salt and freshly ground black pepper

60g (2oz) butter

2 tsp chopped marjoram

juice and grated zest of ½ unwaxed orange

Cook the carrots in boiling, salted water until just tender, about 4–5 minutes, then drain. Melt the butter, toss the carrots in it, adding pepper, marjoram, orange juice, and zest. Cook for 1–2 minutes, then serve.

Sweet marjoram

Beetroot with dill

SERVES 4

300g (10oz) raw beetroot

2 tbsp olive or walnut oil

1 tbsp balsamic vinegar

2–3 tbsp chopped dill

Peel and grate the beetroot (wear gloves if you don't want your hands dyed red). Heat the oil, tip in the beetroot, and fry, stirring and tossing for 5–6 minutes. Put the beetroot into a warmed serving dish and sprinkle over the balsamic vinegar. Stir in most of the dill, keeping a little aside to garnish the top. This can be served warm or as a salad.

Squash purée

The hard-skinned squashes – acorn, butternut, kabocha – make wonderful light purées in varying shades of gold. They respond well to spicing – ginger, cardamom, cinnamon, mace, or clove are all suitable – and to a dose of alcohol.

SERVES 2

1 small–medium squash

salt and freshly ground black pepper

¼–½ tsp ground spice

60–80g (2–3oz) butter

150–200ml (5–7fl oz) crème fraîche

2 tbsp rum or whisky (optional)

Heat the oven to 190°C (375°F/Gas 5). Cut the squash in half and remove the seeds. Bake in the oven for 30–45 minutes, depending on the size and variety. Scoop the flesh out of the skins and purée with salt and pepper, the spice of your choice, and enough butter and cream to make a smooth purée. Stir in the rum or whisky if you are using it. The purée will keep warm, covered, in a low oven for 10–15 minutes.

Pasta, noodles, and grains

Linguine with herbs

This dish is only worth making if you have good, fresh herbs and extra virgin olive oil. Chop the herbs by hand rather than in a processor to achieve a better texture.

SERVES 4

4 sprigs basil

6 sprigs flat-leaf parsley

3 sprigs marjoram

1 sprig rosemary

1 small sprig hyssop

100ml (3½fl oz) extra virgin olive oil

salt and freshly ground black pepper

1 shallot, peeled and finely chopped

3–4 tbsp fresh breadcrumbs

600g (1lb 5oz) fresh or 400g (14oz) dried linguine

Discard the large stalks from the herbs and chop the leaves and fine stalks. Make sure that the sharp leaves of the rosemary and hyssop are chopped small. Infuse the herbs with all but 2 tbsp of the oil in a large serving bowl, and season, giving a good grinding of pepper.

Heat the remaining oil and sauté the shallot and breadcrumbs until the breadcrumbs are crisp. Cook the linguine al dente and drain well. Toss the pasta in the oil and herb mixture, scatter over the shallot and breadcrumbs, and serve.

Liquorice basil

Tunisian rishta with chicken, peas, and broad beans

Rishta is an Arabic word for long ribbons of pasta. If you can't get small young broad beans, buy another 500g (1lb 2oz) of beans in their pods, cook them for a few minutes in boiling water, then drain and remove the skins.

SERVES 6

2 tbsp olive oil

200g (7oz) boneless chicken thighs, cut into small pieces

1 onion, finely chopped

250g (9oz) small broad beans (shelled weight)

200g (7oz) peas (shelled weight)

handful of chopped flat-leaf parsley

500g (1lb 2oz) peeled, deseeded, and chopped tomatoes or a 400g can chopped tomatoes

1 tbsp harissa

salt and freshly ground black pepper

300g (10oz) fettuccine

Heat the olive oil in a heavy-based saucepan and cook the chicken and onion until lightly coloured, stirring occasionally. Add the broad beans, peas, parsley, tomatoes, harissa, and season with salt and pepper. Add 150ml (5fl oz) water and simmer gently for 30 minutes, until the chicken is cooked.

Bring a large pan of salted water to the boil and add the fettuccine. Cook according to the time given on the packet, until al dente. Drain and add the pasta to the chicken and vegetables. Toss and leave to cook for a further 5 minutes, then serve.

Noodles with beef and broccoli

SERVES 2

300g (10oz) lean sirloin steak

3 tbsp soy sauce

2 tbsp rice vinegar

1 tsp chopped garlic

1 tsp chopped fresh root ginger

1 tsp sugar

4 tbsp sunflower oil

250g (9oz) egg noodles

200g (7oz) small broccoli florets

4 spring onions, finely sliced

3 tbsp chopped coriander leaves

1 tbsp toasted sesame seeds

Slice the steak across the grain into thin strips. Combine the soy sauce, vinegar, garlic, ginger, sugar, and 2 tbsp oil, and marinate the beef for 30 minutes.

Cook the noodles in plenty of unsalted boiling water until just tender. Drain and rinse them under cold water.

Heat a wok, pour in the remaining oil, and swirl to coat the bottom and sides. Stir-fry the broccoli for 2 minutes, add the noodles and toss them for 2 minutes, then add the beef and its marinade. Stir-fry for another 2 minutes, stirring in the spring onions and coriander. Turn into a warmed serving bowl, sprinkle over the sesame seeds, and serve.

Laksa

Laksa is a fresh-tasting Malay dish of noodles in a spiced coconut milk broth. Candlenuts are hard, oily nuts with a slightly bitter taste, used as a thickening agent; sweeter macadamia nuts can be substituted. Candlenuts and dried prawns are available from oriental shops.

SERVES 6

400g (14oz) fresh rice noodles

2 garlic cloves

3 stalks lemon grass, lower third only

5cm (2in) piece of fresh root ginger or galangal

3 red chillies, deseeded

8 shallots

2 tsp fresh turmeric or ½ tsp ground

5 candlenuts

2 tbsp dried prawns, soaked in a little water

3 tbsp sunflower oil

200g (7oz) bean sprouts, tails trimmed

600ml (1 pint) fish or chicken stock

600ml (1 pint) coconut milk

400g (14oz) white fish fillet, cut into 4cm (1½in) pieces

300g (10oz) small prawns, cooked and peeled

salt

juice of 1 lime

2 spring onions, finely sliced

2 tbsp chopped rau ram or coriander leaves

Blanch the noodles in a large pan of unsalted, boiling water. Drain and rinse thoroughly in cold water.

To prepare the spice paste, roughly chop the garlic, lemon grass, ginger, chillies, shallots, fresh turmeric, and candlenuts. Blend them in a food processor with the dried prawns (and ground turmeric if that is what you are using). Add a little oil if necessary to make a smooth paste. Blanch the bean sprouts for 1 minute, drain, and rinse – it helps to keep them crisp.

Heat the remaining oil in a large pan or wok. Add the spice paste and fry, stirring constantly, until the paste is fragrant and the oil separates from the solids, about 5 minutes. Add the stock, bring to the boil, and stir to blend it with the paste. Reduce the heat, add the coconut milk, simmer for 2–3 minutes, then add the fish and stir until it is almost cooked. Add the prawns and season with salt and the lime juice.

Serve laksa in deep bowls. Divide the noodles and bean sprouts between them, ladle over some of the broth and seafood. Garnish with spring onion and rau ram.

Stir-fried vegetables with egg noodles

You can vary the vegetables in this dish to suit your taste. Use mushrooms, celery, or fine green beans cut in slivers. If you want a non-vegetarian meal, toss in 300g (10oz) minced pork as soon as the flavourings start to take colour.

SERVES 3–4

300g (10oz) fresh or dried egg noodles

1½ tbsp sesame oil

2 tbsp sunflower oil

3 garlic cloves, finely chopped

3cm (1in) piece of fresh root ginger, finely chopped

2 small chillies, deseeded and chopped (or more to taste)

100g (3½oz) carrots, cut in thin batons

1–2 pak choi or other Chinese greens, leaves separated and sliced if large

1 red pepper, cut in strips

100g (3½oz) mangetout or snow peas

80g (3oz) bean sprouts

2–3 tbsp soy sauce

5–6 spring onions, white part and a little green, cut in slivers

large handful of coriander leaves and small stalks, chopped

Rinse fresh noodles in warm water and then boil in a large pan of unsalted, boiling water. They will be done in 1–4 minutes, depending on their thickness. If you use dried noodles they will take 4–10 minutes. Taste before the recommended cooking time is reached; do not overcook. Drain, then rinse, and drain again to get rid of starch.

If you need to set them aside for some time, place them in a bowl and toss with 1 tbsp sesame oil. To reheat, dip them briefly into a pan of boiling water or pour boiling water over them in a colander.

Heat a large wok, add the sunflower oil, swirl around to coat the sides, and then add the garlic, ginger, and chillies. Stir-fry quickly, making sure the flavourings don't burn. Add the carrots, toss and stir for 1–2 minutes, then put in the pak choi. Stir for another minute or two then, add the pepper and mangetout, continue to stir and then put in the bean sprouts. Stir in the remaining sesame oil and soy sauce and then the noodles, tossing and stirring so that they mix in with the vegetables. Serve in bowls topped with the spring onion and coriander.

Malabar pilaf

This pilaf comes from the southwestern hills of India, where spices grow in profusion. It makes an excellent accompaniment to braised chicken or lamb, or to a vegetable stew. The pilaf is served with its spices but only the cumin seeds are eaten.

SERVES 4–6

500g (1lb 2oz) basmati rice

2 tbsp sunflower oil or clarified butter

1 large onion, chopped

8 green cardamom pods

1 cinnamon stick

8 cloves

1 tsp cumin seeds

12 black peppercorns

1 tsp salt

1–2 tbsp sunflower oil or melted butter (optional)

Measure the rice, wash it in cold water, drain, and rinse until the water runs clear; soak it in cold water for 30 minutes or so.

Heat the oil in a heavy-based saucepan and fry the onion until golden. Bruise the cardamoms lightly and break the cinnamon in three. Add all the spices to the onion and fry gently for about 30 seconds, until the spices are slightly puffed and have darkened a little.

Drain the rice and add it to the pan. Fry for 2–3 minutes, stirring, until the rice becomes translucent. Add 1¼ measures of boiling water for every 1 measure of rice. Season with salt and bring back to the boil. Reduce the heat to very low, cover the pan, and simmer for 15 minutes. The water will be absorbed and the surface of the rice will be covered with tiny steam holes. If you wish, add the oil or butter to the rice now.

Fold a kitchen towel, put it over the pan, put on the lid, and fold up the corners of the towel over the top. Leave the pan on the heat for 5 minutes longer, then turn off the heat and leave to steam undisturbed for a further 5–10 minutes. Turn the rice out onto a warmed serving dish with a wooden fork, fluffing the rice as you do so.

Cloves

Rice with herbs

This is a beautiful dish – the green herbs cling to the rice and the crisp, golden crust on the bottom of the pan is a delightful surprise. Fresh herbs are best for this Iranian dish but you can use dried: 15–20g (½–¾oz) will flavour 500g (1lb 2oz) rice. Fresh herbs must be completely dry when they are added to the rice, so put them through a salad spinner or dry them carefully in a kitchen towel before chopping.

SERVES 4

500g (1lb 2oz) basmati rice

salt

100g (3½oz) butter, or 6 tbsp sunflower oil

80g (3oz) dill, finely chopped

80g (3oz) parsley, finely chopped

80g (3oz) coriander, finely chopped

80g (3oz) chives, finely chopped

Put the rice into a large saucepan, pour over cold water, swirl around, then drain and rinse until the water runs clear. Return the rice to the pan and soak for at least 2 hours in salted water; the longer it soaks, the better.

Drain the rice, then add 1 tbsp salt to 2.5 litres (4½ pints) of water, bring to the boil, and put in the rice, stirring to ensure it does not stick. Boil the rice, uncovered, for 2–3 minutes and test to see whether it is almost tender. It should be soft on the outside but still retain a firm core. Drain and rinse the rice in lukewarm water.

Put half the butter or oil and 3 tbsp water into a non-stick pan if you have one large enough for the rice; otherwise rinse the pan the rice was cooked in and use that. When the butter has melted or the oil is hot, put in a layer of rice, then a third of the mixed herbs. Repeat this layering, making each layer a bit narrower than the one before so that you have a cone-shaped mound in the pan. Finish with a layer of rice. With the handle of a wooden spoon, poke two or three holes through the cone down to the bottom of the pan to allow steam to escape. Pour over the rest of the butter or oil.

Cover the pan with a folded kitchen towel and the lid, flip the ends of the towel up over the lid to keep them away from the heat. Cook on high heat for 3–4 minutes, until the rice is steaming, then turn the heat very low and steam for 30 minutes. The cloth absorbs excess steam and the rice grains will be separate. The rice will keep hot for a further 20–30 minutes, provided the cloth and lid are left in place. To serve, turn the rice into a warmed serving dish with a wooden fork. Lift out the crust with a spatula and put it around the rice.

Arroz al horno

This Spanish dish of rice and chick peas is baked in the oven. Spanish rice is medium grain, but if you can't get Spanish use an Italian rice rather than a long grain rice. The chick peas are cooked in advance (or use canned), then the casserole takes only 30 minutes or so to prepare and cook. It has a whole head of garlic in the centre which flavours the rice beautifully and is mellow to eat.

SERVES 4–6

1 head garlic

80ml (2½fl oz) olive oil

3 tomatoes, peeled and chopped

2 potatoes, thinly sliced

1 tsp smoked paprika

salt

120g (4oz) chickpeas, cooked

750ml (1¼ pints) vegetable or chicken stock

400g (14oz) rice

Heat the oven to 200°C (400°F/Gas 6). Remove any loose outer skin from the garlic but keep the head intact. Wipe it clean. Heat the oil in an ovenproof casserole – in Spain it would be an earthenware casserole – and sauté the garlic.

After 2–3 minutes, add the tomatoes and potatoes. Sauté for a few minutes more, season with paprika and salt, and add the chickpeas. Heat the stock. Tip the rice into the dish and stir well to mix, then pour over the stock. Make sure the garlic is in the centre. Bring to the boil and simmer for 2–3 minutes, then transfer the dish to the oven and cook for about 20 minutes. Check that the rice is done and remove the dish from the oven. Separate the cloves of garlic and serve them with the rice.

VARIATIONS

In some places, small pieces of blood sausage or chorizo are added, sometimes raisins plumped in warm water, elsewhere haricot beans replace the chick peas. Arroz al horno can be interpreted in different ways, but keep the same proportions of rice and chickpeas or beans, and keep the head of garlic.

Artichoke, broad bean, and quinoa salad

Quinoa is from the chenopod family, so it is not strictly a grain, but is used as one. It is native to the Andean region, where I enjoyed it several years ago. I remember bringing back packets to London; now it widely available in supermarkets and health food shops.

SERVES 4

200g (7oz) quinoa

4–5 artichoke hearts

1 tbsp olive oil

300g (10oz) podded broad beans

100g (3½oz) cashew nuts

3 large tomatoes, diced

1 small red onion, finely chopped

handful of mizuna, nasturtium, or other salad leaves

2 tsp ground cumin

salt and freshly ground black pepper

2–3 tbsp wine vinegar

5–6 tbsp extra virgin olive oil

basil leaves, torn, or borage flowers

Rinse the quinoa well and cook in 600ml (1 pint) water for 15–20 minutes until it is well cooked, and the water is absorbed. Drain, rinse under cold water, and spread out on a tray to dry.

Blanch the artichoke hearts, if using frozen. Cut them into strips and sauté gently in 1 tbsp olive oil. Bring the broad beans to the boil in a saucepan of salted water, drain, rinse under cold water, and remove the skins. Lightly toast the cashew nuts in a dry frying pan.

Make a dressing with the cumin, salt and pepper, vinegar, and olive oil and pour into a salad bowl. When the artichokes, beans, and cashews are cold, and the quinoa dry, add the salad leaves to the bowl, and then the rest of the ingredients, except the basil leaves. Toss gently. Scatter the basil leaves or borage flowers over the top.

Lime basil

Couscous with seven vegetables

In this traditional dish the vegetables may be varied: pumpkin, peas, potatoes, artichokes, or other vegetables in season can be used instead of those given below.

SERVES 6

3 tbsp olive oil

1 tsp freshly ground black pepper

1 tbsp paprika

1 tbsp tabil (*p.283*) or ground cumin and coriander

2 onions, coarsely chopped

3 tomatoes, peeled and chopped

60g (2oz) chickpeas, soaked overnight, or ½ can chickpeas, rinsed

2 carrots, thickly sliced

2 courgettes, thickly sliced

3 small white turnips, quartered

200g (7oz) shelled or frozen broad beans

200g (7oz) cabbage heart, cut in pieces

2 red peppers, cut in squares

handful of coriander leaves, chopped

salt

300g (10oz) quick-cooking couscous

harissa (*p.292*)

Heat the oil in a large saucepan, put in the spices and onions, and fry over medium heat for 3–4 minutes; then add the tomatoes and fry for a few minutes more.

If you are using soaked chickpeas, drain them and add to the pan with 900ml (1½ pints) water. Bring to the boil, cover, and leave to boil for 40 minutes. Then add the other vegetables, coriander leaves, and salt, and cook for a further 20–30 minutes, until all the vegetables are ready.

If you are using canned chickpeas, add them with the other vegetables, coriander, and salt to taste. Pour over the same quantity of water as above, bring to the boil, and simmer for 20–30 minutes until all the vegetables are cooked.

Prepare the couscous, according to the instructions on the packet, when the stew is almost ready. To serve, mound the couscous in a warmed serving dish, put the vegetables around it, and spoon over some of the broth. Use a ladleful of broth to thin the harissa, and pour the rest into a separate bowl. Serve the couscous with the extra broth and the harissa.

Cakes and desserts

Marzipan and poppy seed cake

This is a pleasant teatime cake. The marzipan gives it richness and combines well with the mellow, almond-like flavour of the poppy seeds. It will keep for some days in a tin.

FOR a 1kg (2¼lb) cake using a loaf tin

150g (5½oz) butter

120g (4oz) caster sugar

3 eggs, separated

2 tbsp rum

100ml (3½fl oz) soured cream, or single cream mixed with 2 tbsp lemon juice

200g (7oz) marzipan, chilled in the freezer for 30 minutes and grated

150g (5½oz) plain flour

2 tsp baking powder

pinch of salt

60g (2oz) poppy seeds

Heat the oven to 180°C (350°F/Gas 4) and grease and line the base of a 1kg (2¼lb) loaf tin. In a bowl, beat together the butter and sugar until pale and fluffy. Add the egg yolks, one at a time, beating well to incorporate them, then add the rum and cream. Stir in the grated marzipan.

Sift the flour, baking powder, and salt together two or three times. Stir in the poppy seeds. Whisk the egg whites until they stand in peaks and set aside. Mix the flour and poppy seeds into the batter, then add 2–3 tbsp egg whites to loosen it. Fold in the rest of the egg whites with a large metal spoon.

Turn the mixture into the tin and bake for about 1 hour until a skewer pushed into the centre comes out clean. Put the tin on a wire rack for 10 minutes, then lift out the cake and leave to cool on the rack.

Vanilla ice cream

SERVES 6

450ml (15fl oz) full milk or single cream

1 vanilla pod, split lengthways

4 egg yolks

150g (5½oz) caster sugar

150ml (5fl oz) double cream

Put the milk or single cream and the vanilla pod into a heavy-based saucepan and bring slowly to the boil. Remove from the heat, cover, and leave to infuse for 20 minutes. Take out the vanilla pod and scrape the seeds into the liquid.

Beat the egg yolks and sugar until thick and pale. Gently reheat the milk or cream and beat a little of it into the egg yolks. Pour the egg mixture into the cream and return the pan to a low heat. Stir until the custard is thick enough to coat the back of a spoon; it will take several minutes. Do not let it boil.

Remove the pan from the heat and continue to stir until it has almost cooled. Whip the double cream lightly and fold it into the custard. Freeze in an ice cream machine following the maker's instructions.

VARIATION
Cardamom ice cream
Replace the vanilla pod by 8 lightly crushed cardamom pods. Infuse for 30 minutes, then strain and make as above.

Cinnamon ice cream
Replace the vanilla pod by 1 tbsp finely ground cinnamon. There is no need to infuse; just follow the method above.

Lavender ice cream
Replace the vanilla pod by 3 tbsp fresh lavender flowers. Infuse for 1 hour, then strain. Add 1 tsp lavender flowers, chopped finely, just before adding the double cream.

Vanilla

Speculaas

Speculaas are Dutch biscuits which can either be thin and crunchy or more shortbread-like. They are traditional for the Feast of St Nicolas on 5th December. The biscuits may be stamped with an image or figure on one side, or may have been shaped in a traditional wooden mould cut as St Nicolas, or a Dutch symbol such as a windmill.

The traditional spices for speculaas are cinnamon, nutmeg, allspice, cloves, and cardamom. Ginger is sometimes included. This recipe makes the thicker, shortbread-style biscuits.

MAKES 15–20 biscuits depending on the size

2 tsp cinnamon

scant ¼ tsp ground allspice

¼ tsp ground cloves

½ tsp grated nutmeg

scant ¼ tsp ground cardamom seeds, pods discarded

200g (7oz) self-raising flour

100g (3½oz) soft brown sugar

125g (4½oz) butter

flaked almonds (optional)

Mix all the spices and stir them into the sifted flour. Mix in the sugar and butter, gradually, either in a food processor or by hand. If the mixture appears stiff, add a spoonful of water to form a dough. Turn the dough onto a lightly floured surface and roll out to 5mm (¼in) thickness. Heat the oven to 180°C (350°F/Gas 4).

Cut the dough into circles or shapes with a cookie cutter and lay them on a baking sheet lined with greaseproof paper. Sprinkle with flaked almonds, if you wish, and bake for 15–20 minutes or until golden. Cool on a wire rack.

Baked figs with port and cinnamon

If you have figs that aren't quite ripe, this is a good way of using them. The flavourings can be varied: use seeds from 4–5 cardamom pods or 1 tsp lavender flowers instead of the cinnamon, a muscat or other dessert wine instead of the port, and orange juice and a little sugar instead of syrup. Firm peaches and nectarines also bake well.

SERVES 6

60g (2oz) sugar

6 tbsp port

½ stick cinnamon

12 figs

Heat the oven to 200°C (400°F/Gas 6). Heat 100ml (3½fl oz) water and the sugar in a small saucepan until the sugar has dissolved; simmer the syrup for 3–4 minutes.

Pour the syrup into an ovenproof dish just big enough to hold the figs in one layer. Pour in the port. Break the cinnamon in two. Put the figs into the dish and tuck the cinnamon between them.

Bake for 20–30 minutes, depending on the ripeness of the figs. Lift out the figs to a serving dish. Transfer the liquid to a pan, reduce a little, and then strain the sauce over the figs. Serve at once or leave until cold.

Cloves

Index

Entries in *italic* indicate botanical names; page numbers in **bold** indicate illustrations, and page numbers in ***bold italics*** indicate recipes.

Acknowledgments

About the author

Jill Norman is a respected author and editor with a wide knowledge and appreciation of foods from many parts of the world. In the 1970s she created the food and wine list for Penguin Books. This led to travels in pursuit of food and drink, and a passion to discover the origins of herbs and spices and how they are used. She is acknowledged internationally as an authority on herbs and spices. *The Complete Book of Spices* won awards in the UK and the US, and the first edition of *Herbs and Spices* was honoured by the German Academy of Gastronomy. All of her books have been widely translated. Jill was Elizabeth David's publisher and is now literary trustee of the David estate.

Author's acknowledgments

Updated edition 2015: For the second edition, publisher Mary-Clare Jerram was once again instrumental in orchestrating a splendid team. Dawn Henderson, Peggy Vance, and Christine Keilty at DK London and Janashree Singha, Ivy Roy, Navidita Thapa, and Alicia Ingty at DK Delhi have been constructive, helpful, and patient throughout and worked to difficult deadlines. My warmest thanks go to them all.

First edition 2002: Thanks first to my husband, Paul Breman, who helped with research, and encouraged me constantly throughout the writing of the book. He also compiled the index.

Many friends generously provided information or samples from their own part of the world or their own area of expertise; thanks go to Lynda Brown, Vic Cherikoff, Nevin Halıcı, Ian Hemphill, Richard Hosking, Philip Iddison, Aglaia Kremezi, Myung Sook Lee, Maricel Presilla, Diny Schouten, Maria José Sevilla, Margaret Shaida, David Thompson, Yong Suk Willendrup, Paula Wolfert, and Sami Zubaida.

William Penzey of The Spice House in Milwaukee generously provided a wealth of spices and information; Dr P.S.S. Thampi of the Spices Board of India provided useful contacts in Kerala; Summa Navaratnam and N.M. Wickramasinghe helped on cinnamon production; Patricia Raymond of Aust & Hachmann gave help on vanilla; the Hungarian Trade Office and Foods from Spain on paprika and pimentón; Sarah Wain of West Dean Gardens took me through their impressive collection of chillies; Kevin Bateman of MSK provided samples of Kashmiri saffron and bourbon vanilla; Chris Seagon of Laurel Herb Farm provided herbs; Jason Stemm sent me statistics from the American Spice Trade Association, and A.C. Whitely of the Royal Horticultural Society and Dr Mark Nesbitt of the Royal Botanic Gardens at Kew helped me to identify golpar.

At Dorling Kindersley publisher Mary-Clare Jerram, art director Carole Ash, and their team conceived an exciting and ambitious book; Gillian Roberts has been an exemplary managing editor; Frank Ritter and Hugh Thompson have been painstaking and constructive in their editing; Toni Kay and Sara Robin have produced a handsome and imaginative design; and Dave King has produced lively and informative photographs of all the herbs and spices. My thanks go to all of them.

Publisher's acknowledgments

Updated edition 2015: Dorling Kindersley would like to thank Michele Clarke for the index; Dorothy Kikon, Seetha Natesh, Arani Sinha, and Neha Samuel for proofreading.

First edition 2002: Dorling Kindersley would like to thank Marghie Gianni and Jo Gray for design assistance; Sarah Duncan for picture research; Jo Harris for research and styling; Nancy Campbell for research and sourcing items for photography; Jim Arbury for his splendid Hamburg parsley; Patty Penzey of The Spice House; Debbie Yakeley at Richters in Ontario; and all those who helped us in Florida, making it possible to photograph many fresh herbs and chillies when they were unobtainable in the UK – Linda Cunningham in Jacksonville and Maggie at Maggie's Herb Farm, Della and Tim Baldwin at Palm Valley Peppers, and Paul Figura.

Picture acknowledgments

The publisher would like to thank the following for their kind permission to reproduce the photographs:

a=above; b=below; c=centre; l=left; r=right; t=top;

Anthony Blake Photo Library: Sue Atkinson 75br; Martin Brigdale 193r; Graham Kirk 212; Andrew Pini 75 bl.

Jacques Boulay: 151br, 180–181.

Corbis: Jonathan Blair 44bl; Chris Bland 45tl; Michael Busselle 75tr; Dean Conger 192b, 193bl; Ric Ergenbright 180bl; Owen Franken 74b, 151tr, 232tl, 233tl, 233tr; Michael Freeman 150–151b; Lindsay Hebberd 232–233; Chris Hellier 45tr, 150bl; Dave G Houser 212cl; Earl & Nazima Kowall 181tl; Gail Mooney 213tl; Caroline Penn 181tr; Kevin Schafer 150t.

Flowerphotos: Barbara Gray 192tl.

Garden Picture Library: David Cavagnaro 74–75; Brigitte Thomas 151tl; Michel Viard 213tr, 213br, 232tr.

Oxford Scientific Films: Deni Bown 193tl; Alain Christof 44–45; Bob Gibbons 213bl; TC Nature 233br.

All other images © Dorling Kindersley

The Dorling Kindersley picture library contains over 2.5 million images, including travel photography, food, and drink. For more information, visit **www.dkimages.com**